PATENTS, HUMAN RIGHTS, AND ACCESS TO MEDICINES

Patent rights on pharmaceutical products are one of the factors that may contribute to the problem of the lack of access to affordable medicines in developing countries. In this work, Emmanuel Kolawole Oke provides a systematic analysis of the tension between patent rights and human rights law, contending that, in order to preserve their patent policy space and secure access to affordable medicines for their citizens, developing countries should incorporate a model of human rights into the design, implementation, interpretation, and enforcement of their national patent laws. Through a comprehensive analysis of court decisions from three key developing countries (India, Kenya, and South Africa), Oke assesses the effectiveness of national courts in resolving conflicts between patent rights and the right to health, and demonstrates how a model of human rights can be incorporated into the adjudication of patent rights.

Emmanuel Kolawole Oke is a lecturer in International Intellectual Property Law at Edinburgh Law School, University of Edinburgh. His research explores the interface between intellectual property and other branches of international law such as international trade law, international investment law, and international human rights law.

Patents, Human Rights, and Access to Medicines

EMMANUEL KOLAWOLE OKE
University of Edinburgh

CAMBRIDGE
UNIVERSITY PRESS

CAMBRIDGE
UNIVERSITY PRESS

Shaftesbury Road, Cambridge CB2 8EA, United Kingdom

One Liberty Plaza, 20th Floor, New York, NY 10006, USA

477 Williamstown Road, Port Melbourne, VIC 3207, Australia

314–321, 3rd Floor, Plot 3, Splendor Forum, Jasola District Centre, New Delhi – 110025, India

103 Penang Road, #05–06/07, Visioncrest Commercial, Singapore 238467

Cambridge University Press is part of Cambridge University Press & Assessment, a department of the University of Cambridge.

We share the University's mission to contribute to society through the pursuit of education, learning and research at the highest international levels of excellence.

www.cambridge.org
Information on this title: www.cambridge.org/9781108458986

DOI: 10.1017/9781108654685

First published 2022
First paperback edition 2025

A catalogue record for this publication is available from the British Library

Library of Congress Cataloging-in-Publication data
NAMES: Oke, Emmanuel Kolawole, author.
TITLE: Patents, human rights, and access to medicines / Emmanuel Kolawole Oke, Edinburgh Law School, University of Edinburgh.
DESCRIPTION: Cambridge, United Kingdom ; New York, NY : Cambridge University Press, 2022. | Based on author's thesis (doctoral - University College, Cork. Law Department, 2015) issued under title: Preserving patent policy space and securing access to medicines in developing countries : the role of states and pharmaceutical corporations. | Includes bibliographical references and index.
IDENTIFIERS: LCCN 2021039275 (print) | LCCN 2021039276 (ebook) | ISBN 9781108472104 (hardback) | ISBN 9781108458986 (paperback) | ISBN 9781108654685 (epub)
SUBJECTS: LCSH: Drugs–Patents | Drug accessibility–Law and legislation. | Patents (International law) | Foreign trade regulation–Health aspects. | Right to health.
CLASSIFICATION: LCC K1519.D78 O34 2022 (print) | LCC K1519.D78 (ebook) | DDC 346.04/86–dc23
LC record available at https://lccn.loc.gov/2021039275
LC ebook record available at https://lccn.loc.gov/2021039276

ISBN 978-1-108-47210-4 Hardback
ISBN 978-1-108-45898-6 Paperback

Contents

Acknowledgements

This book is a product of my doctoral research at the School of Law, University College Cork, Ireland, which was completed in 2015. I am therefore immensely grateful for the financial support provided for my research by the School of Law. I also convey thanks to my supervisors, Professor Steve Hedley and Professor Louise Crowley, for their excellent guidance and support during my doctoral research. I also acknowledge the support of Professor Conor O'Mahony whilst I was studying in Cork. I am equally grateful to my doctoral examiners, Professor Aurora Plomer and Dr Fidelma White, for their comments and suggestions. I must acknowledge the assistance and support I received from my fellow doctoral researchers during our time together in Cork. I thank Anthony O'Dwyer, Dug Cubie, Fariborz Safari, John McNally, Alejandra Calle-Saldarriaga, Lydia Buckley, and Rachel Hanly.

Since the completion of my doctoral research and prior to the conclusion of work on this book, I have received useful comments and feedback from a number of senior scholars in the field of intellectual property law. In this regard, I am grateful to Professor Brad Sherman, Professor Laurence Helfer, Professor Paul Torremans, Professor Shubha Ghosh, and Professor Peter Yu. I am equally thankful to my colleagues at Edinburgh Law School, especially Dr Smita Kheria, Professor John Cairns, and Professor James Harrison. My thanks also go to Matt Gallaway of Cambridge University Press for his patience with me and kind assistance since the start of this project. Matt has been quite helpful through the various vicissitudes of completing this book.

This book is dedicated to the memory of my late dad, Professor Olubode Oke, who finished his race on this terrain before I finished my work on this book project.

1

Introduction

1.1 THE PROBLEM OF ACCESS TO AFFORDABLE MEDICINES IN DEVELOPING COUNTRIES

Payment for pharmaceutical products has long been identified as one of the potential causes of poverty in developing countries.[1] Moreover, there is a cyclical relationship between poverty and poor health.[2] In relation to developing countries, the health challenges confronting them is exacerbated by the high incidence of both communicable and non-communicable diseases in these countries. According to the Joint United Nations Programme on HIV/AIDS (UNAIDS), as at 2019, it is estimated that about 7.5 million people live with human immunodeficiency virus (HIV) in South Africa[3] and around 1.5 million people live with the same disease in

[1] See Jayashree Watal, 'Access to Essential Medicines in Developing Countries: Does the WTO TRIPS Agreement Hinder It?' (2000) Science, Technology and Innovation Discussion Paper No. 8, Center for International Development, Harvard University, Cambridge, 2, available from www.iatp.org/files/Access_to_Essential_Medicines_in_Developing_Co.pdf (last accessed 21 September 2021), who notes that 'Expenditures on medicines can represent up to 66% of total health spending in developing countries and could be a major cause of household impoverishment, as 50–90% of such expenditures are out-of-pocket expenses.' For a global perspective on out-of-pocket on health generally, see Adam Wagstaff, Patrick Eozenou, and Marc Smitz, 'Out-of-Pocket Expenditures on Health: A Global Stocktake' (2020) 35(2) *The World Bank Research Observer* 123.

[2] See David H. Peters, Anu Garg, Gerry Bloom, Damian G. Walker, William R. Brieger, and M. Hazifur Rahman, 'Poverty and Access to Health Care in Developing Countries' (2008) 1136 *Annals of the New York Academy of Sciences* 161, who noted that, 'Although a lack of financial resources or information can create barriers to accessing services, the causal relationship between access to health services and poverty also runs in the other direction. When health care is needed but is delayed or not obtained, people's health worsens, which in turn leads to lost income and higher health care costs, both of which contribute to poverty … The relationship between poverty and access to health care can be seen as part of a larger cycle, where poverty leads to ill health and ill health maintains poverty.'

[3] UNAIDS, 'South Africa – HIV and AIDS Estimates (2019)', available from www.unaids.org/en/regionscountries/countries/southafrica (last accessed 21 September 2021).

Kenya.[4] Furthermore, in 2020, there were over 1.3 million new cases of cancer in India, over 100,000 new cases in South Africa, and over 42,000 new cases in Kenya.[5] These figures indicate that, in the years to come, poor patients in these and other developing countries will continue to require access to medicines at affordable prices in order to sustain a healthy and productive lifestyle.[6]

It is therefore imperative for the governments of these three developing countries (i.e., India, Kenya, and South Africa), and indeed for the governments of other developing countries facing similar health challenges, to take the necessary steps to facilitate access to medicines at affordable prices for their citizens. However, one crucial impediment that can hinder the ability of governments to make medicines affordable in their countries is the current global system for the protection of intellectual property rights as embodied in the World Trade Organization's (WTO) Agreement on Trade-Related Aspects of Intellectual Property Rights (TRIPS Agreement) which was signed in Marrakesh, Morocco, on 15 April 1994.[7] By making it mandatory for all WTO members (except the least developed countries) to grant patents on pharmaceutical products, the TRIPS Agreement has encroached on the policy space hitherto enjoyed by countries with regard to the design of their national patent laws.[8]

4 UNAIDS, 'Kenya – HIV and AIDS Estimates (2019)', available from www.unaids.org/en/regionscountries/countries/kenya (last accessed 21 September 2021).

5 See International Agency for Research on Cancer (Globocan 2020), 'India', available from https://gco.iarc.fr/today/data/factsheets/populations/356-india-fact-sheets.pdf (last accessed 21 September 2021); International Agency for Research on Cancer (Globocan 2020), 'South Africa', available from https://gco.iarc.fr/today/data/factsheets/populations/710-south-africa-fact-sheets.pdf (last accessed 21 September 2021); International Agency for Research on Cancer (Globocan 2020), 'Kenya', available from https://gco.iarc.fr/today/data/factsheets/populations/404-kenya-fact-sheets.pdf (last accessed 21 September 2021).

6 Writing in relation to cancer in developing countries, Ellen 't Hoen notes that: 'While death rates from cancer in wealthy countries are slightly declining because of early diagnosis and the availability of treatment, this is not the case in low- and middle-income countries. The rates are rising in low- and middle-income countries, partly because of the [ageing] of the population. Currently 14 million people a year are diagnosed with cancer. That will increase to 19 million by 2025, 22 million by 2030 and 24 million by 2035. More than 60 percent of the world's cancer cases occur in Africa, Asia, and Central and South America … In low- and middle-income countries, however, treatment for cancer is not widely available … Health systems are often unable to deal with cancer treatment. Prevention and early detection programmes are weak or non-existent. This situation is exacerbated by the lack of financing for healthcare and low health insurance and social security coverage … In certain cases, the high cost of treatment and in particular the high cost of cancer medication throws up additional barriers' (Ellen 't Hoen, 'Access to Cancer Treatment: A Study of Medicine Pricing Issues with Recommendations for Improving Access to Cancer Medication', Report Prepared for Oxfam (2015), 4, available from http://oxfamilibrary.openrepository.com/oxfam/handle/10546/344070 (last accessed 21 September 2021).)

7 Agreement on Trade Related Aspects of Intellectual Property (TRIPS) 1869 UNTS 299, 33 ILM 1197 (1994).

8 Article 27(1) of the TRIPS Agreement provides, *inter alia*, that 'patents shall be available for any inventions, whether products or processes, in all fields of technology, provided that they are new, involve an inventive step and are capable of industrial application'. The TRIPS Agreement provides for transition periods for developing and least-developed countries to implement the

Patent rights on pharmaceutical products can prevent the sale of patented drugs at competitive prices in the market and empowers the patent owner to sell its patented drug at exorbitant prices. The pricing of patented drugs beyond the reach of poor patients in developing countries can further impoverish poor patients in these countries and this invariably perpetuates the deadly cycle of poverty and ill health.[9] It should, however, be noted that, despite the strictures imposed by the current

Agreement. While developed countries were given one year, developing countries were given a period of five years after the entry into force of the Agreement (i.e., from 1995 till 2000) to implement the Agreement. See Article 65(2), TRIPS Agreement. However, developing countries that had no patent protection for pharmaceuticals were given a transition period of ten years from the entry into force of the Agreement to provide patent protection for pharmaceutical products (i.e. from 1995 till 2005). See Article 65(4), TRIPS Agreement. The transition periods for developing countries with regard to the general implementation of the TRIPS Agreement and the provision of patent protection for pharmaceutical products have since expired. Least-developed countries were initially given ten years to implement the TRIPS Agreement (Article 66(1) of the TRIPS Agreement), but this was later extended till 2013. See WTO Council for TRIPS, 'Extension of the Transition Period under Article 66.1 for Least Developed Country Members', Decision of the Council for TRIPS of 29 November 2005, IP/C/40 (30 November 2005). In June 2013, least-developed countries were granted a further extension till July 2021 with regards to the implementation of the TRIPS Agreement. See WTO Council for TRIPS, 'Extension of the Transition Period under Article 66.1 for Least Developed Country Members', Decision of the Council for TRIPS of 11 June 2013, IP/C/64 (12 June 2013). In July 2021, least-developed countries were granted a further extension till July 2034 with regard to the implementation of the TRIPS Agreement. See, WTO Council for TRIPS, 'Extension of the Transition Period under Article 66.1 for Least Developed Country Members', Decision of the Council for TRIPS of 29 June 2021, IP/C/88 (29 June 2021). In 2002, in a separate arrangement, least-developed countries were granted a further extension till 2016 with respect to the provision of patent protection for pharmaceutical products. See WTO Council for TRIPS, 'Extension of the Transition Period under Article 66.1 of the TRIPS Agreement for Least-Developed Country Members for Certain Obligations with Respect to Pharmaceutical Products', Decision of the Council for TRIPS of 27 June 2002 IP/C/25 (1 July 2002). Furthermore, in November 2015, least-developed countries were granted a further extension till January 2033 with regard to the provision of patent protection for pharmaceutical products. See WTO Council for TRIPS, 'Extension of the Transition Period under Article 66.1 of the TRIPS Agreement for Least Developed Country Members for Certain Obligations with Respect to Pharmaceutical Products', Decision of the Council for TRIPS of 6 November 2015, IP/C/73 (6 November 2015).

9 On the effect of patents on access to pharmaceutical products in developing countries see, Ellen F. M. 't Hoen, 'TRIPS, Pharmaceutical Patents and Access to Essential Medicines: Seattle, Doha and Beyond', in Jean-Paul Moatti, Tony Barnett, Benjamin Coriat, Yves Souteyrand, Jérome Dumoulin, and Yves-Antoine Flori (eds.), *Economics of AIDS and Access to HIV/AIDS Care in Developing Countries – Issues and Challenges* (ANRS, 2003), 39–57. See also Jean Lanjouw, 'A Patent Policy Proposal for Global Diseases', in Boris Pleskovic and Nicholas Stern (eds.), *Annual World Bank Conference on Development Economics 2001/2002* (World Bank and Oxford University Press, 2002), 193, who stated that '… in a poor country even a small price increase due to such a monopoly can greatly reduce the number of people able to purchase patented drugs and the welfare of those who do. This is particularly so since drug purchases in developing countries are largely paid for directly by consumers, without the benefit of insurance'. See further, Henry Grabowski, 'Patents, Innovation and Access to New Pharmaceuticals' (2002) 5 *Journal of International Economic Law* 849, 856, who stated that, 'In the case of patented drugs, their comparatively higher prices can serve as an additional barrier to many individuals in gaining access to the newest medicines.' But *cf.* Amir Attaran and Lee Gillespie-White, 'Do Patents for Antiretroviral Drugs Constrain Access to AIDS Treatment in Africa?' (2001) 286 *JAMA* 1886.

global regime on intellectual property rights, developing countries can still secure access to affordable medicines for their citizens by taking steps to preserve their patent policy space.

1.2 ACCESS TO MEDICINES AND PATENT POLICY SPACE

A very apt description of the term 'policy space' that approximates to a definition is provided by the United Nations Conference on Trade and Development (UNCTAD) in the Sao Paulo Consensus document of 2004.[10] In that document, UNCTAD describes 'policy space' as 'the space for national economic policy, i.e. the scope for domestic policies, especially in the area of trade, investment and industrial development'.[11] Policy space is the freedom that a country has to design its national policies, including intellectual property policy, in a manner that suits its needs and level of economic development.

According to Chang, developing countries experienced 'exceptional economic growth during the 1950s to the 1970s'.[12] During this period, developing countries enjoyed a wider policy space, unlike now.[13] This demonstrates the crucial importance of policy space to economic growth and development. However, between the 1980s and 2000s, there was a shrinkage of the policy space available for developing countries.[14] Several factors have been identified as being responsible for this shrinkage of policy space, including the conditionalities attached to the loans obtained from international financial institutions such as the World Bank and the IMF, the aid policies of developed countries, and the establishment of the WTO in 1995.[15]

10 See UNCTAD, 'Sao Paulo Consensus', UNCTAD TD/410 (25 June 2004).

11 Ibid., para 8.

12 Ha-Joon Chang, 'Policy Space in Historical Perspective with Special Reference to Trade and Industrial Policies' (2006) 41 *Economic and Political Weekly* 627, 629. As Chang points out, 'In the 1960s and the 1970s . . . per capita income in the developing world grew at 3 per cent, a rate two to three times higher than what was experienced by the developed countries in the 19th century during their industrial revolution (1–1.15 per cent). Some countries grew much faster than that . . . Per capita income in countries like Japan (then still a developing country by any reasonable definition), South Korea, Taiwan and Singapore grew at 5–6 per cent per year, doubling the income in 12–13 years . . .' (629–30).

13 Ibid., 629–30.

14 Ibid., 627. Providing a discussion of policy space from a historical perspective, Chang notes that '. . . the phenomenon of shrinking policy space is in fact not new. In the days of imperialism, the stronger countries were able to restrict the policy space of the weaker countries in the most blatant way . . . Therefore, it may be useful to look at the historical experiences in order to put the current debate on policy space in an appropriate historical context' (628).

15 Ibid., 627; Alisa DiCaprio and Kevin P. Gallagher, 'The WTO and the Shrinking of Development Space: How Big Is the Bite?' (2006) 7 *Journal of World Investment and Trade* 781, 785. See further, Sheila Page, 'Policy Space: Are WTO Rules Preventing Development?' Overseas Development Institute, Briefing Paper, (January 2007) 1, who notes that 'Perceived extensions to international rules and controls in the 1980s and 1990s included the new rules in the WTO: those on services; the new provisions on patents and copyright, under Trade Related Intellectual Property (TRIPS); and also the strengthened enforcement mechanism. But some

Even after the establishment of the WTO, developed countries have continued to utilize bilateral and regional free trade agreements to further constrain the ability of developing countries to utilize the policy space available to them within the WTO framework.[16] The globalization of neoliberal policies and the attendant shrinkage of policy space in recent decades has, however, not led to increased economic growth in a number of developing countries.[17] It is noteworthy that at the Summit of the Heads of State and Government of the Group of 77 (G77) held in Bolivia in June 2014, the developing countries adopted a declaration which, among other things, called for 'the international trading system to respect and reinforce the policy space of developing countries for the promotion and growth of [their] industrial development and for the design and implementation of [their] industrial strategies'.[18]

One particular area where there has been a significant shrinkage of policy space is the area of intellectual property (especially patent policy). Prior to the WTO's Agreement on Trade-Related Aspects of Intellectual Property Rights (TRIPS Agreement), countries (both developed and developing) enjoyed wide policy space with regard to intellectual property rights. Specifically, patent laws have always reflected the stage of technological and economic development of each country.[19] Importantly, the level of patent protection usually depended on whether the country was an innovator or an imitator.[20] It was during this period, prior to the emergence of the TRIPS Agreement, that countries like India were able to deny patent protection for pharmaceutical products, and this was one of the crucial factors that assisted

of the most significant threats were seen in proposals for a Multilateral Agreement on Investment, the environmental conventions, bilateral and regional agreements, and, particularly for indebted developing countries, the increased financial power of the World Bank and IMF.'

16 Chang, 'Policy Space in Historical Perspective', 628.

17 According to Chang, '... developing countries have been doing much worse in the last quarter of a century than they used to in the two decades ... during the 1960s and the 1970s ... Income distribution has worsened in the majority of developing countries, while poverty has increased in many of them. Neoliberal policies may not be totally responsible for such poor performance, but at the least we can say that those policies have failed to deliver their central promise of accelerated growth' (ibid., 630).

18 Declaration of the Summit of Heads of State and Government of the Group of 77, 'For a New World Order for Living Well' (Santa Cruz de la Sierra, Plurinational State of Bolivia, 14 and 15 June 2014), para 86, available from www.g77.org/doc/A-68-948(E).pdf (last accessed 21 September 2021).

19 As Shadlen notes, 'National patent regimes have traditionally reflected levels of economic development. Poorer countries, with fewer innovative capacities, have typically made private ownership of knowledge difficult to obtain, and, once granted, the property rights themselves tended to be weaker than in wealthier countries.' Kenneth C. Shadlen, 'Policy Space for Intellectual Property Management: Contrasting Multilateral and Regional-Bilateral Arrangements' (2008) 10 *Economica, Rio de Janeiro* 55, 56.

20 See also DiCaprio and Gallagher, 'The WTO and the Shrinking of Development Space', 789, who note that 'There are different dynamics between innovators and imitators. Innovators have to worry about how to appropriate returns on their R&D investment. Imitators, on the other hand, are concerned with profitably adapting and adopting different technologies.'

the growth of the Indian generic drugs industry.[21] In addition, countries such as Japan and South Korea also made productive use of the wide policy space available in the area of intellectual property law during this period to permit copying and assimilation of foreign patented technology, and this contributed to their growth and development.[22]

All these developments were possible because the Paris Convention for the Protection of Industrial Property of 1883 (Paris Convention),[23] which preceded the TRIPS Agreement, preserved the policy space of state parties in the field of patent law. Under the Paris Convention, countries were permitted to exclude any invention from patent protection, there was no fixed duration for patent rights, and (in comparison to the TRIPS Agreement) there were fewer restrictions on the grant of compulsory licences.

However, the TRIPS Agreement has significantly reduced the policy space that countries have in the area of intellectual property law.[24] Members of the WTO (except least-developed countries) are now required to design their intellectual property laws in accordance with the minimum standards stipulated in the TRIPS Agreement. For instance, prior to the TRIPS Agreement, more than 40 countries did not provide patent protection for pharmaceuticals and many countries provided only process patents but not product patents for pharmaceuticals.[25] This is however not possible anymore because WTO members (except least-developed countries) are forbidden from denying the grant of patent protection for pharmaceutical products by virtue of Article 27 of the TRIPS Agreement. Thus, the freedom hitherto enjoyed by countries to design their intellectual property laws in a manner that corresponds with their level of economic and technological development has been

[21] See, section 5 of the Indian Patents Act 1970. See also Jean O. Lanjouw, 'The Introduction of Pharmaceutical Product Patents in India: "Heartless Exploitation of the Poor and Suffering?"' (1998) NBER Working Paper 6366; Sudip Chaudhuri, *The WTO and India's Pharmaceuticals Industry: Patent Protection, TRIPS, and Developing Countries* (Oxford University Press, 2005).

[22] See Carlos M. Correa, 'Intellectual Property Rights and Inequalities in Health Outcomes', in Ronald Labonte, Ted Schrecker, Corinne Packer, and Vivien Runnels (eds.), *Globalization and Health: Pathway, Evidence and Policy* (Routledge, 2009), 265, who notes that, 'In fact, the most successful cases of industrial and technological development in recent history took place in a flexible framework of [intellectual property rights] protection, such as witnessed in Japan and Korea.'

[23] Paris Convention for the Protection of Industrial Property, 1883, as last revised at Stockholm in 1967 and as amended in 1979, 828 UNTS 305.

[24] See Shadlen, 'Policy Space for Intellectual Property Management', 56.

[25] See, WHO, 'Network for Monitoring the Impact of Globalization and TRIPS on Access to Medicines' (Health Economics and Drugs, EDM Series No. 11, WHO/EDM/PAR/2002.1, 2002) 15, available from https://apps.who.int/iris/bitstream/handle/10665/67194/WHO_EDM_PAR_2002.1.pdf (last accessed 21 September 2021). According to Correa, 'In many European countries (such as France, Germany, and Switzerland) that are proponents of strong patent protection today, pharmaceutical product patents were only recognized after the 1960s. Portugal, Spain, and the Nordic countries waited until the 1990s' (Correa, 'Intellectual Property Rights and Inequalities in Health Outcomes', 265).

significantly reduced. There has been a shrinkage of intellectual property policy space, including patent policy space.[26]

Though there has been shrinkage of policy space in the general area of intellectual property law, the focus of this book is on the shrinkage of patent policy space. Specifically, the focus is on the effects of the shrinkage of patent policy space on access to medicines in developing countries. It needs to be stressed, however, that, even though intellectual property policy space has been reduced, the TRIPS Agreement does not completely eliminate policy space in the area of intellectual property law.[27] Countries are still free to utilize the limited intellectual property policy space that still exists within the framework of the TRIPS Agreement.

In this regard, it is pertinent to note that the TRIPS Agreement contains certain flexibilities that countries can use to facilitate access to affordable medicines and address the health challenges in their countries. Such flexibilities include the freedom to exclude new forms of known drugs from patent protection, the freedom to adopt the principle of international exhaustion of patent rights to facilitate the parallel importation of drugs (Article 6), regulatory review exemption for producers of generic drugs, research exception, compulsory licences (Article 31), and delinking the grant of marketing approval for generic drugs from the patent status of branded drugs.

However, several developing countries have failed to utilize the available policy space (or flexibilities) in the TRIPS Agreement due to political and economic pressure from certain developed countries.[28] In addition, some developed countries have continued to take steps to ratchet up the current global standards on intellectual property rights through the use of bilateral and regional free trade agreements.[29]

[26] As Sheila Page notes, 'The introduction of rules on patents and copyright in the Uruguay Round was probably one of the most important sources of concern over policy space (and certainly was one of the first subjects where the words were used) . . . Policy space was indeed reduced: countries needed to change their rules . . .' (Page, 'Policy Space', 3)

[27] See Shadlen, 'Policy Space for Intellectual Property Management', 56.

[28] See, Rachel Hermann, 'Developing Countries Are Not Making the Most of TRIPS Flexibilities because of Political Pressure' (2011) 343 *British Medical Journal* d7706. It is also possible that some developing countries choose not to exploit the patent policy space available in the TRIPS Agreement due to a perceived need to preserve their international competitiveness. As noted by the United Nations Department of Economic and Social Affairs (UNDESA), '. . . Global competitive pressures tend to restrict a country's policy choices and often have an adverse effect on social development, since decisions or actions required to advance social policies and social equality are usually perceived as unnecessary costs. Put simply, social development policies are often mistakenly considered to be in conflict with the preservation of a country's international competitiveness . . . [E]xternal competitive pressures have restricted the ability of some countries to pursue certain aspects of social policy and have therefore undermined the progress of social development.' See UNDESA, '*Report on the World Situation: The Inequity Predicament*' (UNDESA, 2005), 106.

[29] See Meri Koivusalo, Ted Schrecker, and Ronald Labonte, 'Globalization and Policy Space for Health and Social Determinants of Health', in Ronald Labonte, Ted Schrecker, Corinne Packer, and Vivien Runnels (eds.), *Globalization and Health: Pathway, Evidence and Policy*

Developing countries need to muster the political will to preserve and utilize the existing policy space available to them under the TRIPS Agreement and steadfastly resist pressures to implement intellectual property standards that are incongruent with their current state of economic and technological development. In this regard, it is necessary to highlight some of the reasons why developing countries need to preserve their patent policy space.

Firstly, the current shrinkage of patent policy space affects the ability of developing countries to discharge their human rights obligations, especially their right to health obligations.[30] The right to health is recognized in several international instruments, including Article 12 of the International Covenant on Economic, Social and Cultural Rights (ICESCR).[31] One of the essential components of the right to health is access to essential medicines.[32] In General Comment No. 14 on Article 12, the UN Committee on Economic, Social, and Cultural Rights (CESCR) explained that state parties are obliged to respect, protect, and fulfil the right to health.[33] The CESCR further noted that one of the core obligations of state parties in relation to the right to health, from which no derogation is permissible,[34] is the provision of essential drugs.[35]

States who are parties to the ICESCR, including developing countries, therefore have an obligation to provide access to essential medicines for their citizens. But, as Carlos Correa rightly points out, the current global regime on intellectual property 'has increasingly limited the room left to countries to exercise their sovereign rights and discharge their obligations in public health, including those subsumed under

(Routledge, 2009), 108–9, who note that 'Bilateral and regional agreements, often between industrialized and developing countries, are increasing in number and importance, particularly as they generally go beyond requirements within WTO agreements. This is notably the case with respect to intellectual property rights.' See also Correa, 'Intellectual Property Rights and Inequalities in Health Outcomes', 264, who notes that 'Negotiating such agreements has allowed the United States to gain concessions on a bilateral basis that were unlikely to be reached in a multilateral framework where developing countries have become increasingly reluctant to support a further elevation of [intellectual property rights] standards.'

30 See Correa, 'Intellectual Property Rights and Inequalities in Health Outcomes', 263.

31 See also, The Constitution of the WHO (1946); The Universal Declaration of Human Rights, G.A. Res. 217A (III) (1948), Article 25.

32 See CESCR, 'General Comment No. 14, The Right to the Highest Attainable Standard of Health' E/C.12/2000/4 (2000), para 12; UN Human Rights Council, 'Access to Medicines in the Context of the Right of Everyone to the Enjoyment of the Highest Attainable Standard of Physical and Mental Health', A/HRC/RES/23/14 (2013).

33 CESCR, 'General Comment No. 14, para 33.

34 Ibid., para 47.

35 Ibid., para 43(d). According to the World Health Organization (WHO), essential drugs are drugs that 'satisfy the priority health care needs of the population' and 'are intended to be available within the context of functioning health systems at all times in adequate amounts ... and at a price the individual and the community can afford'. See, WHO, 'Essential Medicines', available from www.who.int/topics/essential_medicines/en/ (last accessed 21 September 2021).

the right to health'.[36] Patent rights have an impact on the enjoyment of the right to health, especially in developing countries where the monopoly rights conferred by patent law on producers of pharmaceutical products enable them to inflate the price of drugs[37] and prevent competition from producers of cheaper generic drugs. Thus, in order to fulfil their right to health obligations in relation to the provision of access to essential medicines, it is imperative for developing countries to preserve their patent policy space.[38] In this book, it will be contended that developing countries can preserve their patent policy space by incorporating a *model of human rights* into the design, implementation, interpretation, and enforcement of their national patent laws.

Secondly, the current global patent regime primarily serves as an incentive for the production of drugs for diseases affecting patients in rich countries.[39] Thus, developing countries need to think outside the 'patent box' in order to address the problems of neglected diseases affecting poor patients in their countries. The current global patent regime not only impedes access to essential medicines in developing countries, it also fails to incentivize the production of drugs for the treatment of diseases primarily affecting poor patients in developing countries. It could be argued that there would be no new drugs in the absence of patent rights. But this argument, as Sunder rightly points out, 'denies that patents are but one among many alternatives for stimulating and rewarding innovation, including prizes and subsidies. Furthermore, drug companies often benefit from enormous public investment,

[36] Correa, 'Intellectual Property Rights and Inequalities in Health Outcomes', 263. See also Philippe Cullet, 'Patents and Medicines: The Relationship between TRIPS and the Human Right to Health' (2003) 79 *International Affairs* 139, 160, who notes that, 'While states must endeavour as far as possible to reconcile their different international obligations, there seem to be some cases where the implementation of TRIPS directly implies a reduction in access to drugs and thus a step back in the implementation of the right to health. This appears to be unacceptable under the [ICESCR] Covenant and countries in this situation would be expected to give priority to their human rights obligations.'

[37] See Sarah Joseph, 'Trade and the Right to Health', in A. Clapham and M. Robinson (eds.), *Realizing the Right to Health*, Swiss Human Rights Book Series, Vol. 3 (Ruffer & Rub, 2009), 360.

[38] According to para 50 of General Comment No. 14, '…the adoption of laws or policies that interfere with the enjoyment of any of the components of the right to health; and the failure of the State to take into account its legal obligations regarding the right to health when entering into bilateral or multilateral agreements with other States, international organizations and other entities' constitute a violation of a country's obligation to respect the right to health. See CESCR, 'General Comment No. 14', para 50.

[39] Peter Drahos with John Braithwaite, *Information Feudalism: Who Owns the Knowledge Economy?* (Earthscan, 2002), 80, who note that, 'The patent system has not … stimulated the invention and production of the kind of drugs that developing countries need. Pharmaceutical companies carry out R&D in those markets where the returns are likely to be the greatest. This market rationality explains why only 1 per cent of the new chemical entities marketed between 1975 and 1997 related to tropical diseases.'

including basic research conducted in universities and research supported by non-profit foundations and governments.'[40]

Thirdly, encouraging the production of drugs for diseases primarily affecting patients in developing countries requires a lot more than the implementation of patent laws. Developing countries need to channel their limited funds into areas such as the training of local scientists and the funding of scientific research in their educational institutions. As Correa notes, 'in countries lacking capital and required scientific and technological infrastructure, patents operate as a levy collection mechanism and not as a stimulus of local R&D'.[41] In fact, high levels of patent protection can impede technological development in countries with lesser technical capacity because, as Sunder points out, 'patents may impede their ability to gain technical knowledge by copying more advanced industries abroad'.[42] The importance of investing in scientific research and technological infrastructure has been further highlighted by the current COVID-19 pandemic. Crucially, in the absence of domestic manufacturing capacity to produce the needed medicines and vaccines, most of the flexibilities available under the TRIPS Agreement are of no use to developing countries during pandemics such as COVID-19.

1.3 HISTORICAL BACKGROUND

1.3.1 *Patent Policy Space Prior to the TRIPS Agreement*

The globalization of patent law is inextricably and remotely linked with the growth of cross-border trade in the nineteenth century and the growing desire of inventors at that time to obtain patent protection for their inventions outside their own countries.[43] However, the immediate reasons for the globalization of patent law can be traced to the 1873 World Exposition in Vienna. American and German inventors refused to participate in the exposition due to fears that their inventions would not be adequately protected.[44] In order to allay the fears of the American and German inventors and encourage them to participate in the exposition, the Austrian

[40] Madhavi Sunder, *From Goods to a Good Life: Intellectual Property and Global Justice* (Yale University Press, 2012), 175.

[41] Correa, 'Intellectual Property Rights and Inequalities in Health Outcomes', 272.

[42] Sunder, *From Goods to a Good Life*, 176. Sunder further notes that, 'Simply put, the elusive promise of a patent will not spur the creation of new treatments if a country lacks technical know-how. Thus patents in the developing world not only inhibit technology transfer to poor countries; they also engender dependence on developed countries and their drug companies – companies that ... are not particularly interested in serving the populations of the developing world.'

[43] Holger Hestermeyer, *Human Rights and the WTO: The Case of Patents and Access to Medicines* (Oxford University Press, 2007), 33; Susan Sell, *Power and Ideas: North–South Politics of Intellectual Property and Antitrust* (State University of New York Press, 1998), 108.

[44] Christopher May and Susan Sell, *Intellectual Property Rights: A Critical History* (Lynne Rienner Publishers, 2006), 118; Hestermeyer, *Human Rights and the WTO*, 40.

government adopted a temporary law that provided protection for foreign inventors for the duration of the exposition.[45]

The Austrian government subsequently convened a conference in the same year with the objective of establishing a system where states would recognize and protect the rights of foreign inventors.[46] The venue for subsequent conferences on the establishment of an international patent system was Paris, where three conferences were held in 1878, 1880, and 1883. At the 1883 conference, the Paris Convention for the Protection of Industrial Property (covering patents, trademarks, and industrial designs) was approved and signed.[47] The Paris Convention is currently administered by the World Intellectual Property Organization (WIPO).[48] The Paris Convention has subsequently been revised in 1900 (Brussels), 1911 (Washington), 1925 (The Hague), 1934 (London), 1958 (Lisbon), and 1967 (Stockholm).[49]

The Paris Convention contains several provisions aimed at ensuring that inventors can obtain patent protection in multiple countries. For instance, the principle of national treatment is contained in Article 2(1) of the Paris Convention.[50] The principle of national treatment requires that all member states are to ensure that both citizens and foreigners enjoy the same level of patent protection and legal remedy against any infringement of their rights.[51] Thus, under the Paris Convention, a country is not permitted to grant patent protection for pharmaceutical products

45 May and Sell, *Intellectual Property Rights*, 118; Hestermeyer, *Human Rights and the WTO*, 40.

46 May and Sell, *Intellectual Property Rights*, 118–19; Hestermeyer, *Human Rights and the WTO*, 40.

47 May and Sell, *Intellectual Property Rights*, 119; Hestermeyer, *Human Rights and the WTO*, 40.

48 See WIPO, 'WIPO-Administered Treaties', available from www.wipo.int/treaties/en/ (last accessed 21 September 2021).

49 See WIPO, 'Paris Convention for the Protection of Industrial Property', available from www.wipo.int/treaties/en/text.jsp?file_id=288514 (last accessed 21 September 2021)

50 Article 2(1) of the Paris Convention states that 'Nationals of any country of the Union shall, as regards the protection of industrial property, enjoy in all the other countries of the Union the advantages that their respective laws now grant, or may hereafter grant, to nationals; all without prejudice to the rights specially provided for by this Convention. Consequently, they shall have the same protection as the latter, and the same legal remedy against any infringement of their rights, provided that the conditions and formalities imposed upon nationals are complied with.'

51 In his commentary on the Paris Convention, Bodenhausen (a former Director of the United International Bureaux for the Protection of Intellectual Property now known as the World Intellectual Property Organization) notes that 'the advantages which the nationals of the countries of the Union may claim in any other member country consist in the application, without any discrimination, of the national law as applied to nationals of the country itself . . . this means that no reciprocity of protection can be required by the States party to the Convention'. G. H. C. Bodenhausen, *Guide to the Application of the Paris Convention for the Protection of Industrial Property* (United International Bureaux for the Protection of Intellectual Property, 1969), 29. Dominique Guellec notes that the principle of national treatment was 'preferred to the principle of reciprocity (foreign residents would be treated in any country as foreigners are treated in their own country) favoured by the US'. Dominique Guellec, 'Historical Insights', in Dominique Guellec and Bruno van Pottelsberghe de la Potterie (eds.), *The Economics of the European Patent System: IP Policy for Innovation and Competition* (Oxford University Press, 2007), 25.

belonging to its citizens while refusing to grant the same protection to pharmaceutical products belonging to foreigners.

It needs to be stressed, however, that the Paris Convention does not really attempt to harmonize the substantive patent laws of the various member countries.[52] For instance, Article 4*bis* of the Paris Convention specifically provides that patents applied for in the various member states by nationals of the member states shall be independent of patents obtained for the same invention in other countries, whether or not those other countries are members of the Paris Convention.[53] In other words, even though an inventor obtains a patent on the same invention from two different countries, both patents may not necessarily last for the same duration. More importantly, this means that, under the Paris Convention, member states are free to specify their own grounds for nullifying a patent.[54]

The Paris Convention also contains provisions on compulsory licences. Article 5A (2)[55] of the Paris Convention provides that member states 'shall have the right to take legislative measures providing for the grant of compulsory licenses to prevent the abuses which might result from the exercise of the exclusive rights conferred by the patent, for example, failure to work'. Article 5A(2) of the Paris Convention thus permits member states to grant a compulsory licence in order to prevent a patentee from abusing his exclusive rights by, for instance, failing to work the patented invention in the country where the patent was granted. This provision therefore permits member states to incorporate 'local working requirements' into their patent law and deems the failure to work a patented invention as an abuse of a patent right.[56] However, the grant of a compulsory licence is circumscribed by the

[52] Hestermeyer, *Human Rights and the WTO*, 35.

[53] According to Bodenhausen, 'the principle of the mutual independence of patents obtained for the same invention in the various countries of the Union . . . was introduced into the Additional Act to the Convention adopted at the Revision Conference of Brussels in 1900 . . . The provision obliges the member States . . . to consider their patents independent of other patents for the same invention, even if those patents are granted in non-Member States' (Bodenhausen, *Guide to the Application of the Paris Convention*, 61–2).

[54] As Bodenhausen notes, 'the independence of patents granted for the same invention concerns their normal duration as well as the possibilities of earlier termination. Such possibilities exist not only in cases of forfeiture or nullity but also if prescribed fees for the maintenance of a patent are not paid' (ibid., 62).

[55] Commenting on the provisions of Article 5A of the Paris Convention, Bodenhausen notes that '. . . the original text of the Convention of 1883 only contained a provision stating that in the case of importation of patented articles . . . the patentee remained under the obligation to exploit his patent in accordance with the laws of the country into which he introduced the patented articles. The Revision Conference of Brussels in 1900 added a more general provision concerning the non-working of a patent: Article 2 of the Additional Act adopted in Brussels. This regulation was elaborated further by the following Revision Conferences of Washington (1911), The Hague (1925), London (1934) and Lisbon (1958) . . .' (ibid., 68).

[56] According to Bodenhausen, under the Paris Convention, 'The member States are also free to define what they understand by "failure to work." Normally, working a patent will be understood to mean working it industrially, namely, by manufacture of the patented product, or industrial application of a patented process. Thus, importation or sale of the patented article, or

provisions of Article 5A(4) of the Paris Convention which provides that a compulsory licence 'may not be applied for on the ground of failure to work or insufficient working before the expiration of a period of four years from the date of filing of the patent application or three years from the date of the grant of the patent, whichever period expires last . . .'. In addition, pursuant to the same Article 5A(4), a compulsory licence can be refused if the patentee justifies his inaction (i.e., failure to work or insufficient working) by legitimate reasons.

The Paris Convention does not attempt to supplant the substantive patent rules of member states, neither does it impose any minimum standards of patent protection on the member states. It is noteworthy that two of the original signatories to the Paris Convention, Switzerland and the Netherlands, did not have patent laws at the time they signed the Convention.[57] Furthermore, the Paris Convention permits member states to utilize compulsory licences to facilitate the transfer of technology[58] to their territories by ensuring that failure to work a patented invention constitutes a valid ground for encroaching on the exclusive rights granted to patentees. Thus, even though the Paris Convention created an easier path for inventors seeking to obtain patent protection for their inventions in multiple jurisdictions, it equally preserves the policy space of member states to design their patent laws to suit their domestic needs.

Compared to the current TRIPS Agreement, the Paris Convention is an extremely flexible agreement that imposes minor constraints on member states. There are at least six key flexibilities in the Paris Convention: one, freedom to determine the substantive criteria for granting patents; two, freedom to decide whether to exclude certain subject matter from patent protection; three, freedom to determine the duration of patent rights; four, freedom to grant compulsory licences for failure to work a patented invention within a country; five, freedom to

of the article manufactured by a patented process, will not normally be regarded as "working" the patent.' (ibid., 71).

57 See Ha-Joon Chang, 'Intellectual Property Rights and Economic Development: Historical Lessons and Emerging Issues' (2001) 2 *Journal of Human Development* 287, 292.

58 As Michael Halewood notes, 'Working requirements and compulsory licences are important mechanisms by which a patent granting country can compel foreign patentees to transfer technology to within its jurisdiction . . . [the local working requirement] has the effect of forcing foreign patentees to situate production facilities within the patent granting country. Such transfers of technology are desirable from the patent granting country's point of view because they contribute to a variety of public policy goals such as employment creation, industrial and technological capacity building, national balance of payments, and economic independence . . . In the absence of controls such as compulsory licensing and mandatory local working, patent granting countries are left in the unenviable position of having to trust that foreign patent holders will decide on the basis of their own self interests to transfer technology to within their jurisdictions.' See Michael Halewood, 'Regulating Patent Holders: Local Working Requirements and Compulsory Licences at International Law' (1997) 35 *Osgoode Hall Law Journal* 243, 245–6.

determine what constitutes failure to work a patented invention; and six, freedom to determine whether to grant compulsory licences in the public interest.[59]

1.3.2 *Attempts to Reclaim Patent Policy Space at the Multilateral Level*

The TRIPS Agreement mandates all the members of the WTO to provide minimum levels of protection for certain intellectual property rights, such as copyright and related rights, trademarks, patents, geographical indications, industrial designs, layout designs of integrated circuits, and undisclosed information. The provisions of the TRIPS Agreement that deal with patents are located in Articles 27–34. According to Article 27.1 of the TRIPS Agreement:

> ... patents shall be available for any inventions, whether products or processes, in all fields of technology, provided that they are new, involve an inventive step and are capable of industrial application ... [and] patents shall be available and patent rights enjoyable without discrimination as to the place of invention, the field of technology and whether products are imported or locally produced.

In other words, all forms of inventions are covered by this provision, including pharmaceutical products, once all the requirements for patentability are satisfied.[60] Thus, apart from the permissible exceptions contained in Articles 27.2 and 27.3,[61] the scope of patentable subject matter under the TRIPS Agreement is quite broad.

59 See Warren Landau, 'Multinational Corporations and Lesser Developed Countries – Foreign Investment, Transfer of Technology, and the Paris Convention: Caveat Investor' (1980) 5 *University of Dayton Law Review* 105, 149. See also Poku Adusei, *Patenting of Pharmaceuticals and Development in Sub-Saharan Africa: Laws, Institutions, Practices, and Politics* (Springer, 2013), 69, who notes that 'It is ... significant to point out that, in spite of the Paris Convention's pro-harmonization stance, it left issues of compulsory licensing to individual countries to legislate. Also the Paris Convention did not obligate its members to provide patent protection to pharmaceutical products ... These domestic flexibilities allowed a number of Paris Union-members to exclude pharmaceutical products and processes from patent protection in accordance with their public policy objectives to promote innovation and development. Specifically, until the 1970s and 1980s, a number of western countries including Switzerland, Japan, Canada, Italy, Germany, and Sweden did not grant patent protection to pharmaceutical products, albeit some protected pharmaceutical processes. Spain and Portugal declined to grant patents to pharmaceutical products until 1992.'

60 Hiroko Yamane, *Interpreting TRIPS: Globalisation of Intellectual Property Rights and Access to Medicines* (Hart, 2011), 164.

61 Article 27(2) & (3) of the TRIPS Agreement provides that:

(2) Members may exclude from patentability inventions, the prevention within their territory of the commercial exploitation of which is necessary to protect *ordre public* or morality, including to protect human, animal or plant life or health or to avoid serious prejudice to the environment, provided that such exclusion is not made merely because the exploitation is prohibited by their law.

(3) Members may also exclude from patentability:

(a) diagnostic, therapeutic and surgical methods for the treatment of humans or animals;

(b) plants and animals other than micro-organisms, and essentially biological processes for the production of plants or animals other than non-biological and microbiological processes.

Article 28 of the TRIPS Agreement confers on the patentee the exclusive rights to prevent third parties from making, using, offering for sale, selling, or importing the patented product without its consent. If the patent is on a process (as opposed to a product), the patentee has the exclusive right to prevent third parties from using the process without its consent, and from using, offering for sale, selling, or importing the product obtained directly by that process. Article 33 provides that the duration of a patent shall be at least 20 years from the filing date.

Even though the TRIPS Agreement has as one of its principles in Article 8.1 that 'members may, in formulating or amending their laws and regulations, adopt measures necessary to protect public health and nutrition', it soon became obvious to some developing countries (particularly Brazil and South Africa) that this may not necessarily be the case in practice. For instance, flexibilities that were not prohibited by the TRIPS Agreement and which could be used by developing countries to address public health challenges such as the local working requirements contained in Brazil's Industrial Property Law of 1996[62] and the provision on parallel importation of drugs introduced into South Africa's Medicines and Related Substances Control Act in 1997[63] were opposed by the United States and the pharmaceutical industry.[64]

However, Members shall provide for the protection of plant varieties either by patents or by an effective *sui generis* system or by any combination thereof. The provisions of this subparagraph shall be reviewed four years after the date of entry into force of the WTO Agreement.

62 Article 68 of the Brazilian Industrial Property Law of 1996 provides for the grant of a compulsory licence if a patentee exercises his rights in an abusive manner or engages in the abuse of economic power as determined by an administrative or judicial decision. One of the grounds for the grant of a compulsory licence in Brazil (as contained in Article 68(1)(I) of the Brazilian Industrial Property Law) is failure to satisfy the local working requirements.

63 In 1997, South Africa introduced a special regime for the parallel importation of medicines into the country via an amendment to the country's Medicines and Related Substances Control Act. According to Heinz Klug, 'the new government [of Nelson Mandela] published a national drug policy in January 1996. As a way of attacking the comparatively high cost of drugs in the South African market, the new policy promoted the use of generic drugs and suggested several ways to reduce unacceptably high retail prices, including allowing the state to facilitate the availability of affordable drugs in the private sector. It was that policy imperative that led to the passage of the Medicines and Related Substances Control Amendment Act in December 1997 ... with the aim of bringing down the cost of medicines.' Heinz Klug, 'Access to Medicines and the Transformation of the South African State: Exploring the Interactions of Legal and Policy Changes in Health, Intellectual Property, Trade, and Competition Law in the Context of South Africa's HIV/AIDS Pandemic' (2012) 37 *Law & Social Inquiry* 297, 312.

64 In 1998, thirty-nine pharmaceutical companies lodged a complaint at the Pretoria High Court in South Africa, alleging that the 1997 amendment to the Medicines and Related Substances Control Act was, *inter alia*, incompatible with the TRIPS Agreement. However, after significant public outcry by NGOs, the legal action was withdrawn. See, Haochen Sun, 'The Road to Doha and Beyond: Some Reflections on the TRIPS Agreement and Public Health' (2004)15 *European Journal of International Law* 123, 131. Furthermore, in 2000, the United States initiated dispute settlement proceedings in the WTO against Brazil because of the local working requirements contained in Article 68(1)(I) of the Brazilian Industrial Property Law. The dispute was, however, not resolved by the WTO as both countries reached a settlement

The opposition faced by Brazil and South Africa prompted other developing countries in 2001 to demand for a discussion on the relationship between intellectual property rights and access to medicines at the WTO Council for TRIPS (TRIPS Council). The developing countries wanted to clarify and confirm the flexibilities within the TRIPS Agreement that they could use to facilitate access to medicines in their countries. The first special discussion on intellectual property and access to medicines at the TRIPS Council was held during their meeting of 18–22 June 2001.[65]

During this special discussion, the African Group (a group composed of all African WTO members) proposed that there should be a special declaration on the TRIPS Agreement and access to medicines at the next WTO Ministerial Conference which was scheduled for November 2001.[66] They proposed that the special declaration should affirm that 'nothing in the TRIPS Agreement should prevent Members from taking measures to protect public health'.[67] The African Group also presented its own interpretation of certain key provisions in the TRIPS Agreement. The African Group adopted the position that 'each provision of the TRIPS Agreement should be interpreted in the light of the objectives and principles set forth in Articles 7 and 8' of the TRIPS Agreement.[68]

The least-developed countries (LDCs) also presented their own concerns about the TRIPS Agreement. Essentially, the LDCs were concerned about the implications of Article 31(f) of the TRIPS Agreement,[69] which states that compulsory licences can only be used 'predominantly for the supply of the domestic market of the Member'. This means that countries with insufficient or no local manufacturing capacity would not be able to use compulsory licences to import patented products in large quantities from other countries. Conversely, countries could not grant compulsory licences in order to export large quantities of patented products to other countries. Compulsory licences could only be granted for the 'predominant' purpose of supplying the domestic market of the country where the compulsory licence was granted. This foreclosed the option of granting compulsory licences on patented drugs for many LDCs that could not afford to locally manufacture patented drugs.

and the United States withdrew its claim in 2001. See WTO, 'Brazil – Measures Affecting Patent Protection – Request for Consultations by the United States,' WT/DS199/1, G/L/385, IP/D/23 (8 June 2000). See further, WTO, 'Brazil – Measures Affecting Patent Protection – Notification of Mutually Agreed Solution,' WT/DS199/4, G/L/454, IP/D/23/Add.1 (19 July 2001).

65 See WTO Council for TRIPS, 'Special Discussion on Intellectual Property and Access to Medicines', IP/C/M/31 (18–22 June 2001) (hereinafter: TRIPS Council, 'Special Discussion').

66 Ibid., 4.

67 Ibid.

68 Ibid.

69 Ibid., 29.

The second special discussion on intellectual property and access to medicines at the TRIPS Council was held during their meeting of 19–20 September 2001.[70] At this meeting, the African Group and other developing countries (including Brazil and India) presented the text of a draft WTO Ministerial Declaration on the TRIPS Agreement and public health.[71] A list of the fourteen demands made by the developing countries and contained in their Draft Ministerial Declaration is reproduced in Table 1.1.

It should be noted that some of these demands had already been addressed within the provisions of the TRIPS Agreement.[72] In other words, to satisfy some of the demands, it would not be necessary to amend the TRIPS Agreement.[73] However, some of the other demands do not concern issues specifically addressed by the TRIPS Agreement[74] and, in order to satisfy at least one of them that is, the fifth demand, an amendment to the TRIPS Agreement would be required.[75]

[70] WTO Council for TRIPS, 'Minutes of Meeting', IP/C/M/33 (19–20 September 2001).

[71] See WTO Council for TRIPS, Proposal by the African Group, Bangladesh, Barbados, Bolivia, Brazil, Cuba, Dominican Republic, Ecuador, Haiti, Honduras, India, Indonesia, Jamaica, Pakistan, Paraguay, Philippines, Peru, Sri Lanka, Thailand, and Venezuela, 'Ministerial Declaration on the TRIPS Agreement and Public Health' IP/C/W/312; WT/GC/W/450 (4 October 2001) (hereinafter, TRIPS Council, 'Ministerial Declaration on the TRIPS Agreement and Public Health' Proposal by the African Group and other Developing Countries).

[72] The first demand is addressed in Article 8.1, the second demand can be found in Article 6, the third demand is derived from Article 31, the fourth demand merely reproduces part of the provisions of Article 31(b), the sixth demand reproduces part of Article 31(k), and the eighth demand is arguably already addressed by Article 39.3.

[73] See John Odell and Susan Sell, 'Reframing the Issue: The WTO Coalition on Intellectual Property and Public Health, 2001', in John Odell (ed.), *Negotiating Trade: Developing Countries in the WTO and NAFTA* (Cambridge University Press, 2006), 99, who note that, 'The [developing countries] chose to aspire to a goal that [they] felt was feasible . . . There was some thought of attempting to amend TRIPS formally, perhaps article 8, 27 or 31. But this would have required ratification by national legislatures . . . If [they] had chosen a more radical negotiating objective for Doha, its gains might well have been smaller.'

[74] For instance, the seventh, tenth, eleventh, and fourteenth demands are not really issues that are addressed or required by the TRIPS Agreement.

[75] The ninth demand is interesting in this regard. Essentially, the ninth demand requires that Article 30 of the TRIPS Agreement be construed as permitting what is now being referred to in the academic literature as a 'manufacturing for export' exception to patent rights. Depending on how one interprets Article 30, this demand may or may not require an amendment to the TRIPS Agreement. For a recent scholarly debate on the 'manufacturing for export' exception, see Xavier Sueba, Luis Genovesi, and Pedro Roffe, 'A Manufacturing for Export Exception', in Bryan Mercurio and Daria Kim (eds.), *Contemporary Issues in Pharmaceutical Patent Law: Setting the Framework and Exploring Policy Options* (Routledge, 2017), 161; Eric Solovy and Deepak Raju, 'A Manufacturing-for-Export Exception to Patent Protection: A Proposal for Exporting Violations of the TRIPS Agreement and Beyond?' (2018) 13(1) *Journal of Intellectual Property Law & Practice* 68. The twelfth demand concerns the applicability of non-violation and situation complaints to disputes under the TRIPS Agreement, an issue on which WTO members have not yet reached any consensus. In this regard, see: WTO, '"Non-Violation' Complaints (Article 64.2)" available from www.wto.org/english/tratop_e/trips_e/nonviolation_e.htm (last accessed 21 September 2021); WTO, 'Non-Violation Complaints under the TRIPS Agreement,' Communication from the United States, IP/C/W/599, (10 June 2014); WTO, 'Non-

TABLE 1.1. *List of Demands made by Developing Countries in their Proposed Draft Ministerial Declaration*

1	Nothing in the TRIPS Agreement shall prevent Members from taking measures to protect public health.
2	Each Member retains the right to establish its own policy and rules regarding the exhaustion of intellectual property rights.
3	Each Member has the right to allow other use of the subject-matter of a patent without the authorization of the right holder, including use by the government or third parties authorized by the government, and to determine the grounds upon which such use is allowed.
4	In the case of a national emergency or other circumstances of extreme urgency or in cases of public non-commercial use, Members may grant compulsory licences without prior efforts on the part of the user to obtain authorization from the right holder.
5	A compulsory licence issued by a Member may be given effect by another Member. Such other Member may authorize a supplier within its territory to make and export the product covered by the licence predominantly for the supply of the domestic market of the Member granting the licence. Production and export under these conditions do not infringe the rights of the patent holder.
6	Members are not obliged to apply the conditions set forth in subparagraphs (b) and (f) of Article 31 of the TRIPS Agreement where use of the subject-matter of a patent is permitted to remedy a practice determined after judicial or administrative process to be anti-competitive.
7	Nothing in the TRIPS Agreement shall prevent Members from establishing or maintaining marketing approval procedures for generic medicines and other healthcare products, or applying summary or abbreviated marketing approval procedures based on marketing approvals granted earlier for equivalent products.
8	Nothing in the TRIPS Agreement shall prevent Members from disclosing or using information held by its authorities or the patent holder where it is so required for reasons of public interest, including where such disclosure or use is necessary to implement effectively any compulsory licences or other measures adopted by public authorities in the public interest.
9	Under Article 30 of the TRIPS Agreement, Members may, among others, authorize the production and export of medicines by persons other than holders of patents on those medicines to address public health needs in importing Members.
10	Each Member shall, within or beyond the framework of the WTO, refrain from imposing or threatening to impose sanctions and refrain from employing the grant of incentives or other benefits in a manner which could curtail the ability of developing and least-developed country Members to avail themselves of every possible policy option to protect and promote public health.
11	Members shall exercise utmost restraint in initiating and pursuing dispute settlement proceedings relating to measures adopted or implemented, particularly by developing and least-developed country Members, to protect and promote public health.
12	In its examination of the scope and modalities for the possible application of subparagraphs 1(b) and 1(c) of Article XXIII of GATT 1994 to the settlement of disputes under the TRIPS Agreement, and without prejudice to recommendations that the

Council for TRIPS may adopt and submit to the Ministerial Conference on other relevant aspects, in no event shall such subparagraphs be rendered applicable to measures adopted and implemented by Members, particularly developing and least-developed country Members, to protect and promote public health.

13 In view of the special needs and requirements of developing and least-developed country Members, their economic, financial and administrative constraints, and their need for flexibility to create a viable technological base, the transition period provided for their benefit under Articles 65.4 and 66.1 of the TRIPS Agreement shall be extended for another period of five (5) years from the expiration of the transition periods provided thereunder, particularly in respect of the obligation to render available patent protection on products or processes relating to public health, without prejudice to further extensions.

14 The TRIPS Council shall monitor and evaluate on an ongoing basis, in collaboration with relevant international organizations, the effects of the TRIPS Agreement on health, with particular emphasis on access to medicines and research and development on medicines for the prevention and treatment of diseases predominantly affecting people in developing and least-developed countries.

The 'Doha Declaration on the TRIPS Agreement and Public Health' (Doha Declaration)[76] was adopted at the WTO Ministerial Conference on 14 November 2001 and addressed only some of the demands of developing countries. The seven paragraphs contained in the Doha Declaration are reproduced in Table 1.2.

When compared with the original fourteen demands made by developing countries in their proposed Draft Ministerial Declaration, the Doha Declaration can only really be regarded as a modest achievement, at least from the perspective of developing countries. Crucially, out of the fourteen demands made by developing countries, only the first to fifth and thirteenth demands were addressed by the Doha Declaration. Also, even with regard to the thirteenth demand, only the aspect of that demand that involved least-developed countries was addressed by the Doha Declaration. The remaining eight demands made by developing countries were

Violation and Situation Nullification or Impairment under the TRIPS Agreement,' Communication from Argentina and others, IP/C/W/385/Rev.1, (27 May 2015); Nirmalya Syam, 'Non-Violation and Situation Complaints under the TRIPS Agreement Implications for Developing Countries' South Centre Research Paper No. 109 (May 2020). Moreover, the thirteenth demand is a request for an extension of the transition periods available to both developing countries and least-developed countries under the TRIPS Agreement. In this regard, while Article 66.1 of the TRIPS Agreement already envisages that least-developed countries can request for extensions of their transition periods, Article 65 does not provide for such requests for extensions by developing countries. Thus, to meet this demand, at least as it relates to developing countries, an amendment to the TRIPS Agreement would have been required.

76 See WTO Ministerial Conference, 'Declaration on the TRIPS Agreement and Public Health', Adopted on 14 November 2001, WT/MIN(01)/DEC/2 (20 November 2001). This book takes the view that, regardless of its legal status, the Doha Declaration is relevant to both the interpretation and implementation of the TRIPS Agreement.

TABLE 1.2. *Doha Declaration on the TRIPS Agreement and Public Health*

1	We recognize the gravity of the public health problems afflicting many developing and least-developed countries, especially those resulting from HIV/AIDS, tuberculosis, malaria, and other epidemics.
2	We stress the need for the WTO Agreement on Trade-Related Aspects of Intellectual Property Rights (TRIPS Agreement) to be part of the wider national and international action to address these problems.
3	We recognize that intellectual property protection is important for the development of new medicines. We also recognize the concerns about its effects on prices.
4	We agree that the TRIPS Agreement does not and should not prevent members from taking measures to protect public health. Accordingly, while reiterating our commitment to the TRIPS Agreement, we affirm that the Agreement can and should be interpreted and implemented in a manner supportive of WTO members' right to protect public health and, in particular, to promote access to medicines for all. In this connection, we reaffirm the right of WTO members to use, to the full, the provisions in the TRIPS Agreement, which provide flexibility for this purpose.
5	Accordingly and in the light of paragraph 4 above, while maintaining our commitments in the TRIPS Agreement, we recognize that these flexibilities include: a. In applying the customary rules of interpretation of public international law, each provision of the TRIPS Agreement shall be read in the light of the object and purpose of the Agreement as expressed, in particular, in its objectives and principles. b. Each member has the right to grant compulsory licences and the freedom to determine the grounds upon which such licences are granted. c. Each member has the right to determine what constitutes a national emergency or other circumstances of extreme urgency, it being understood that public health crises, including those relating to HIV/AIDS, tuberculosis, malaria, and other epidemics can represent a national emergency or other circumstances of extreme urgency. d. The effect of the provisions in the TRIPS Agreement that are relevant to the exhaustion of intellectual property rights is to leave each member free to establish its own regime for such exhaustion without challenge, subject to the MFN and national treatment provisions of Articles 3 and 4.
6	We recognize that WTO members with insufficient or no manufacturing capacities in the pharmaceutical sector could face difficulties in making effective use of compulsory licensing under the TRIPS Agreement. We instruct the Council for TRIPS to find an expeditious solution to this problem and to report to the General Council before the end of 2002.
7	We reaffirm the commitment of developed-country members to provide incentives to their enterprises and institutions to promote and encourage technology transfer to least-developed country members pursuant to Article 66.2. We also agree that the least-developed country members will not be obliged, with respect to pharmaceutical products, to implement or apply Sections 5 and 7 of Part II of the TRIPS Agreement or to enforce rights provided for under these Sections until 1 January 2016, without prejudice to the right of least-developed country members to seek other extensions of the transition periods as provided for in Article 66.1 of the TRIPS Agreement. We instruct the Council for TRIPS to take the necessary action to give effect to this pursuant to Article 66.1 of the TRIPS Agreement.

not addressed by the Doha Declaration. What follows is an analysis of how the Doha Declaration responded to those demands that were addressed in the Declaration. In this regard, the focus will be on the first to fifth demands contained in the proposed Draft Ministerial Declaration submitted by the developing countries prior to the adoption of the Doha Declaration.

Concerning the first demand, paragraph 4 of the Doha Declaration provides that:

> the TRIPS Agreement does not and should not prevent members from taking measures to protect public health. Accordingly ... the Agreement can and should be interpreted and implemented in a manner supportive of WTO members' right to protect public health and, in particular, to promote access to medicines for all.

Paragraph 4 further affirms the right of WTO Members to use, to the full, the flexibilities in the TRIPS Agreement. In addition, paragraph 5(a) of the Doha Declaration states that 'each provision of the TRIPS Agreement shall be read in the light of the object and purpose of the Agreement as expressed, in particular, in its objectives [Article 7] and principles [Article 8]'.

One unique feature of paragraph 4 of the Doha Declaration is that it contains a statement that the TRIPS Agreement 'should be interpreted and implemented in a manner supportive of WTO Members' right to protect public health and, in particular, to promote access to medicines for all'. As noted in Section 1.2, one of the essential components of the right to health is access to essential medicines.[77] It was further noted in Section 1.2 that one of the core obligations of state parties in relation to the right to health, from which no derogation is permissible,[78] is the provision of essential drugs.[79]

Paragraph 4 of the Doha Declaration therefore goes one step further than Article 8.1 of the TRIPS Agreement, which states that WTO members 'may, in formulating or amending their laws and regulations, adopt measures necessary to protect public health and nutrition' without mentioning the need to promote access to medicines. By providing that the TRIPS Agreement should be interpreted and implemented in a manner supportive of the right of countries to promote access to medicines, paragraph 4 of the Doha Declaration therefore permits WTO members to incorporate a right to health perspective into the interpretation and implementation of the TRIPS Agreement at the national level. This is because access to medicines is an integral component of the right to health, and the promotion and provision of access to essential medicines is a non-derogable obligation for countries that are parties to the ICESCR.

Concerning the second demand, paragraph 5(d) of the Doha Declaration states that the 'effect of the provisions in the TRIPS Agreement that are relevant to the

77 See CESCR, 'General Comment No. 14', para 12; UN Human Rights Council, 'Access to Medicines in the Context of the Right of Everyone to the Enjoyment of the Highest Attainable Standard of Physical and Mental Health', A/HRC/RES/23/14 (2013).

78 CESCR, 'General Comment No. 14', para 47.

79 Ibid., para 43(d).

exhaustion of intellectual property rights is to leave each Member free to establish its own regime for such exhaustion without challenge'. The Doha Declaration therefore affirms the right of countries to engage in parallel importation. With regard to the third demand, paragraph 5(b) of the Doha Declaration provides that each member 'has the right to grant compulsory licences and the freedom to determine the grounds upon which such licences are granted'. Thus, the Doha Declaration supports the view that countries can, for instance, grant compulsory licences on the grounds of the failure of a patentee to satisfy local working requirements.

In relation to the fourth demand, while the Doha Declaration does not directly address the question about whether countries should obtain prior authorization from a patentee before issuing a compulsory licence in an emergency situation, a combined reading of paragraphs 4, 5(a), and 5(c) of the Declaration reveals that it affirms the waiver contained in Article 31(b) of the TRIPS Agreement. Article 31(b) provides that countries need not seek authorization from a patentee before issuing a compulsory licence during an emergency or other circumstances of extreme urgency or in cases of public non-commercial use. Since paragraph 4 of the Doha Declaration affirms the right of countries to use to the full the flexibilities contained in the TRIPS Agreement, the Doha Declaration therefore affirms the waiver contained in Article 31(b) with respect to emergency situations. Furthermore, paragraph 5(c) of the Doha Declaration provides that each country 'has the right to determine what constitutes a national emergency or other circumstances of extreme urgency, it being understood that public health crises, including those relating to HIV/AIDS, tuberculosis, malaria and other epidemics, can represent a national emergency or other circumstances of extreme urgency'. Thus, for the purposes of applying the waiver in Article 31(b), countries are free to define what they deem to be an emergency, which can cover all types of crises from natural disasters to epidemics.

However, these first four demands have already been addressed by the TRIPS Agreement and, in this regard, the Doha Declaration merely confirms the provisions of the TRIPS Agreement. The only exception in this regard is the unique statement in paragraph 4 of the Doha Declaration that the TRIPS Agreement should be interpreted and implemented in a manner that supports the right of countries to promote access to medicines.

The fifth demand is addressed by paragraph 6 of the Doha Declaration. Paragraph 6 of the Doha Declaration acknowledges that WTO members with insufficient or no manufacturing capacities in the pharmaceutical sector could face real difficulties in making effective use of compulsory licences under the TRIPS Agreement. The TRIPS Council was therefore directed to find a solution to this problem and report back before the end of 2002. But it was not until 2003 that the WTO General Council adopted a decision that waived the requirements of Article 31(f) and permitted member countries to export drugs manufactured under compulsory licenses to countries that lacked local capacity to produce such drugs[80] This became known as the 'Paragraph 6 Solution' after paragraph 6 of the Doha Declaration.[81] Thus, in a hypothetical scenario, country A (a country with insufficient or no domestic capacity to manufacture pharmaceutical products) can obtain essential drugs through a compulsory licence that allows importation from country B (a country with sufficient manufacturing capabilities).[82]

The waiver under the 'Paragraph 6 Solution' was subsequently codified as an amendment to the TRIPS Agreement and it is contained in Article 31*bis* of the Agreement.[83] However, there are strenuous requirements that must be satisfied before this waiver can be used. There are onerous requirements on eligibility, notification, and provision of safeguards to prevent diversion of the drugs to other countries.[84] There are different requirements to be fulfilled by the importing country and the exporting country. Thus, this waiver has failed to achieve its aim as it has only been used once by Canada to supply anti-retroviral drugs to Rwanda. This failure can be blamed on the cumbersome procedures that countries are required to follow before they can utilize the waiver.[85]

Thus, the attempt made by developing countries to re-shape the TRIPS Agreement and reclaim some patent policy space only yielded marginal gains in the form of the confirmation of the flexibilities that are already contained in the TRIPS Agreement and the introduction of a waiver system that is more burdensome and less beneficial to both developing and least-developed countries. The experience of developing countries with regard to their attempt to re-shape the TRIPS Agreement demonstrates how difficult it is for developing countries to re-shape the global patent system at the multilateral level. Apart from the fact that it is quite difficult for developing countries to re-shape the global patent law system at the

80 WTO General Council, 'Implementation of Paragraph 6 of the Doha Declaration on the TRIPS Agreement and Public Health', Decision of the General Council of 30 August 2003, WT/L/540 and Corr. 1 (1 September 2003) (Hereinafter, August 2003 Decision).

81 Marla L. Mellino, 'The TRIPS Agreement: Helping or Hurting Least Developed Countries' Access to Essential Pharmaceuticals?' (2010) 20 *Fordham Intellectual Property, Media & Entertainment Law Journal* 1349, 1362.

82 Ibid.

83 This amendment to the TRIPS Agreement entered into force on 23 January 2017 after its ratification by two-thirds of WTO members.

84 See K. M. Gopakumar, 'The WTO Deal on Cheap Drugs: A Critique' (2004) 7 *The Journal of World Intellectual Property* 99.

85 See Peter Drahos, 'Four Lessons for Developing Countries from the Trade Negotiations over Access to Medicines' (2007) 28 *Liverpool Law Review* 11, 13; Erin M. Anderson, 'Unnecessary Deaths and Unnecessary Costs: Getting Patented Drugs to Patients Most in Need' (2009) 29 *Boston College Third World Law Journal* 85; Brook K. Baker, 'Arthritic Flexibilities for Accessing Medicines: Analysis of WTO Action Regarding Paragraph 6 of the Doha Declaration on the TRIPS Agreement and Public Health' (2004) 14 *Indiana International Comparative Law Review* 613; Muhammad Zaheer Abbas and Shamreeza Riaz, 'Compulsory Licensing and Access to Medicines: TRIPS Amendment Allows Export to Least-Developed Countries' (2017) 12(6) *Journal of Intellectual Property Law and Practice* 451.

multilateral level, developed countries have continued to ratchet up the global patent law standards through the extensive use of bilateral and plurilateral trade agreements.

Nevertheless, the statement contained in paragraph 4 of the Doha Declaration to the effect that the TRIPS Agreement should be interpreted and implemented in a manner that supports the right of countries to promote access to medicines offers an avenue for developing countries to preserve their patent policy space. In other words, paragraph 4 of the Doha Declaration provides a linchpin that developing countries can use to preserve their patent policy space as it sanctions the incorporation of a right to health perspective, and invariably the incorporation of a *model of human rights*, into the design, implementation, interpretation, and enforcement of their national patent laws. How developing countries can preserve their patent policy space and secure access to affordable medicines through the incorporation of a *model of human rights*, and more specifically through the incorporation of a right to health perspective, into their national patent law framework is therefore the central focus of this book.

1.4 THE ROADMAP FOR THE REST OF THE BOOK

Flowing from the analysis above, this book answers two key questions: (1) How should the relationship between patent rights and human rights be conceptualized? (2) In resolving the tension between patent rights and the right to health and in trying to discharge their right to health responsibilities, what should inform the design, implementation, interpretation, and enforcement of patent rights by the organs of the state in developing countries? In answering these two key questions, this book adopts a combination of methodologies. Thus, the book adopts a socio-centric view of intellectual property rights and a human rights framework in answering these two basic questions.

This book contends that, while inventions are usually understood from a creator-centric perspective, inventions should be properly approached from a socio-centric perspective because inventors usually draw and build on the efforts of other members of society. Thus, properly construed, patent law should be viewed from a socio-centric perspective, and this should inform the design, interpretation, and enforcement of patent rights.

This book examines how three select developing countries (i.e., India, Kenya, and South Africa) have reacted to the impact of the TRIPS Agreement on access to medicines in their countries. Essentially, the book examines how these countries have addressed the tension between patent rights and the right to health in their respective jurisdictions. These countries have been selected for analysis primarily because they all face, in varying degrees, similar challenges with regard to facilitating access to affordable medicines. Furthermore, all these three countries are members of the WTO and are thus obligated to provide patent protection for pharmaceutical products. In addition, the right to health is a justiciable right in all three countries. Thus, these three countries serve as ideal jurisdictions for the purposes of investigating how developing countries can address the tension between patent rights and the right to health in the design, implementation, interpretation, and enforcement of their patent laws.[86]

Importantly, the three selected countries are key actors in their respective regions of the world, and one of them (i.e., India) is a key actor at the global level. India is considered as the 'pharmacy of the developing world' because of its strong generic drug industry.[87] Kenya is a key actor in eastern Africa[88] and South Africa is a key actor in Africa.[89] While it is true that there are other countries that equally have to confront the tension between patent rights and human rights in their attempts to facilitate access to medicines,[90] factors such as language barriers, and constraints of time and space render it impracticable to include these countries within the scope of this book. Furthermore, this book adopts the view that it is preferable to conduct in-depth case-studies on three key countries with a view to distilling key principles that can be of general application to all the developing countries confronted with the tension between patent rights and human rights instead of engaging in a cursory overview of the laws and court decisions from a large number of countries.

With regard to the application of a human rights framework in answering the two key questions outlined above, as Yamin notes, '[t]o assert that health is an issue of rights is to assert that the state and other actors bear some responsibility in ensuring fair distributions of the social determinants of health as well as availability and access

86 This naturally excludes countries where there is no justiciable right to health from the scope of this book. See generally, Colleen M. Flood and Aeyal Gross, 'Litigating the Right to Health: What Can We Learn from a Comparative Law and Health Care Systems Approach' (2014) 16 (2) *Health and Human Rights Journal* 62, 68–9.

87 See Simon Reid-Henry and Hans Lofgren, 'Pharmaceutical Companies Putting Health of World's Poor at Risk' *The Guardian* (26 July 2012), available from www.theguardian.com/global-development/poverty-matters/2012/jul/26/pharmaceutical-companies-health-worlds-poor-risk (last accessed 22 September 2021), who state that 'India is often called the pharmacy of the developing world ... as more than 50% of its $10bn annual generic medicine production is exported.'

88 See Jon Rosen, 'Strategic Posture Review: Kenya' (World Politics Review, 21 January 2014), available from www.worldpoliticsreview.com/articles/13509/strategic-posture-review-kenya (last accessed 22 September 2021), describing Kenya as 'East Africa's most significant diplomatic and economic actor'.

89 See Romy Chevallier, 'South Africa: An International Actor and Partner for the EU' (*South African Institute of International Affairs*, 24 July 2008), available from www.saiia.org.za/opinion-analysis/south-africa-an-international-actor-and-partner-for-the-eu (last accessed 22 September 2021).

90 See generally, H. Brennan, R. Distler, M. Hinman, and A. Rogers, 'A Human Rights Approach to Intellectual Property and Access to Medicines' Global Health Justice Partnership Policy Paper 1, Yale Law School and Yale School of Public Health (September 2013), discussing, *inter alia*, court cases that deal with patent rights and access to medicines from countries such as Chile, India, Colombia, South Africa, Argentina, Kenya, Peru, and Thailand.

to care.'[91] Yamin further contends that, in applying a human rights framework to health, 'our starting point should be to take suffering seriously' because doing so will challenge us 'to reconfigure our approaches to both health and rights'.[92] Jochnick contends that

> [t]he real potential of human rights lies in its ability to change the way people perceive themselves *vis-à-vis* the government and other actors. Rights rhetoric provides a mechanism for reanalysing and renaming 'problems' as 'violations', and, as such, something that need not and should not be tolerated . . . Rights make it clear that violations are neither inevitable nor natural, but arise from deliberate decisions and policies.[93]

The application of a human rights framework to health helps to define the relationship between rights-holders and duty bearers and it equally enables the establishment of mechanisms of accountability.[94]

Applying a human rights framework to health compels us to challenge our narrow conception of health as the mere absence of disease or infirmity; it compels us to shift from the biomedical paradigm to a broader paradigm that understands health in the social, political, historical, and economic contexts in which people live.[95] In addition, applying a human rights framework to health equally compels us to challenge our narrow conception of rights; it challenges us to move away from a narrow conception of rights to a broader perspective.[96] This book therefore agrees

91 Alicia E. Yamin, 'Will We Take Suffering Seriously? Reflections on What Applying a Human Rights Framework to Health Means and Why We Should Care' (2008) 10 (1) *Health and Human Rights* 45.

92 Ibid., 46.

93 Chris Jochnick, 'Confronting the Impunity of Non-State Actors: New Fields for the Promotion of Human Rights' (1999) 21 *Human Rights Quarterly* 56, 60.

94 Yamin, 'Will We Take Suffering Seriously?', 49.

95 Ibid., 47. As Yamin notes, 'The biomedical paradigm is so entrenched in both research and training of physicians and other health professionals, as well as in public discourse about health, that it is widely taken for granted . . . [T]he two facets of this paradigm . . . can be summarized as follows: first, health and disease are defined by experts as scientifically and objectively ascertainable in isolation from the broader context in which people live; and, second, the judgments prescribed by those experts come to instantiate a truth that is beyond question by either individual patients or by the public in general . . . In contrast, rights-based approaches present a more fundamental critique of this paradigm's portrayal of reality . . . in a rights framework, health is produced, experienced, and understood in the social, political, historical, and economic contexts in which we live. This perspective forces us to see the suffering that is not the result of "natural" biological causes but rather stems from human choices about policies, priorities, and cultural norms, about how we treat each other and what we owe each other.'

96 As Yamin contends, 'Despite impressive advances in clarifying the content of the right to health as well as other economic, social, and cultural rights (ESC rights) under positive international law, narrow conceptions of rights continue to be reflected in public discourse and underpin neoliberal paradigms of economic development and globalization. Such restricted conceptions of rights are far from emancipatory for . . . "the destitute sick." Using rights to advance the health of impoverished and marginalized peoples around the world requires more than

with Barratt that it is impossible to resolve the tension between patent rights and access to medicines by relying only on the internal principles contained in intellectual property law and that the best way to resolve this tension is by utilizing the norms contained in the human rights system.[97] This book therefore contends that developing countries should incorporate a *model of human rights* into the design, implementation, interpretation, and enforcement of their national patent laws.

As noted in Section 1.3, countries are permitted to incorporate a *model of human rights* into their national patent law system because paragraph 4 of the Doha Declaration provides that the TRIPS Agreement can and should be interpreted and implemented in a manner that supports the right of countries to promote access to medicines. At this point, it is helpful to examine the views expressed by WTO members about the nature of the relationship between patent rights and the human right to health during the discussions that preceded the emergence of the Doha Declaration. This should provide a better understanding of the unique statement in paragraph 4 of the Doha Declaration that the TRIPS Agreement should be interpreted and implemented in a manner that supports the right of countries to promote access to medicines.

During the first special discussion on intellectual property and access to medicines at the TRIPS Council that was held on 18–22 June 2001, the Indian delegation stated that 'affordable access to medicines for what are life-threatening diseases for people in developing countries is a fundamental human right'.[98] The Indian delegation further noted that the 'governments in these countries therefore have a duty and responsibility to ensure both availability and affordable prices for medicines'.[99] The relationship between access to medicines, the human right to health, and patent rights was further explored by the Kenyan delegation in its statement thus:

> [P]harmaceutical products cannot be regarded as ordinary goods or products, because access to essential, life-saving and vitally needed drugs are an integral part of the realization of a fundamental human right, i.e. the right to health. It means that policies pursued by all concerned in the sector must aim to make drugs available for all who need to have them and at affordable prices. Patents affect prices by creating market monopolies, greatly hindering access to the patented products by those who need them, predominantly poor people who lack health insurance. Price is a key factor to health delivery, and it becomes to us a health

reference to positive norms; it also demands critiquing and expanding limited understandings of rights in theory and practice. Implicitly, doing so also requires challenging underlying premises about justice and power' (ibid., 46).

97 See Amanda Barratt, 'The Curious Absence of Human Rights: Can the WIPO Development Agenda Transform Intellectual Property Negotiation?' (2010) 14 *Law, Democracy & Development* 14, 24.

98 TRIPS Council, 'Special Discussion', 21.

99 Ibid.

> concern when it impedes access to health care. This special impediment must be overcome as a priority in order to reverse the human suffering we are faced with.[100]

The relationship between access to medicines, the human right to health, and patent rights was equally emphasized by other developing countries from Latin America, Asia, and Africa.[101] However, it needs to be stressed that, during these discussions that preceded the Doha Declaration, developing countries did not seem to make any clear demand that the nature of the relationship between access to medicines, patent rights, and human rights should be clarified. Nevertheless, it is significant to note that the concerns expressed by these countries about how patent rights under the TRIPS Agreement should be interpreted and implemented is reflected in paragraph 4 of the Doha Declaration. Thus, the statement in paragraph 4 of the Doha Declaration that the TRIPS Agreement 'can and should be interpreted and implemented in a manner supportive of WTO members' right ... to promote access to medicines for all' can be construed as a response to the concerns expressed by developing countries about the impact of patent rights on access to medicines and the human right to health.

Thus, the overriding question remains this, why is it crucial for developing countries to incorporate a *model of human rights* into their national patent law

[100] Ibid., 54.

[101] See the statements by Venezuela (ibid., 14), noting that 'When some countries' interpretation of a failure to observe patent rights leads them to claim violation of the TRIPS Agreement, they are not taking into consideration the fact that developing countries are entitled to take the necessary measures to promote and protect health pursuant to Articles 2 and 12 of the International Covenant on Economic, Social and Cultural Rights and the [Universal] Declaration of Human Rights.'; Bolivia (ibid., 31), noting that 'It should be recalled in this connection that access to medicines is a public health priority which prevails over purely commercial considerations in that it is one of the human rights, i.e. the right to health.'; Cuba (ibid., 51), noting that 'Ongoing research into new medicines for both longstanding and new diseases must not be the cause of, or effectively result in, the side-lining of the most sacred of all human rights, the right to life ...'; Ecuador (ibid., 59), noting that '... Ecuador repeats that it considers health to be a basic human right which must be recognized and applied without any conditions or limitations. In other words, the protection of the right to health cannot be made contingent on the protection of intellectual property rights or, to put it another way, the application of intellectual property rights must be of benefit to society as a whole and cannot aim merely to protect private rights. Access to medicines is a prerequisite to the full exercise of the right to health. This access must be general, and not limited to a certain type of medicines.'; Dominican Republic (ibid., 62), noting that 'Our delegation is particularly eager to ensure that this discussion does not turn into a mere public relations exercise aimed at "demonstrating" our solidarity with the poor people of this earth, whose human rights are at issue when doubts are expressed on the way in which our countries have exercised their multilateral intellectual property rights. And I speak of human rights because, as the distinguished Ambassador of Bolivia rightly pointed out, human rights include the right to health.'; Sri Lanka (ibid., 65), noting that '... access to essential drugs is part of human rights to health.'; Uganda (ibid., 77), noting that 'I cannot but agree with the statement made by the Ambassador of India earlier that the cry for affordable access to medicines for what are life-threatening diseases for people in developing countries is a cry of a fundamental human right of nature.'

systems? Since patent rights have an impact on access to medicines,[102] there exists a tension between patent rights and the right to health (as the right to have access to medicines is an integral component of the right to health).[103] According to Barratt, it is impossible to resolve the tension between patent rights and access to medicines by relying only on internal principles contained in intellectual property law. She suggests that the best way to resolve this problem is by using external norms contained in the human rights system. According to her:

> Negotiations over patents and public health are impossible to finalise using only internal principles of intellectual property law because the debate straddles the tension inherent in the patent system – benefits of patent monopolies versus consequent social costs. Intellectual property law does not tell us when the social costs of the system become legally unacceptable. States need, in addition, to use an 'external' argument and look for norms outside of intellectual property law and principles to resolve this impasse. The human rights system provides clear standards and benchmarks which give legal content to the term 'public benefit' and demarcate a bottom line below which the social costs of the international patent system become non-negotiable and potentially unlawful.[104]

Barratt further contends that human right norms 'provide specific limitations on what is negotiable, while identifying precise minimum conditions that are beyond negotiation'.[105] Thus, unlike the internal principles contained in intellectual property law which are quite ambiguous and open to multiple interpretations, human right norms contain certain minimum core obligations that are beyond negotiation. More importantly, with the elucidation provided by the CESCR on certain economic and social rights through its various General Comments, it is now very difficult to argue that economic and social rights such as the right to health are vague rights with no identifiable obligations. General Comment No. 14 has clarified the essential components of the right to health. It is, therefore, beyond negotiation that states have an obligation to provide access to medicines for their citizens and to ensure that their legal framework on patent rights does not impede the enjoyment of the right to health.

Incorporating a *model of human rights* into a country's patent law system will not only help to preserve the country's patent policy space, it will also help to facilitate access to medicines. By relying on both paragraph 4 of the Doha Declaration and

[102] See Joseph, 'Trade and the Right to Health', 360.

[103] See CESCR, 'General Comment No. 14', para 12; UN Human Rights Council, 'Access to Medicines in the Context of the Right of Everyone to the Enjoyment of the Highest Attainable Standard of Physical and Mental Health', A/HRC/RES/23/14 (2013).

[104] See Barratt, 'The Curious Absence of Human Rights', 24.

[105] Ibid., 32; Mac Darrow, *Between Light and Shadow: The World Bank, the International Monetary Fund and International Human Rights Law* (Hart, 2003).

their obligations under Article 12 of the ICESCR, it is possible for developing countries to incorporate a *model of human rights* into the design, implementation, interpretation, and enforcement of their patent laws at the national level. In order to demonstrate how this can work in practice, in subsequent chapters of this book, the incorporation of a *model of human rights* into the national patent law system of three developing countries (India, Kenya, and South Africa) will be critically examined.

The remainder of this book is made up of six chapters. Chapters 2 and 3 focus on the first key question identified here regarding how the relationship between patent rights and human rights should be conceptualized. Chapter 2 contends that the appropriate justification for patent rights is one that is constructed on a socio-centric approach to patent law. It critically examines some of the popular theoretical justifications that have hitherto been postulated as explanations for the existence of intellectual property rights in general and patent rights in particular, and it concludes with the view that the regulatory theory of intellectual property is the only theory that adopts a broad socio-centric approach. The broad socio-centric approach of the regulatory theory of intellectual property law permits the incorporation of a *model of human rights* into a country's patent law system.

Building on the discussion in Chapter 2, Chapter 3 deals with the nature of the relationship between patent rights and the right to health under international human rights law. Chapter 3 proceeds to answer two key questions that are integral to the issues addressed in this book. First, are patent rights human rights? Second, is the incorporation of a *model of human rights* compatible with the TRIPS Agreement? Chapter 3 concludes with the view that patent rights cannot be considered as human rights under international human rights law, and that the *model of human rights* is compatible with the TRIPS Agreement. There is therefore nothing that prohibits a developing country from insisting on the primacy of human rights obligations when attempting to resolve the tension between patent rights and the right to health at the national level.

Chapters 4–6 thereafter proceed to address the second key question identified here, that is, in resolving the tension between patent rights and the right to health and in trying to discharge their right to health responsibilities, what should inform the design, implementation, interpretation, and enforcement of patent rights by the organs of the state in developing countries? The analyses contained in Chapters 4–6 focus mainly on how the national courts and tribunals in Kenya, South Africa, and India, respectively, have incorporated a *model of human rights* into their decisions when adjudicating disputes that involve a tension between patent rights and the right to health. The cases examined in these three chapters demonstrate that the incorporation of a *model of human rights* into the adjudication of such disputes can be useful in preserving patent policy space and securing access to medicines.

The final chapter of this book, Chapter 7, contains the concluding thoughts based on the answers provided to the two key questions that this book addresses. This book provides a systematic analysis of court decisions from three key developing countries and it assesses how the national courts in these countries resolve the tension between patent rights and the right to health. Essentially, the book demonstrates how a *model of human rights* can be incorporated into the adjudication of disputes involving patent rights in national courts.

2

Patent Policy, Access to Medicines, and the Regulatory Theory of Patent Rights

2.1 INTRODUCTION

The central focus of this chapter is the identification of the appropriate theoretical justification for patent rights. Since patent law deals with inventions, it is important to have a proper understanding of how inventions are made. In this regard, one of the objectives of this chapter is to determine the most appropriate explanation for the development of inventions between the creator-centric (heroic) theory of invention and the socio-centric theory of invention. This will serve as a background to the discussion of the issue that is the central focus of this chapter: identifying the appropriate theoretical justification for patent rights.

Currently, the requirements for the grant of a patent in most (if not all) countries is structured around a creator-centric (heroic) theory of invention. As Diamond notes, the heroic theory of invention 'is encouraged by patent law, because an applicant for a patent must prove the novelty of the invention submitted ... From a patent lawyer's perspective, the ideal invention is one that arises without any precursors, like Athene springing fully formed from the forehead of Zeus'.[1] The heroic theory of invention gives a single person all the credit for a particular invention.[2] Under the heroic theory of invention, as described by Epstein, an 'invention is

[1] Jared Diamond, *Guns, Germs, and Steel: The Fates of Human Societies* (W. W. Norton & Company, 2005), 244.

[2] See Ralph Epstein, 'Industrial Invention: Heroic, or Systematic?' (1926) 40 *The Quarterly Journal of Economics* 232, 237. Examples of biographical accounts that adopted the heroic theory of invention include: Gilbert French, *The Life and Times of Samuel Crompton* (Simpkin, Marshall & Co., 1859); Samuel Smiles, *Lives of Boulton and Watt* (2nd ed., John Murray, 1866). For a discussion on why inventors rose to heroic stature in Victorian Britain, see Christine MacLeod, *Heroes of Invention: Technology, Liberalism and British Identity, 1750–1914* (Cambridge University Press, 2007).

conceived to have flashed virtually from [one man's] brain alone, or to have been worked out by him as a result of his peculiar inspiration or genius'.[3]

However, there are few, if any, inventions with no precursors. For instance, the steam engine 'invented' by James Watt in 1769 was an improvement on Thomas Newcomen's steam engine. The precursor to Newcomen's steam engine was the steam engine patented by Thomas Savery in 1698. Savery's engine was preceded by the steam engine designed by Denis Papin around 1680, which was in turn preceded by the ideas of Christiaan Huygens.[4] The same can be said about the 'invention' of the incandescent bulb by Thomas Edison, the airplane invented by the Wright brothers, and the telegraph invented by Samuel Morse.[5] All these inventions were preceded by earlier inventions. In rejecting the heroic theory of invention, Diamond rightly concludes, *inter alia*, that 'technology develops cumulatively, rather than in isolated heroic acts'.[6]

The socio-centric theory of invention, however, does not ignore the role played by individual inventors in the creation and production of inventions. Rather, from a socio-centric perspective, inventions are regarded as the products of both individual inventors and the society in which they live.[7] According to Ogburn and Thomas, 'there are two factors in the making of inventions, namely, mental ability and the existing status of culture'.[8] Ogburn and Thomas demonstrate the importance of 'the existing status of culture' by referring to the fact that electrical appliances could not have been invented in the fifteenth century.[9]

3 Epstein, 'Industrial Invention', 237. Epstein further notes that '[s]uch accounts of the course of invention are commonly found in biographies. The biographer makes a hero of his subject and imputes to him qualities of vision and accomplishment which enable him to do what other men, men of lesser mold can not do.' (237–8).

4 Diamond, *Guns, Germs, and Steel*, 244–5. See also Epstein, 'Industrial Invention', 242–3; William Ogburn and Dorothy Thomas, 'Are Inventions Inevitable? A Note on Social Evolution' (1922) 37 *Political Science Quarterly* 83, 90–1; Robert Thurston, *A History of the Growth of the Steam Engine* (4th ed., D. Appleton & Co., 1902).

5 Diamond, *Guns, Germs, and Steel*, 245.

6 Ibid.

7 As Epstein points out, 'Quite opposed to the heroic theory ... are the views of a number of historians, psychologists, and economists. These emphatically assert that no single man, even if he is a genius, is responsible for the sum total of his abilities, and for the overt acts and accomplishments in which his abilities become crystallized. To the *society* and the generation into which he is born and lives, the inventor owes a debt that stretches back to the life of other generations which have preceded. Thus regarded, a given invention is merely the culmination of a train of efforts reaching back into the past and brought to fruition in the present' (Epstein, 'Industrial Invention', 242; emphasis added).

8 Ogburn and Thomas, 'Are Inventions Inevitable?', 86.

9 Ogburn and Thomas note that, '... the elements of the material culture at any one time have a good deal to do with determining the nature of the particular inventions that are made. For instance, a few discoveries regarding electricity made possible a great many inventions in which these fundamental discoveries were used or applied. The many electrical appliances could not have been invented in ... the fifteenth century, because the fundamental discoveries regarding electricity had not been made ... The fact that so many electrical inventions followed so

Thus, unlike the advocates of the creator-centric theory of invention who, as Epstein notes, always contend 'that without the one man whose life they are chronicling, a particular invention could not, or would not readily have been forthcoming',[10] the socio-centric theory of invention reveals that inventions are inevitable once the social conditions are right and that no one person is indispensable with regard to the development of any invention.[11] As Ogburn and Thomas point out, even though James Watt was a great man, he 'does not seem to have been indispensable to the perfection of the steam engine. It would be an absurdity to conclude that, even if he had died in infancy, the Industrial Revolution would not have occurred'.[12]

To demonstrate the point that no single individual is indispensable to the development of any invention, Ogburn and Thomas provide a list of 148 inventions and discoveries that were discovered, more or less, simultaneously and independently by two or more persons.[13] Some of the simultaneous inventions include the telephone, the phonograph, the telegraph, the sewing machine, the steamboat, and the typewriter. Essentially, inventions are inevitable in any society that is prepared for them, and no society has to wait for the birth of a single rare genius before certain inventions can be developed.[14]

The creator-centric notion of the heroic inventor under patent law is quite similar to the notion of solitary romantic authorship under copyright law, which has been criticized by scholars such as Boyle, Woodmansee, and Jaszi.[15] According to Woodmansee, '[t]he notion that the writer is a special participant in the production process – the only one worthy of attention – is of recent provenience. It is a by-product of the Romantic notion that significant writers break altogether with tradition to create something utterly new, unique – in a word, "original".'[16]

quickly after certain researches in electricity had been made, suggests the inevitability of these inventions' (ibid., 87–8).

10 Epstein, 'Industrial Invention', 238.

11 According to Ogburn and Thomas, 'a specific invention depends upon a certain cultural preparation, and could not be made without the existence of the constituent cultural elements that make the invention' (Ogburn and Thomas, 'Are Inventions Inevitable?', 92).

12 Ibid., 91.

13 Ibid., 93–8.

14 According to Ogburn and Thomas, 'The fact that so many electrical inventions followed so quickly after certain researches in electricity had been made, suggests the inevitability of these inventions. And also the fact that most of the major electrical inventions were made by two or more inventors leads one to think that electrical development was more dependent on cultural preparation than on genius' (ibid., 88).

15 See James Boyle, 'A Theory of Law and Information: Copyright, Spleens, Blackmail, and Insider Trading' (1992) 80 *California Law Review* 1413; James Boyle, *Shamans, Software, and Spleens: Law and the Construction of the Information Society* (Harvard University Press, 1996); Martha Woodmansee, 'On the Author Effect: Recovering Collectivity' (1992) 10 *Cardozo Arts & Entertainment Law Journal* 279; Peter Jaszi, 'On the Author Effect: Contemporary Copyright and Collective Creativity' (1992) 10 *Cardozo Arts & Entertainment Law Journal* 293.

16 Woodmansee, 'On the Author Effect', 280.

Aoki points out that the 'originary concept of Romantic Authorship emerged at a particular point in the 18th century'.[17] Woodmansee further notes that if 'we move backward in time, the collective, corporate, or collaborative element in writing ... becomes even more pronounced' and that during the period spanning from 'the Middle Ages right through the Renaissance new writing derived its value and authority from its affiliation with the texts that preceded it'.[18]

Building on the work of Boyle and Jaszi, Aoki extends the criticism of the concept of romantic authorship in copyright law to the notion of the heroic inventor embedded in patent law. According to Aoki, '[o]riginality, the romantic author's shibboleth, appears as an even stronger component in patent law's requirement that an inventor seeking a patent must come up with something substantially new.'[19] Relying on the works of Kuhn (on the history of science)[20] and Merton (on the sociology of science),[21] Aoki argues,

> As with the romantic author, the image of the originary scientific genius is an extremely historically contingent formation, running counter to many recent accounts of the history and sociology of scientific invention and progress. The latter stress the great degree to which absolute scientific originality is more myth than reality. However, as in copyright law, potent traces of reasoning premised on the image of the ground-breaking inventive genius remain secreted in patent law's interstices. Also like copyright, where the myth of solitary authorial originality persists, despite the humdrum nature and broad scope of what is potentially

[17] Keith Aoki, 'Authors, Inventors and Trademark Owners: Private Intellectual Property and the Public Domain – Part I' (1993–1994) 18 *Columbia-VLA Journal of Law & The Arts* 1, 72.

[18] Woodmansee, 'On the Author Effect', 281. See also Jaszi, 'On the Author Effect', 304, who noted, 'faith in solitary, originary Romantic "authorship" blinds decision-makers to the advantages of non-conforming cultural production. Copyright law, with its emphasis on rewarding and safeguarding "originality," has lost sight of the cultural value of what might be called "serial collaborations" – works resulting from successive elaborations of an idea or text by a series of creative workers, occurring perhaps over years or decades. Before copyright law's acceptance of Romantic "authorship" was complete, for example, copyright actually encouraged the creation of popular adaptations of preexisting work ... But where the law formerly envisioned the possibility of improving existing works by redaction or expansion, modern copyright is more myopic, focussing exclusively on the potential for harm to the interests of the original "author." Today, the privilege of producing "derivative works" that re-work or incorporate protected preexisting texts generally is reserved to those who have obtained copyright permission.' See further, Aoki, 'Authors, Inventors and Trademark Owners – Part I', 72, who noted that, 'The figure of the author conveniently focuses our attention on the individual creator and conceals to a great extent the degree to which all cultural production has a strongly collective and incremental history, extending other people's ideas, work and expressions.'

[19] Keith Aoki, 'Authors, Inventors and Trademark Owners: Private Intellectual Property and the Public Domain – Part II' (1993–1994) 18 *Columbia-VLA Journal of Law & The Arts* 191, 214.

[20] Thomas Kuhn, *The Structure of Scientific Revolutions* (2nd ed., The University of Chicago Press, 1970).

[21] Robert K. Merton, 'The Normative Structure of Science', in Norman W. Storer (ed.), *The Sociology of Science: Theoretical and Empirical Investigations* (The University of Chicago Press, 1973), 267, 277–8.

> copyrightable, there is an odd gap between the palimpsest or trace of the inventive genius and the prosaic technical nature of most patented inventions.[22]

This chapter therefore adopts the view that the best explanation for the development of inventions is the socio-centric theory of invention.[23] If inventions are socio-centric, it follows that the patent law system (which is designed to regulate the exclusive rights granted to inventors) should also be socio-centric and not creator-centric. In this regard, this chapter builds on the work of Shubha Ghosh, who contends that intellectual property law and policy should be user-centred and not creator-centric.[24] Ghosh's definition of 'users' is in accordance with a socio-centric approach to intellectual property rights in general and patent rights in particular. According to Ghosh, users are 'a highly differentiated group' which includes 'individuals who need to negotiate intellectual property in pursuing their own creative objectives, professional tasks, or ordinary life experiences'.[25] In this regard, Ghosh notes that users would include, *inter alia*, 'bloggers, medical professionals, documentary filmmakers, parodists, news commentators, fans of creative works, cultural critics, remixers, inventors, artists, consumers, entrepreneurs, academics, and cultural preservationists'.[26] Users would also include patients who require access to medicines.[27] As Ghosh points out, this list is not exhaustive.[28] Thus, other users can be included in the list.

Building on Ghosh's definition of 'users', this chapter contends that the adoption of a socio-centric approach in the design and implementation of a country's intellectual property law and policy (including patent law and policy) would facilitate the incorporation of the interests of users of inventions, such as patients who need access to medicines on one hand and manufacturers of generic drugs,

22 Aoki, 'Authors, Inventors and Trademark Owners – Part II', 216–17.

23 See also George Basalla, *The Evolution of Technology* (Cambridge University Press, 1988) (Basalla challenges the notion that technological advances are the results of the efforts of a few heroic individuals who produce revolutionary inventions that owe little or nothing to the technological past).

24 Shubha Ghosh, 'Managing the Intellectual Property Sprawl' (2012) 49 *San Diego Law Review* 979, 1017. According to Ghosh, 'we should view intellectual property law and policy as user centered, and not a balancing of interests between creative persons and the rest of us. This argument follows from what I hope is the uncontroversial observation that we are all users of the intellectual property subject matter ... [In order] to engage the intellectual property policy debate fully, I argue that intellectual property policy should center the user in the debate and structure rights with users in mind' (ibid., 981). Ghosh was writing in response to Robert Merges' book (Robert Merges, *Justifying Intellectual Property* (Harvard University Press, 2011)). Ghosh contends that Merges, in his book, adopts a creator-centric approach in his attempt to justify intellectual property rights. Ghosh therefore seeks to shift Merges' argument 'from one centered on creative persons to one centered on the much more broad and relevant class of users' (ibid.).

25 Ibid., 984.

26 Ibid.

27 Ibid., 1030.

28 Ibid., 984.

who play a huge role in facilitating access to cheaper medicines, on the other hand. A socio-centric approach to patent law does not seek to underestimate or undermine the role of inventors or patent owners; rather, it aims to 'include a wide range of constituencies who benefit from [patent] law'.[29] Within a socio-centric framework, the interests of inventors and corporate actors who own patents on pharmaceutical products will be considered alongside those of poor patients, manufacturers of generic drugs, and 'other groups who are caught in the web of patent policy and practice.[30] As inventors and owners of patents are also 'users' of the patent system, it implies that, within a socio-centric framework, as Ghosh points out, 'the perspective of users as a whole would be the unifying policy' of patent law.[31]

This chapter examines some of the popular theoretical justifications that have hitherto been postulated as explanations for the existence of intellectual property rights in general and patent rights in particular. Constraints of time and space make it practically impossible to examine all the available theories on intellectual property, and the focus will be limited to the Lockean theory, the Hegelian theory, the utilitarian theory, and the regulatory theory. The rest of this chapter is structured into four sections. Sections 2.2 and 2.3 examine the Lockean and Hegelian theories, respectively, while Sections 2.4 and 2.5 focus on the utilitarian and regulatory theories, respectively. The chapter concludes with the view that the regulatory theory of intellectual property is the only theory that adopts a broad socio-centric approach. Thus, any developing country that seeks to preserve its patent policy space and secure access to medicines for its citizens should treat intellectual property rights (including patent rights) as instruments that regulate the exclusive rights granted to inventors.

2.2 THE LOCKEAN THEORY AND PATENT RIGHTS

John Locke, in his *Second Treatise of Government*, develops an argument on how property held in common can be converted into personal property. In Locke's view, God has given the whole earth to mankind in common.[32] Within Locke's framework, the only way an individual can appropriate any part of the earth as his personal property is through the difficult, if not impossible, means of seeking the consent of all the rest of mankind. Locke therefore sought to demonstrate 'how men might come to have a property in several parts of that which God gave to mankind in common, and that without any express compact of all the commoners'.[33]

29 Ibid., 1016.

30 Ibid.

31 Ibid., 1032.

32 John Locke, *Second Treatise of Government* (first published 1690), section 25.

33 Ibid., section 25. As Daniel Attas points out, 'A theory of property such as [Locke's] must advance a positive principle of original acquisition. Some action on the part of the individual must make it the case that certain parts of the natural world become his property and must be

Locke argues that an individual can appropriate any part of that which God has given to mankind in common without obtaining the consent of the rest of mankind by mixing his labour with it. According to Locke, each individual owns his body, and therefore each individual equally owns what his body does, that is, his labour.[34] Furthermore, in the Lockean framework, since each individual owns his labour, each individual also owns what he joins his labour with.[35] Thus, anything that an individual mixes his labour with belongs to him without the need to seek the consent of the rest of mankind.[36] Locke includes two provisos within his framework for the appropriation of property. One, there has to be 'enough, and as good, left in common for others'.[37] Two, an individual can only appropriate as much as he 'can make use of to any advantage of life before it spoils ... whatever is beyond this, is more than his share, and belongs to others' because God did not make anything 'for man to spoil or destroy'.[38] In Locke's view, it is human labour that gives objects value.[39]

recognized as such.' See Daniel Attas, 'Lockean Justifications of Intellectual Property', in Axel Gosseries, Alain Marciano, and Alain Strowel (eds.), *Intellectual Property and Theories of Justice* (Palgrave Macmillan, 2008), 37.

34 See Edwin Hettinger, 'Justifying Intellectual Property' (1989) 18 *Philosophy & Public Affairs* 31, 37.

35 Ibid.

36 In the words of Locke, 'Though the earth ... be common to all men, yet every man has a property in his own person: this no body has any right to but himself. The labour of his body, and the work of his hands, we may say, are properly his. Whatsoever then he removes out of the state that nature hath provided, and left it in, he hath mixed his labour with, and joined to it something that is his own, and thereby makes it his property. It being by him removed from the common state nature hath placed it in, it hath by this labour something annexed to it, that excludes the common right of other men: for this labour being the unquestionable property of the labourer, no man but he can have a right to what that is once joined to ...' (Locke, *Second Treatise of Government*, section 27). According to Daniel Attas, 'The [Lockean] principle of self-ownership states that every individual owns his own body, in the same way he might own an animal. Thus, he enjoys all the rights of control, income and transfer with respect to his own body ... By the same token he would own any of his body products (hair, fingernails, blood, etc.), as well as the activity of his body ... [W]ere there a way to extend the kind of privileged status one has with respect to one's body so that it might also encompass parts of the natural world, we could see how one might come to own not only one's body and its products, but also some external resources. For Locke, labour provides such a means. By labouring on the natural world one mixes one's labour, in Locke's notorious phrase, with some unowned resources. If private property in the newly created object is not respected, in so far as that object contains some self-owned labour, one's self-ownership is violated. Thus one can come to acquire private property in natural resources by infusing them with self-owned substance' (Attas, 'Lockean Justifications of Intellectual Property', 37–8).

37 Locke, *Second Treatise of Government*, section 27.

38 Ibid., section 31.

39 In the words of Locke: '... it is labour indeed that puts the difference of value on every thing; and let any one consider what the difference is between an acre of land planted with tobacco or sugar, sown with wheat or barley, and an acre of the same land lying in common, without any husbandry upon it, and he will find, that the improvement of labour makes the far greater part of the value. I think it will be but a very modest computation to say, that of the products of the earth useful to the life of man nine tenths are the effects of labour: nay, if we will rightly

There are several problems with relying on Locke's theory as a justification for intellectual property rights, including patent rights. The first problem with the application of the Lockean framework to intellectual property rights (including patent rights) concerns the inherent differences between the nature of the commons in the context of tangible property and the nature of the commons in the context of intellectual ideas (or the intellectual commons). As Daniel Attas points out, the structure of the commons within the Lockean framework, which was developed in relation to 'a material conception of assets, seems unsuited to the sphere of ideas'.[40] It is not clear what would constitute the intellectual commons in the context of intellectual property. If the intellectual commons refers to the 'historical basic knowledge available to all' then it will be difficult to argue that, by developing new ideas based on this historical basic knowledge, 'one comes to own the previously unowned foundational knowledge at the basis of these new ideas'.[41]

The second problem concerns the question of the value of an invention. If indeed it is human labour that endows an object with value, it becomes necessary to determine whose labour gives an intellectual object such as an invention its value. If one adopts the creator-centric theory of invention, it can possibly be argued that the inventor's labour is what gives an invention its value. However, as noted in Section 2.1, the socio-centric theory of invention provides a better explanation for the development of inventions. From a socio-centric perspective, the value of an invention cannot be attributed solely to the labours of any particular inventor (or group of inventors).[42] As Edwin Hettinger notes, an invention does not 'operate in a vacuum', and 'intellectual activity is not creation *ex nihilo*'.[43] Inventions (and other intellectual products) are social products that depend on the ideas of those who came before the inventors.[44] It is difficult, if not impossible, to separate the labour of an inventor from that of his precursors.[45]

estimate things as they come to our use, and cast up the several expences about them, what in them is purely owing to nature, and what to labour, we shall find, that in most of them ninety-nine hundredths are wholly to be put on the account of labour.' (ibid., section 40).

40 Attas, 'Lockean Justifications of Intellectual Property', 41.

41 Ibid.

42 As Daniel Attas points out, '... the phenomena of multiple inventions support the idea that inventions and discoveries cannot be considered the product of a lone inventor. Much of their substance is owed to circumstances, common knowledge, a social problem awaiting a solution, a methodology of technological innovation based primarily on imitation and piecemeal improvement, and chance' (ibid., 43).

43 Hettinger, 'Justifying Intellectual Property', 38.

44 Ibid.

45 According to Daniel Attas, 'it would be difficult even in theory to pinpoint the individual to whom we could attribute the production of [an] idea. Although we could imagine a first and solitary human being gathering and hunting to satisfy his needs, it is more difficult to form a coherent image of a person inventing or making discoveries in a social-scientific vacuum. A theory of appropriation that depends on a one-to-one relation between producer and product is useless in the case of intellectual products' (Attas, 'Lockean Justifications of Intellectual Property', 44). As Hettinger further points out: 'Separating out the individual contribution of

A related but different issue is the gap between the claim that an inventor has a right to possess and use his invention, on one hand, and the claim that an inventor ought to receive the full market value of the invention by selling the invention in the market, on the other hand.[46] As Ghosh notes, focusing on labour 'as the source of property rights, and hence social and economic value, distorts our understanding of markets'.[47] Even if it is possible to separate the labour of an inventor from that of his precursors, the Lockean theory does not provide a justification for the claim that an inventor is entitled to receive the market value of his invention.[48] Market value, as Hettinger points out, 'is a socially created phenomenon, depending on the activity (or nonactivity) of other producers, the monetary demand of purchasers, and the kinds of property rights, contracts, and markets the state has established and enforced'.[49] Thus, while the Lockean framework may allow an inventor to possess and use his invention for his own benefit, it does not give the inventor a right to make profits from his invention through sales in the market.[50]

A third problem with the Lockean framework and patent rights concerns the application of the two Lockean provisos in the context of patent rights. As noted, the first Lockean proviso is that there has to be 'enough, and as good, left in common for others'. This proviso has been interpreted to mean that there should be no loss to others when property is being acquired.[51] However, by making it impossible for subsequent inventors, who independently invent a product, to obtain a patent after an earlier inventor has obtained a patent on the same invention, contemporary

the inventor, writer, or manager from this historical/social component is no easy task. Simply identifying the value a laborer's labor adds to the world with the market value of the resulting product ignores the vast contributions of others. A person who relies on human intellectual history and makes a small modification to produce something of great value should no more receive what the market will bear than should the last person needed to lift a car receive full credit for lifting it. If laboring gives the laborer the right to receive the market value of the resulting product, this market value should be shared by all those whose ideas contributed to the origin of the product' (Hettinger, 'Justifying Intellectual Property', 38).

46 Hettinger, 'Justifying Intellectual Property', 40.

47 Ghosh, 'Managing the Intellectual Property Sprawl', 1006. Ghosh further notes, 'To be fair, Locke develops a political theory rather than an economic one . . . Labor is one factor in the marketplace. Market negotiations involve a complex set of transactions among laborers, owners of financial assets, consumers, managers of organizations, and stewards of natural resources. To reduce the value that markets produce to labor is to ignore the role of technologies, finance, taste, pure chance, and a host of other factors. All of these factors shape the scope and influence of property rights either directly or indirectly and consequently affect the transactions that drive markets' (1006).

48 Hettinger, 'Justifying Intellectual Property', 38.

49 Ibid.

50 Ibid., 40.

51 Lawrence Becker, *Property Rights: Philosophic Foundations* (Routledge & Kegan Paul Ltd, 1977), 42–3; referred to by Hettinger, 'Justifying Intellectual Property', 44. See also Attas, 'Lockean Justifications of Intellectual Property', 47, who noted that, 'According to contemporary understandings of the "enough and as good" proviso, an original acquisition is permitted if it does not worsen anyone's material well-being'.

patent law is in breach of the first proviso in the Lockean framework.[52] These subsequent independent inventors obviously suffer a loss because of the first patent grant, because their own inventions are also a product of their labours.[53] There seems to be no reason why they should be prohibited from selling and deriving profits from the product of their labours. As pointed out in Section 2.1, the research of Ogburn and Thomas confirms that it is not unusual for multiple persons to independently invent a particular product. While these independent inventors should, strictly speaking, be entitled to exploit their inventions within a Lockean framework, this is impossible under the current patent law in most jurisdictions.

In addition, there are also difficulties with the application of Locke's second proviso, specifically in the context of patent rights. According to Locke's second proviso, an individual can only appropriate as much as he 'can make use of to any advantage of life before it spoils' and 'whatever is beyond this, is more than his share'. As Locke himself explains, 'if either the grass of his enclosure rotted on the ground, or the fruit of his planting perished without gathering, and laying up, this part of the earth, notwithstanding his enclosure, was still to be looked on as waste, and might be the possession of any other'.[54] Daniel Attas notes that Locke's proviso against spoilage

> is motivated not by the aesthetic of rotting fruit or the insult to the Creator, but by what is denied to other needy people. Thus it does not understand waste as the ruin or perishing of foodstuffs, but the non-use, abuse or misuse, that is to say, the criminally inefficient use, of resources.[55]

In relation to patents, Hettinger points out that, since inventions are non-exclusive, 'this requirement prohibiting waste can never be completely met by intellectual property', because, when patentees charge fees for the use of their inventions, 'certain beneficial uses of these intellectual products are prevented', and this is 'wasteful, since everyone could use and benefit from intellectual objects concurrently'.[56]

With regard to access to medicines, the breach of Locke's proviso against spoilage is not just a theoretical possibility. Several poor patients in developing countries are unable to obtain access to the drugs they need because of the exorbitant prices charged by the pharmaceutical companies that own the patents on these drugs. In some cases, access to these patented drugs could be enhanced if generic production

52 Hettinger, 'Justifying Intellectual Property', 44.
53 Ibid.
54 Locke, *Second Treatise of Government*, section 38.
55 Attas, 'Lockean Justifications of Intellectual Property', 46.
56 Hettinger, 'Justifying Intellectual Property', 44–5. See also, Attas, 'Lockean Justifications of Intellectual Property', 47, who noted that, 'if we understand waste not as the ruin or rotting of perishables, but as the recklessly suboptimal use of resources, then the appropriation of intellectual products can definitely be checked by a non-waste proviso. Intellectual property widely and routinely denies use from all those who cannot or will not pay for it.'

is permitted. However, since patent rights confer the exclusive right of production on patent owners, where there is no competition from manufacturers of generic drugs, several patients who would benefit from using those patented drugs can be prevented from doing so.[57]

2.3 THE HEGELIAN THEORY AND PATENT RIGHTS

Hegel's personality theory, as further refined by Margaret Radin, is another theory that has been used to justify both property rights and intellectual property rights.[58] Hegel argues that an individual can only realize his self-identity when he is given an opportunity to exercise his will on external objects.[59] According to the Hegelian personality theory of property rights, property serves as a means for self-actualization.[60] 'The premise underlying the personhood perspective', as Margaret Radin points out, 'is that to achieve proper self-development – to be a *person* – an individual needs some control over resources in the external environment' and the 'necessary assurances of control take the form of property rights'.[61] Essentially, the personality theory of property advocates that everyone should be given a threshold amount of property that will make it possible for them to function as free individuals and also facilitate the development of their personality.[62]

In Hegel's view, 'property is the embodiment of personality'.[63] In the Hegelian framework, as Tom Palmer points out, 'personality does not simply require external objects for its development', more importantly, personality is developed when it becomes objectified 'through externalization of its will'.[64] Unlike the Lockean theory which relies strongly on labour, in the Hegelian framework, occupancy or

57 As Daniel Attas explains, commercial firms 'will typically adopt a pricing strategy that maximises their profits, not one that maximises their sales. Consequently, some technology will be made available only to the few who can afford it, even though more people could conceivably enjoy it with its production still viable. That is to say, in many cases the technology can be more widely shared without jeopardising the economic basis of its production. This is exacerbated by the monopolistic control held by the owners of intellectual property. Lacking any competition, their maximising strategy will tend to restrict even further the user base. In one intuitive sense, therefore, intellectual property can lead to waste.' Attas, 'Lockean Justifications of Intellectual Property', 47.

58 See G. W. F. Hegel, *Philosophy of Right* (first published 1821, Thomas Knox tr, Oxford University Press, 1967); Margaret Radin, 'Property and Personhood' (1982) 34 *Stanford Law Review* 957; Ofer Tur-Sinai, 'Beyond Incentives: Expanding the Theoretical Framework for Patent Law Analysis' (2012) 45 *Akron Law Review* 243, 274.

59 Tur-Sinai, 'Beyond Incentives', 274.

60 See Justin Hughes, 'The Philosophy of Intellectual Property' (1988) 77 *The Georgetown Law Journal* 287, 330.

61 Radin, 'Property and Personhood', 957 (emphasis in the original).

62 Tur-Sinai, 'Beyond Incentives', 274.

63 Hegel, *Philosophy of Right*, para 50.

64 Tom Palmer, 'Are Patents and Copyrights Morally Justified? The Philosophy of Property Rights and Ideal Objects' (1990) 13 *Harvard Journal of Law & Public Policy* 817, 838.

taking possession is the means by which external objects are transformed into property.[65] Anything is capable of being the subject of property in the Hegelian framework and, as Drahos notes, there is no predetermination of 'what can and cannot be the subject of property. Personality is left free to range over the world'.[66] In other words, whatever the will decides to occupy becomes property.[67] Hegel, however, notes that occupancy of objects can be conditioned by physical strength, cunning, and dexterity.[68] Furthermore, the effectiveness of our occupation is contingent on the nature of the object that we are seeking to occupy. According to Hegel, '[o]wing to the qualitative differences between natural objects, mastery and occupancy of these has an infinite variety of meanings and involves a restriction and contingency that is just as infinite'.[69] For instance, food can be completely appropriated, while elements cannot be completely appropriated.[70]

In the Hegelian framework, property can also be alienated or abandoned through the same means by which it was occupied, that is, through an act of will.[71] However, only things that are external by nature can be alienated or abandoned.[72] In the words of Hegel,

> The reason I can alienate my property is that it is mine only in so far as I put my will into it. Hence I may abandon ... as a *res nullius* anything that I have or yield it to the will of another and so into his possession, provided always that the thing in question is a thing external by nature.[73]

What are things not 'external by nature'? According to Hegel, 'those goods, or rather substantive characteristics, which constitute my own private personality and the universal essence of my self-consciousness are inalienable and my right to them is imprescriptible. Such characteristics are my personality as such, my universal freedom of will, my ethical life, my religion'.[74]

It should, however, be noted that what is not 'external by nature' can be made external within the Hegelian framework and, therefore, even personality can be alienated.[75] Personality can be alienated voluntarily or through force, for instance through slavery. According to Hegel, slavery, serfdom, disqualification from holding property, and encumbrances on property are examples of the alienation of personality.[76] Hegel notes further that intelligence, rationality, morality, ethical life, and

[65] Ibid., 838.
[66] Peter Drahos, *A Philosophy of Intellectual Property* (Ashgate, 1996), 78.
[67] Ibid., 78.
[68] Hegel, *Philosophy of Right*, para 52.
[69] Ibid., para 52.
[70] Drahos, *A Philosophy of Intellectual Property*, 78.
[71] Ibid.
[72] Ibid., 78–9.
[73] Hegel, *Philosophy of Right*, para 65.
[74] Ibid., para 66.
[75] Drahos, *A Philosophy of Intellectual Property*, 79.
[76] Hegel, *Philosophy of Right*, para 66.

religion can be alienated by, for instance, 'ceding to someone else full power and authority to fix and prescribe what actions are to be done (as when an individual binds himself expressly to steal or to murder ... or to a course of action that may involve crime), or what duties are binding on one's conscience or what religious truth is'.[77] Personality can, however, be regained through the negation of the actions that made it external in the first place and which enabled another person to possess it.[78] Drahos distils from this that the 'clear implication of Hegel's argument is that property functions as a survival or defence mechanism. The free-willing mind occupies things in the world, including personality, so that others will not do so and rob it of its powers of determination and self-development'.[79]

With regard to intellectual property, Hegel appears to have adopted a utilitarian approach. According to Hegel, 'The purely negative, but most basic, means of furthering the sciences and arts is to protect those who work in them against *theft* and to provide them with security for their property, just as the earliest and most important means of furthering commerce and industry was to protect them against highway robbery.'[80] Nevertheless, Hegel appears to situate his analysis of intellectual property within a socio-centric context. Hegel stresses the fact that the main purpose of intellectual products is the education of other people in the society[81] and that innovation is essentially incremental and socio-centric in nature.[82]

77 Ibid., para 66.

78 Drahos, A *Philosophy of Intellectual Property*, 79. According to Hegel, 'The right to what is in essence inalienable is imprescriptible, since the act whereby I take possession of my personality, of my substantive essence, and make myself a responsible being, capable of possessing rights and with a moral and religious life, takes away from these characteristics of mine just that externality which alone made them capable of passing into the possession of someone else. When I have thus annulled their externality, I cannot lose them through lapse of time or from any other reason drawn from my prior consent or willingness to alienate them. This return of mine into myself, whereby I make myself existent as Idea, as a person with rights and moral principles, annuls the previous position and the wrong done to my concept and my reason by others and myself when the infinite embodiment of self-consciousness has been treated as something external, and that with my consent. This return into myself makes clear the contradiction in supposing that I have given into another's possession my capacity for rights, my ethical life and religious feeling; for either I have given up what I myself did not possess, or I am giving up what, so soon as I possess it, exists in essence as mine alone and not as something external' (Hegel, *Philosophy of Right*, para 66).

79 Drahos, A *Philosophy of Intellectual Property*, 79.

80 G. W. F. Hegel, *Elements of the Philosophy of Right* (first published 1821, Allen Wood ed. and Hugh Nisbet tr., Cambridge University Press, 1991), para 69 (emphasis in the original).

81 Drahos, A *Philosophy of Intellectual Property*, 82.

82 According to Hegel, '... the destiny [*Bestimmung*] of a product of the intellect [*Geistesprodukt*] is to be apprehended by other individuals and appropriated by their representational thinking, memory, thought, etc. Hence the mode of expression whereby these individuals in turn make *what they have learned* ... into an *alienable thing* will always tend to have some distinctive *form*, so that they can regard the resources which flow from it as their property, and may assert their right to reproduce it. The propagation of the sciences in general, and the specific business of teaching in particular ... consist in the *repetition* of established thoughts, all of which have

Commenting on Hegel's analysis, Drahos notes that the reworking of established thoughts into new forms occurs through the social process of the transmission of knowledge.[83] Intellectual products therefore facilitate this social process by making it possible for people to learn from what others have created or invented. 'At any given moment', Drahos notes, 'individuals are engaged in personal, incremental contributions or modification of [the existing] stock of knowledge. Existing forms of knowledge are revised by individuals of different generations and so are thus both propagated and perhaps advanced for the benefit of others.'[84]

Hegel, however, fails to state the extent or degree to which an individual can appropriate ideas from the existing stock of knowledge and claim property rights in the new works that emerge from the social process of the transmission of knowledge.[85] This implies, as Drahos points out, that every society has 'to work out legal boundaries within their intellectual systems that ensure those systems serve the learning needs of others and future generations'.[85] In other words, if the main purpose of intellectual products is to facilitate learning and incremental innovation in society, the intellectual property system (including the patent system) must be designed in a way that enables this purpose to be achieved. The intellectual property system must therefore not stifle the social process of the transmission of knowledge, as this can in turn stifle innovation in society.

Hegel has been described as 'one of the most difficult writers in world history' and a writer that is 'difficult to understand'.[87] This probably explains why there is a divergence of opinion amongst intellectual property law scholars on the application of Hegel's theory to intellectual property. For instance, Schroeder contends that 'Hegel's project is completely antithetical to Radin's theory of property and personhood' and that 'Hegel's logic has absolutely nothing to say on the issue of whether society *should* adopt a positive law of intellectual property'.[88] While this might be regarded as an extreme view which may or may not be correct, it will be contended in this chapter (for reasons which will be shortly examined) that relying on the

already been expressed and acquired from external sources ...' (Hegel, *Elements of the Philosophy of Right*, para 69; emphasis in the original).

83 Drahos, *A Philosophy of Intellectual Property*, 82.

84 Ibid.

85 Ibid. In this regard, Hegel merely states that, 'As for the extent to which the existing store of knowledge, and in particular the thoughts of other people who retain external ownership of their intellectual products, become, by virtue of the new *form* which they acquire through repeated expression, a special intellectual [*gestiges*] property of the individual who reproduces them and thereby give him (or fail to give him) the right to make them his external property in turn – the extent to which this is so cannot be precisely determined, nor therefore defined in terms of right and the law' (Hegel, *Elements of the Philosophy of Right*, para 66; emphasis in the original).

86 Drahos, *A Philosophy of Intellectual Property*, 82.

87 Jeanne Schroeder, 'Unnatural Rights: Hegel and Intellectual Property' (2006) 60 *University of Miami Law Review* 453, 458.

88 Ibid., 457–8 (emphasis in the original).

Hegelian framework to justify intellectual property rights is highly problematic from a socio-centric perspective.

Another question that has been raised with regard to the application of the Hegelian framework to intellectual property rights concerns whether it is best applied to literary works as opposed to scientific inventions. Hughes contends that the Hegelian personality justification is best applied to the arts.[89] Hughes argues that certain 'categories of intellectual property seem to be receptacles for personality; others seem as if they do not manifest any "personality" of their creators. Poems, stories, novels, and musical works are clearly receptacles for personality. The same can be said for sculpture, paintings, and prints'.[90] According to Hughes, the Hegelian personality framework becomes problematic when applied to, *inter alia*, the 'technological categories of intellectual property: patents, microchip masks, and engineering trade secrets' noting that we usually do not consider these items as 'manifesting the personality of an individual, but rather as manifesting a raw, almost generic insight'.[91]

The analysis of Hughes, however, seems to be based on a misconstruction of Hegel's statement that 'property is the embodiment of personality'.[92] Drahos makes the crucial point that, within the Hegelian framework, all types of property constitute 'part of the explanation for the way personality begins to actualize itself in the world' and, to achieve this self-actualization, individuals can place their will into anything.[93] According to Hegel, 'A person has the right to place his will in any thing ... [t]he thing thereby becomes *mine* and acquires my will as its substantial end'.[94] Drahos contends that artistic objects do not enjoy any privileged status within the Hegelian framework and the 'imposition of artistic form is simply one means by which we can take possession of something'.[95] It will therefore appear that, within the Hegelian framework, individuals can place their will into both artistic objects and scientific inventions.

The biggest challenge with applying the Hegelian framework to intellectual property rights is neither with Hegel's comments on intellectual property (which, as noted above, are based on a socio-centric approach) nor with his analysis on

89 Hughes, 'The Philosophy of Intellectual Property', 330.

90 Ibid., 340.

91 Ibid., 341. Hughes, however, points out that, 'It is an oversimplification to think that some genres of intellectual property *cannot* carry personality. This oversimplification avoids the true issue of the constraints of economy, efficiency, and physical environment which limit the range of personal expression. Such constraints exist to some degree in every genre ... Subtle manifestations of personality may be visible only to people knowledgeable in that field. Just as chess players can recognize particular moves as reflecting the personality of certain players, particular moves in a computer program or a chemical process may be characteristic of a particular inventor or group' (342–3; emphasis in the original).

92 Hegel, *Philosophy of Right*, para 50. Drahos, *A Philosophy of Intellectual Property*, 79.

93 Drahos, *A Philosophy of Intellectual Property*, 80.

94 Hegel, *Elements of the Philosophy of Right*, para 44 (emphasis in the original).

95 Drahos, *A Philosophy of Intellectual Property*, 80.

personality per se. The biggest problem with applying the Hegelian framework to intellectual property, as Drahos points out, is with Hegel's theory of state.[96] In the Hegelian framework, 'the state represents the highest form of freedom an individual can attain' and the 'potentiality which begins with subjective free will and personality becomes concrete actuality in the state'.[97] In a manuscript, which was unpublished during his lifetime, titled *The German Constitution*, Hegel argues that the task of the state is to defend the property of its citizens.[98]

Drahos contends that 'the evolution of intellectual property rights' within Hegel's analysis of state and property, 'may exacerbate the problems of poverty and economic development rather than help them'.[99] This is based on Hegel's statement to the effect that, 'as right *in itself* becomes law in civil society, so too does my individual ... right, whose existence ... was previously *immediate* and *abstract*, acquire a new significance when its existence is recognized as part of the existent ... universal will and knowledge'.[100] The implication of this is that, as Drahos points out, property 'which, at the level of abstract right, was a relation between a thing and an individual will becomes in civil society a formal and posited relation of recognition between individuals'.[101] Drahos contends that the formal recognition of property rights in the Hegelian framework can inhibit the self-development of individuals in a society.[102] Applying this criticism to intellectual property rights, Drahos contends that intellectual property rights 'represents an extension of property rights to an almost indefinite range of objects – scientific ideas, art, the genetic codes of nature – all of which fall within intellectual property's ever expanding domain'.[103] Drahos argues that the extension of property rights to abstract objects such as scientific ideas, based on the Hegelian account of property in civil society, is likely to have negative prospects.[104]

96 Ibid. Drahos notes that Hegel's theory of state 'helps us to understand the organic role of intellectual property and the dangers that intellectual property rights may pose for community'.

97 Ibid., 83.

98 G. W. F. Hegel, 'The German Constitution', in Laurence Dickey and Hugh Nisbet (eds.), *Political Writings* (Cambridge University Press, 1999).

99 Drahos, *A Philosophy of Intellectual Property*, 86.

100 Hegel, *Elements of the Philosophy of Right*, para 217 (emphasis in the original).

101 Drahos, *A Philosophy of Intellectual Property*, 86.

102 According to Drahos, 'Implicit in Hegel's analysis is that the actualizing possibilities of individuals within civil society are conditioned by formal property relations. There is a negative and positive aspect to this. On the positive side the existence of formal property relations means that the embodiment of my will in things is recognized. The negative is that a pattern of formal recognition of property rights can limit my possibilities. The fact that others have property rights as well as the matrix of individual property relations within the social system means that some objects are put beyond my will. Contract can overcome this restrictive aspect of property in that I can acquire the property of others through agreement. The basic point, however, remains unchanged. Property conditions the development potentialities of individuals and communities in both negative and positive ways' (ibid., 87).

103 Ibid., 87.

104 Ibid. As Drahos points out, 'Property in abstract objects increases the capacity of owners to place restrictions on the use of physical objects. The more objects that are removed from the possibility of direct occupation by personality, the greater the reliance by individuals on the

One good example, which illustrates the problem with the Hegelian framework with regard to its application to intellectual property, is the problem of access to patented pharmaceutical products in developing countries. The Hegelian framework relies on the use of contracts as a means for individuals to gain access to objects that they need. This means that individuals who cannot afford to pay for the objects that they need may be left with no other viable alternatives. This has grave implications for poor patients in developing countries who cannot afford to pay the exorbitant prices charged by those who own patents on some of these medicines.

Thus, a developing country that is interested in fostering human development in general and facilitating access to affordable medicines in particular may not find the Hegelian framework to be a suitable framework on which to base its policy on patent rights. While Hegel situates his comments on intellectual property within a sociocentric framework, other aspects of his work relating to the relationship between the state and property can potentially lead to negative consequences in terms of human and economic development. Invariably, the interests of inventors and patent owners are given the centre-stage while the interests of other users of patented goods in society are neglected within the broader Hegelian framework.

2.4 UTILITARIANISM AND PATENT RIGHTS

The typical explanation for the utilitarian justification, particularly in relation to patent rights, is that the grant of exclusive rights on inventions is necessary because inventions, due to their public goods nature, are costly to produce but can be easily appropriated.[105] According to Kenneth Dam, the primary problem that the patent system solves is the 'appropriability problem,' that is, '. . . if a firm could not recover the costs of invention because the resulting information were available to all, then we could expect a much lower and indeed suboptimal level of innovation . . . the patent system prevents others from reaping where they have not sown and thereby promotes research and development (R&D) investment in innovation'.[106] As Burk and Lemley point out, from the utilitarian perspective, patent rights are 'justifiable if they offer a

contract mechanism to gain access. Contract, when it operates within the atomistic setting of civil society, is hardly likely to remedy unequal property distribution. The poor are unlikely to be able to bargain their way to a more equitable distribution of property, or even to negotiate just access and use' (87–8).

105 See Dan Burk and Mark Lemley, 'Policy Levers in Patent Law' (2003) 89 *Virginia Law Review* 1575, 1580. Public goods are goods which are non-rivalrous and non-excludable. A non-rivalrous good is a good that can be enjoyed by multiple consumers at the same time without any consumer detracting from the benefits enjoyed by other consumers. Non-excludability means that it is impossible or impractical to prevent free-riders from enjoying the benefits of a good. See Daphna Lewinsohn-Zamir, 'Consumer Preferences, Citizen Preferences, and the Provision of Public Goods' (1998) 108 *Yale Law Journal* 377. See also Paul Samuelson, 'The Pure Theory of Public Expenditure' (1954) 36 *The Review of Economics and Statistics* 387–9.

106 Kenneth Dam, 'The Economic Underpinnings of Patent Law' (1994) 23 *Journal of Legal Studies* 247.

net benefit to society [by] trading the disutility of restricted output and higher prices for the greater social utility of inventions that might otherwise not be produced'.[107]

The utilitarian justification for intellectual property rights, including patent rights, therefore posits that it is necessary to 'strike an optimal balance between, on the one hand, the power of exclusive rights to stimulate the creation of inventions and works of art and, on the other hand, the partially offsetting tendency of such rights to curtail widespread public enjoyment of those creations'.[108] In other words, utilitarian theorists believe that patent rights should be designed in a manner that achieves a balance between the need to incentivize creative people to invent on the one hand, and the interests of the public in obtaining access to beneficial inventions on the other hand. In sum, utilitarians contend that, without patent rights, there will be no incentives for inventors to produce new and beneficial inventions.[109]

There are a number of problems with the utilitarian justification for patent rights. Firstly, the utilitarian theory is constructed on the assumption that the production of innovative products is dependent on the existence of patent rights or that the grant of patent rights is the best way to stimulate the production of inventions. There is, however, no conclusive evidence[110] indicating that inventors cannot be stimulated to produce inventions through the use of other incentives such as monetary rewards, profits resulting from lead time, tax credits, subsidies, and the prestige that is associated with engaging in scientific innovation.[111] Furthermore, it is not every inventor that is stimulated by a desire for economic gain.[112]

[107] Burk and Lemley, 'Policy Levers in Patent Law', 1580.

[108] William Fisher, 'Theories of Intellectual Property', in Stephen Munzer (ed.), *New Essays in the Legal and Political Theory of Property* (Cambridge University Press, 2001), 169.

[109] Hettinger sums up the utilitarian argument for intellectual property rights thus, 'Without the copyright, patent, and trade secret property protections, adequate incentives for the creation of a socially optimal output of intellectual products would not exist. If competitors could simply copy books, movies, and records, and take one another's inventions and business techniques, there would be no incentive to spend the vast amounts of time, energy, and money necessary to develop these products and techniques. It would be in each firm's self-interest to let others develop products, and then mimic the result. No one would engage in original development, and consequently no new writings, inventions, or business techniques would be developed.' Hettinger, 'Justifying Intellectual Property', 47–8.

[110] As Robert Merges points out, 'The sheer practical difficulty of measuring or approximating all the variables involved means that the utilitarian program will always be at best aspirational. Like designing a perfect socialist economy, the computational complexities of this philosophical project cast grave doubt on its fitness as a workable foundational for the field. In my research, I have become convinced that with our current tools we will never identify the "optimal number" of patented, copyrighted, and trademarked works ... Try as I might, I simply cannot justify our current IP system on the basis of verifiable data showing that people are better off with IP law than they would be without it. Maximizing utility, I have come to see, is not a serviceable first-order principle of the IP system. It is not just what IP is really all about at the deepest level.' Merges, *Justifying Intellectual Property*, 3.

[111] See Fisher, 'Theories of Intellectual Property', 180; Wendy Gordon, 'Intellectual Property', in Peter Cane and Mark Tushnet (eds.), *The Oxford Handbook of Legal Studies* (Oxford University Press, 2003), 632.

[112] Writing in the context of copyright law (but with equal application to and implications for patent law), Rebecca Tushnet notes that, '... the desire to create can be excessive, beyond

Secondly, the utilitarian framework provides a very narrow view of the role of intellectual property (including patents) in the society. As Sunder points out, 'intellectual property today is more than simply a tool for incentivizing creative production in the form of more things'.[113] Current intellectual property laws, as Sunder notes, impacts 'the ability of humankind to flourish, affecting everything from the developing world's access to food, textbooks, and essential medicines, to the ability of citizens everywhere to democratically participate in political and cultural discourse'.[114]

Viewed from a socio-centric perspective, the utilitarian framework does not ignore the interests of other members of the society even though its main goal is to find ways to incentivize creative people to produce useful inventions. Thus, the utilitarian framework tries to find a way to facilitate access to intellectual goods and this problem is typically reduced to two values, that is, incentives and access.[115] Nevertheless, the emphasis is still usually on how to provide incentives while the issue of access is typically treated as a secondary issue. As Sunder points out, 'the prevailing vision is an incentive vision'.[116] But as Sunder rightly argues, it is crucial for intellectual property to 'consider values beyond simply the value of incentivizing production'.[117]

Sunder's argument can be extended further by stating that intellectual property in general, and patent law in particular, should adopt a broader paradigm that also considers the impact of intellectual property on human rights. For instance, patent rights empower patent owners to charge exorbitant prices for certain essential drugs and this has an impact on the enjoyment of the right to health in a number of developing countries. Since access to medicines is a component of the right to health, any activity that hinders access to medicines invariably impedes the enjoyment of the right to health. This is, however, not an issue that can be adequately addressed within the narrow utilitarian framework as its emphasis is on incentivizing

rationality, and free from the need for economic incentive. Psychological and sociological concepts can do more to explain creative impulses than classical economics.' Rebecca Tushnet, 'Economies of Desire: Fair Use and Marketplace Assumptions' (2009) 51 *William and Mary Law Review* 513, 515.

[113] Madhavi Sunder, *From Goods to a Good Life: Intellectual Property and Global Justice* (Yale University Press, 2012), 24.

[114] Ibid.

[115] Ibid., 30.

[116] Ibid., 31. Sunder further notes that, 'By and large, the fight is over the proper economic analysis to incentivize production or sometimes more broadly ... to correct market failure in information production' (31).

[117] Ibid., 31. According to Sunder, '... intellectual property law must adopt broader social and cultural analysis. The fundamental failure in the economic story of intellectual property has to do with information's role in cultural life and human flourishing ... Thus rather than narrowly viewing intellectual property as incentives-for-creation – that is, as merely economic or technology policy – we must understand intellectual property as social and cultural policy. Increasingly in the Knowledge Age, intellectual property laws come to bear on giant-sized values, from democracy and development to freedom and equality' (31–2).

the production of inventions, while access to patented goods is treated as a secondary or subsidiary issue.[118]

Furthermore, it is even doubtful whether relying on the utilitarian framework to justify patent rights serves the health needs of developing countries. As Sunder rightly notes, 'the evidence shows that patents offer no incentive for developing drugs for neglected diseases that predominantly afflict the poor'.[119] Thus, besides failing to adequately address the access needs of poor patients in developing countries, the utilitarian framework equally fails to incentivize the production of drugs for the treatment of diseases that predominantly affect poor patients in developing countries.[120]

2.5 THE REGULATORY THEORY OF PATENT RIGHTS

None of the theoretical justifications that have been assessed thus far, when critically examined from a socio-centric perspective, can be said to provide a sufficient justification or explanation for the existence of intellectual property rights, nor do they adequately recognize the interests of other users of the intellectual property system apart from creators. The deontological frameworks derived from both the Lockean and Hegelian theories both focus almost exclusively on the interests of the creators. While the utilitarian framework appears to spare some thought for the interests of other users in society who require access to intellectual products, it still

[118] As Sunder points out, 'The *intellectual-property-as-incentives* approach fails to account for the wide range of values at stake in global intellectual production today. Even the well-intentioned critics of maximalist intellectual property cannot address the giant-sized values implicit in current debates, from democracy to development, purely from within the traditional economic framework. The fundamental value of the intellectual-property-as-incentives approach is maximizing cultural production. This narrow theory presumes that maximizing cultural production in the aggregate will lead to the greatest good for the greatest number of people' (ibid., 44; emphasis in the original).

[119] Ibid., 198.

[120] As Chidi Oguamanam notes, 'When creativity is dictated by, or exclusively fused with the pursuit of commercial success and the profit motive, innovation in the nobler public interest areas that have little or no direct commercial overflows is fundamentally jeopardized ... Such logic yields an innovation and creative agenda that targets the needs of those who can afford them in accordance with market/economic considerations. In this dynamic, basic or platform research with no immediate, visible, direct or short term commercial application are fundamentally undermined ... [I]ntellectual property's emphasis on profit and reward has yielded a pharmaceutical research agenda that aims at a "cosmetic society," a healthcare research priority and a healthcare system that ignore the sick and needy but cater to the wealthy and healthy who can afford to keep investments in cosmetic drugs and procedures viable. Recent pharmaceutical and "cosmecuetical" research and development in libido-enhancing drugs and anti-ageing products and procedures have been less problematic from the business perspective, in comparison to the controversy surrounding funding and access in regard to dedicated research and benefits regarding autism, Downs syndrome, malaria, typhoid, meningitis, yellow fever, river blindness, chistosomaisis, HIV/AIDS, and other major health care challenges of our time.' Chidi Oguamanam, 'Beyond Theories: Intellectual Property Dynamics in the Global Knowledge Economy' (2009) 9 *Wake Forest Intellectual Property Law Journal* 104, 121, 123–4.

places the interests of the creators and patent owners in a pre-eminent position and treats the interests of other users in the society as a secondary issue. There is thus a need to explore alternative theoretical frameworks that can be used to design a country's patent system in accordance with a socio-centric paradigm.

Shubha Ghosh has suggested that intellectual property should be understood through the lens of regulatory justice.[121] According to Ghosh, 'intellectual property can best be understood as a system of laws meant to define and regulate creative activity'[122] and 'intellectual property establishes a system of rights and obligations that order the processes of creating novel products and services that are valuable to society'.[123] Ghosh further contends that, if intellectual property is a system that defines and regulates creative activity, this implies that intellectual property is not about things but about activities.[124] Viewing intellectual property through this perspective, according to Ghosh, also facilitates a 'deeper consideration of the normative goals driving the structure of intellectual property law', and these normative goals are termed 'regulatory justice'.[125] In other words, Ghosh is suggesting that understanding intellectual property as the regulation of creative activities is desirable for certain normative reasons.[126]

There are two questions to consider with regard to Ghosh's regulatory theory of intellectual property. First, what does it mean to conceptualize intellectual property through the lens of regulatory justice? Second, what are the normative implications of conceptualizing intellectual property through the lens of regulatory justice?

In answering the first question, Ghosh criticizes the treatment of intellectual property as a species of property rights. Indeed, the deontological theories of Locke and Hegel can only be successfully applied to intellectual property if intellectual property is understood as a species of property rights. Furthermore, the utilitarian framework is based on the assumption that the grant of exclusive rights, similar to property rights, to inventors and creators is the right elixir needed to incentivize the

[121] Shubha Ghosh, 'When Property Is Something Else: Understanding Intellectual Property through the Lens of Regulatory Justice', in Axel Gosseries, Alain Marciano, and Alain Strowel (eds.), *Intellectual Property and Theories of Justice* (Palgrave Macmillan, 2008), 106. See generally, Shubha Ghosh, 'Patents and the Regulatory State: Rethinking the Patent Bargain Metaphor after Eldred' (2004) 19 *Berkeley Technology Law Journal* 1315; Shubha Ghosh, 'Patent Law and the Assurance Game: Refitting Intellectual Property in the Box of Regulation' (2005) 18 *Canadian Journal of Law and Jurisprudence* 307; Shubha Ghosh, 'The Intellectual Property Incentive: Not So Natural as to Warrant Strong Exclusivity' (2006) 3 *SCRIPT-ed* 96; Shubha Ghosh, 'Decoding and Recoding Natural Monopoly, Deregulation, and Intellectual Property' (2008) 2008 *University of Illinois Law Review* 1125. For a regulatory conception of copyright law, see, Stephen Zimmermann, 'A Regulatory Theory of Copyright: Avoiding a First Amendment Conflict' (1986) 35 *Emory Law Journal* 163.

[122] Ghosh, 'When Property Is Something Else', 106.

[123] Ibid., 106–7.

[124] Ibid., 107.

[125] Ibid.

[126] Ibid.

production of intellectual products. Ghosh argues that 'it would be wrong to reduce patent and copyright law to a species of property law',[127] as this reductionist approach overlooks several aspects of patent and copyright law.[128]

With regard to patents, Ghosh points out that there is only a superficial resemblance between patents and property and that 'it would be wrong to assume from that family resemblance that patent law is simply a branch of property law'.[129] He further contends that it is impossible to comprehend several crucial features of patent law by merely appealing to the 'category of property and its attendant principles'.[130] One of the aspects of patent law that Ghosh refers to is the on sale bar, which prohibits the grant of a patent on an invention if the patent applicant has sold or publicly disclosed the invention for a certain period of time before seeking to apply for a patent on the invention. Ghosh also discusses how the resolution of patent infringement suits demonstrates the incongruity between patent law and property law.

With regard to the on sale bar, in most jurisdictions, patent applicants can only apply for a patent within 12 months after publicly disclosing or publicly working their inventions.[131] If intellectual property rights are a species of property rights, the on sale bar appears to be incongruous with the nature of property rights. As Ghosh contends, one crucial hallmark of being the owner of a property is 'the ability to alienate and dispose of one's property as one sees fit, absent harm to others'.[132] However, the on sale bar can be viewed as one of the regulatory features of the patent system as it seeks to facilitate the early disclosure of new inventions to the public. Facilitating the early disclosure of new inventions by encouraging inventors to quickly file for patents is justified, according to Ghosh, 'by the benefits of public disclosure of the invention and the protection of reliance interests vested in members of the public who have bought and used the invention and face the risk of forfeiting that right if a patent is subsequently granted on the invention'.[133]

Ghosh equally contends that patent infringement suits also illustrate the incongruity between patent law and property law.[134] In order to succeed in a patent infringement suit, the patentee must establish that the infringing invention falls within the scope of the claimed description of his own patent and this process shares a superficial resemblance with suits alleging trespass to land.[135] Just as judges resolve suits alleging trespass to land by referring to the legal description of the land to

[127] Ibid., 108.
[128] Ibid., 107.
[129] Ibid., 108.
[130] Ibid.
[131] See, for instance, section 32 of the Indian Patents Act of 1970 (as amended in 2005) and section 23(4) of the Kenyan Industrial Property Act of 2001.
[132] Ghosh, 'When Property Is Something Else', 109.
[133] Ibid.
[134] Ibid.
[135] Ibid.

determine the metes and bounds of the land in order to establish if indeed there has been a trespass, judges dealing with patent infringement suits usually rely on the claims in a patent as setting forth the metes and bounds of the patentee's interest – a process termed claim construction or interpretation of claims in a patent.[136]

However, as Ghosh rightly points out, reliance on the analogy of trespass to land is merely 'metaphorical' as there are differences between a patent infringement suit and an action for trespass to land.[137] While the legal description of land refers to natural boundaries, patent claims are mere 'verbal descriptions of the underlying conception that the patent owner has invented'.[138] Ideally, as Wagner and Petherbridge note, 'patent claims might function approximately like the title documents to the real property they weakly resemble and thus have a clear and specific analytic framework'.[139] Realistically, this is not possible because patent claims 'cover intangible concepts rather than physical locations or objects; the precision of real-space descriptions cannot be replicated for the products of human creativity'.[140] The legal descriptions contained in patents are, according to Ghosh, entirely linguistic in nature and this helps to explain why there is 'heated scholarly and judicial debates over the proper interpretation of claims'.[141]

It is undeniable that categorizing patents as property captures some aspects of patent rights such as its alienability, but, as Ghosh contends, treating patents (and other forms of intellectual property) as property shifts the focus away from the activity of creating to the thingness of intellectual property.[142] In Ghosh's view, the features of the patent system, such as the on sale bar and claim construction, indicate that the patent law system is best described and understood as a system that

[136] Ibid. According to Wagner and Petherbridge, 'Claims are thus the touchstone of the patent grant, both establishing the boundaries of the patentee's statutory right to exclude, and defining the scope of the invention for evaluation under the requirements of the Patent Act ... Claim "construction," then, is the process whereby the language found in the claims is, in essence, translated into a meaningful context – either to determine whether infringement has occurred ... or whether the patent claim itself is valid'. Polk Wagner and Lee Petherbridge, 'Did Phillips Change Anything? Empirical Analysis of the Federal Circuit's Claim Construction Jurisprudence', in Shyamkrishna Balganesh (ed.), *Intellectual Property and the Common Law* (Cambridge University Press, 2013) 124–5.

[137] Ghosh, 'When Property Is Something Else', 109.

[138] Ibid.

[139] Wagner and Petherbridge, 'Did Phillips Change Anything?', 125. For another criticism of treating intellectual property like property see, Mark Lemley, 'Property, Intellectual Property, and Free Riding,' (2005) 83 *Texas Law Review* 1031.

[140] Wagner and Petherbridge, 'Did Phillips Change Anything?', 125.

[141] Ghosh, 'When Property Is Something Else', 109. See also Polk Wagner and Lee Petherbridge, 'Is the Federal Circuit Succeeding? An Empirical Assessment of Judicial Performance' (2004) 152 *University of Pennsylvania Law Review* 1105, 1133–4; Kristen Osenga, 'Linguistics and Patent Claim Construction' (2006) 38 *Rutgers Law Journal* 61; Peter Menell, 'Informal Deference: A Historical, Empirical, and Normative Analysis of Patent Claim Construction' (2013) 108 *Northwestern University Law Review* 1.

[142] Ghosh, 'When Property Is Something Else', 111.

regulates creative activity rather than the acquisition and management of things or objects.[143]

It is contended here that Ghosh's regulatory theory of intellectual property is compatible with a socio-centric approach to intellectual property including patents. Unlike the deontological and utilitarian justifications considered above which treat intellectual property rights as a species of property rights from a creator-centric perspective, the regulatory theory of intellectual property provides an alternative and more realistic account of the nature of intellectual property. As Ghosh contends, conceptualizing intellectual property as a species of property 'suggests that intellectual property law should protect the autonomous decisions of the intellectual property owner in managing, alienating and devising the subject matter of intellectual property'.[144] The treatment of patents and other forms of intellectual property rights as property is usually situated within a creator-centric framework which is incompatible with the true nature of creative and intellectual products.

Treating intellectual property as regulation, in the words of Ghosh, 'situates intellectual property law beyond the domain of individual decision-making and control'.[145] Within the regulatory framework, patents and other forms of intellectual property are 'understood to have a social dimension' as they are viewed as 'the means to a social-end beyond the protection of individual self-interest'.[146] Thus, the regulatory theory of patents moves us beyond the creator-centric framework found within the theoretical accounts that treat patents as a species of property rights to a socio-centric framework.

While Ghosh's argument that intellectual property should be conceptualized through the lens of regulatory justice and not as a species of property rights is accepted as valid, Ghosh's description of the regulatory theory will be adopted with some slight modification in this chapter. As noted above, Ghosh adopts the view that intellectual property should be conceptualized as a system of laws meant to define and regulate *creative activity*. It is, however, suggested here that it is perhaps better to describe intellectual property as a policy instrument or set of laws meant to define and regulate the *grant of exclusive rights to creators*. There are two reasons for the adoption of this modification to the regulatory theory in this chapter.

Firstly, while it is indeed possible that intellectual property laws can encourage (or even discourage) creative activity, the focus of the protection granted under intellectual property law is usually on the products of creative activity and not really on the creative activity per se. Secondly, describing intellectual property as a system of laws for defining and regulating *creative activity* might be misunderstood as implying that intellectual property laws determine what can and what cannot be created.

143 Ibid.

144 Ibid., 114.

145 Ibid.

146 Ibid.

In other words, some might misconstrue this to mean that intellectual property laws define the bounds of what can be created. It is true that some creative works might be excluded from protection under intellectual property laws, for instance, on the grounds of morality or public order (for example, as provided for under Article 27(2) of the TRIPS Agreement). Also, an invention might not be protected under a country's patent law on the grounds of failure to fulfil any of the criteria for patent protection. However, the exclusion of certain works or inventions from protection under intellectual property law does not prevent creators from producing those works or inventions. It only really means that those creators will not enjoy the benefits that flow from being granted exclusive rights over what they have created.

It is therefore suggested here that intellectual property is best described as a policy instrument or set of laws that define and regulate the *grant of exclusive rights to creators*. Regulation in this context connotes defining the scope of the exclusive rights granted to creators and it does not imply defining the scope of creative activity. This description of the regulatory theory fits better with a socio-centric view of intellectual property because, rather than focusing on the *creative activity* of creators, it focuses on the policy goals that a state might desire to achieve through the grant of exclusive rights to creators.

At this point, it is now appropriate to consider the second question (identified above) with regard to Ghosh's regulatory theory of intellectual property, that is, what are the normative implications of conceptualizing intellectual property (including patents) through the lens of regulatory justice? Ghosh identifies four possible normative implications that flow from viewing intellectual property through the lens of regulatory justice. He refers to these normative implications as models viz., (1) the model of expertise; (2) the model of civic participation; (3) the model of market failure; and (4) the model of management.[147] Each of these models will be examined here.

The *model of expertise* is premised on the assumption that knowledge and information is not distributed equally among people in any society.[148] It also admits the possibility that those who are more knowledgeable or better informed can, and most likely will, use their superior advantage for their own private gain.[149] The *model of expertise* therefore demands that the interests of society should trump private gain and those who possess superior knowledge should use this superior advantage in a manner that is beneficial to the society as a whole.[150]

What are the implications of the *model of expertise* for regulation? According to Ghosh, the *model of expertise* implies that 'rules and institutions are structured in a way that imposes obligations on the better informed and sophisticated. The rules

147 Ibid.

148 Ibid. In this regard Ghosh builds on the work of Stephen Breyer. See Stephen Breyer, *Breaking the Vicious Cycle: Toward Effective Risk Regulation* (Harvard University Press, 2004).

149 Ghosh, 'When Property Is Something Else', 114.

150 Ibid.

and institutions serve to redistribute the fruits of knowledge so that the more sophisticated do not harm the less'.[151] In other words, the *model of expertise* demands that regulation should be designed in a manner that imposes obligations on those who are better informed and to prevent the exploitation of those who are less informed.[152]

Ghosh refers to health and safety regulations and environmental regulations as instances of regulations that are built on the *model of expertise*.[153] According to Ghosh, 'in many instances some parties will be better informed or in a better position to be informed about the harmful effects of a product or service' and the *model of expertise* demands that 'those who are in a position to prevent or mitigate the harmful consequences of a product or service must be accountable for their superior position'.[154] Ghosh contends that, since intellectual property provides a mechanism for knowledge creation, intellectual property can also be understood through the *model of expertise*.[155] If intellectual property becomes too proprietary, it can hinder the dissemination of knowledge and information in the society[156] and it can result in the continuous exploitation of those who are less informed in the society. Thus, the *model of expertise*, Ghosh argues, 'can help us understand intellectual property in terms of the limits that must be placed on exclusion for knowledge creation to be effective'.[157]

The *model of expertise* can therefore help to understand some of the exceptions and limitations that are built into patent law. For instance, patent law draws a distinction between discoveries and inventions. Patent protection is provided for inventions but not for discoveries. Thus, in most countries, the mere discovery of a scientific principle or the formulation of an abstract theory or the discovery of any living thing or non-living substance occurring in nature are not regarded as patentable inventions.[158] The exclusion of discoveries from the scope of patent protection is connected with the knowledge creation role of the patent system. The grant of exclusive rights on scientific theories and things that exist in nature can stifle the growth of science and technology as these discoveries constitute the building blocks of technological innovation in any society.[159]

An example which illustrates this point is the decision of the United States Supreme Court in the case of *Association for Molecular Pathology v. Myriad*

[151] Ibid., 115.
[152] Ibid.
[153] Ibid.
[154] Ibid.
[155] Ibid.
[156] Ibid.
[157] Ibid.
[158] See section 3(c) of the Indian Patents Act; section 25(2) of the South African Patents Act; and section 21(3) of the Kenyan Industrial Property Act.
[159] See generally, Michael Heller and Rebecca Eisenberg, 'Can Patents Deter Innovation? The Anticommons in Biomedical Research' (1998) 280 *Science* 698.

Genetics, Inc.,[160] where the court had to decide the question of the patent eligibility of naturally occurring DNA. In that case, in a unanimous decision, the Supreme Court held that laws of nature, natural phenomena, and abstract ideas are not patentable because they constitute the basic tools of scientific and technological work that are outside the scope of patent protection.[161] The Supreme Court further noted that 'without this exception, there would be considerable danger that the grant of patents would "tie up" the use of such tools and thereby impede future innovation premised upon them' and 'this would be at odds with the very point of patents, which exist to promote creation'.[162] In other words, no matter the amount of time, energy, and resources that one expends to discover a scientific theory or a natural phenomenon, these things ought not to be granted patent protection so as not to impede the dissemination of knowledge and future creativity. The Supreme Court therefore held that 'genes and the information they encode are not patent eligible ... simply because they have been isolated from the surrounding genetic material'.[163]

Furthermore, even where patent protection has been granted on an invention, in certain jurisdictions, patents are still subject to certain exceptions and limitations which facilitate further creativity and innovation. A typical example is the research exception which permits those engaged in research activity to use patented inventions for purposes of research and experimentation. For instance, section 47(3) of the Indian Patents Act provides that the use of a patented invention for purposes of experiment or research including the imparting of instructions to pupils will not constitute an infringement of the patented invention.[164] Exceptions such as these help to fulfil the knowledge-dissemination role of the patent system under the *model of expertise*.

Another implication of the *model of expertise* for patent law is the implied obligation imposed on patent owners to ensure that their inventions are reasonably affordable. As noted above, the *model of expertise* demands that regulation should be designed in a manner that imposes obligations on those who are better informed and to prevent the exploitation of those who are less informed. This implies that the privileges that are conferred upon patent owners also come with certain obligations. The obligations that can be imposed on patent owners, such as pharmaceutical companies, can include obligations to ensure that patented products are not priced beyond the reach of poor people, particularly where the inventions (such as medicines) are vital to the prevention of harm or death.

[160] *Association for Molecular Pathology* v. *Myriad Genetics, Inc.*, 569 US 2013 (decided 13 June 2013).
[161] Ibid., 11.
[162] Ibid.
[163] Ibid., 18.
[164] See also section 58(1) of the Kenyan Industrial Property Law.

The Indian Patents Act provides a good example of a patent system that incorporates the *model of expertise* in this regard as it contains certain general principles applicable to the working of patented inventions in India. For instance, section 83 (d) of the Indian Patents Act states that patents should 'not impede protection of public health and nutrition and should act as instrument to promote public interest specially in sectors of vital importance for socio-economic and technological development of India'. In addition, section 83(g) of the Indian Patents Act equally provides that 'patents are granted to make the benefit of the patented invention available at reasonably affordable prices to the public'.

The Indian Patents Act also provides a mechanism for enforcing these obligations via the provisions dealing with the grant of compulsory licences. Thus, one of the grounds for the grant of a compulsory licence is that 'the patented invention is not available to the public at a reasonably affordable price'.[165] Another ground for the grant of a compulsory licence is the failure of a patentee to satisfy the reasonable requirements of the public with respect to the patented invention.[166] The provisions relating to the grant of a compulsory licence were applied by the Indian Controller of Patents and the Indian Intellectual Property Appellate Board in the case of *Bayer* v. *Union of India* where both tribunals ruled that a compulsory licence could be granted on Bayer's anti-cancer drug, Nexavar, because of Bayer's failure, *inter alia*, to make the patented drug available to the public at a reasonably affordable price.[167]

The *model of civic participation* is grounded in the notion that in the absence of transparency and openness, legislative processes can be captured by special interests.[168] In order to prevent this from happening, the *model of civic participation* therefore demands that regulation is necessary to ensure that legislative processes are subject to public scrutiny and review.[169] Ghosh contends that 'the existence of administrative institutions like the Patent Office' demonstrate 'a commitment to governmental review and criticism of what type of products count as innovative' for the purposes of patent law.[170] Administrative agencies also enable individuals in society to participate in 'the process of innovation and invention by helping to set standards for the creative and inventive processes'.[171]

[165] Section 84(1)(b) of the Indian Patents Act.

[166] Section 84(1)(a) of the Indian Patents Act.

[167] See *Natco* v. *Bayer*, Compulsory License Application No.1 of 2011, decision of the Indian Controller of Patents (9 March 2012); See *Bayer* v. *Union of India & Others*, OA/[illegible]/2012/PT/MUM, decision of the Indian Intellectual Property Appellate Board (4 March 2013).

[168] Ghosh, 'When Property Is Something Else', 115. In this regard Ghosh builds on the works of Jerry Mashaw and Mariano-Florentino Cuéllar. See Jerry Mashaw, *Greed, Chaos, and Governance: Using Public Choice to Improve Public Law* (Yale University Press, 1997); Mariano-Florentino Cuéllar, 'Rethinking Regulatory Democracy' (2005) 57 *Administrative Law Review* 411.

[169] Ghosh, 'When Property Is Something Else', 115.

[170] Ibid., 116.

[171] Ibid.

An example of the *model of civic participation* is the provisions permitting both pre-grant opposition and post-grant opposition to patent applications in India. Pre-grant opposition to pending patent applications is provided for in section 25(1) of the Indian Patents Act. Section 25(1) allows any person to make this pre-grant opposition. The grounds for making a pre-grant opposition include lack of novelty or inventive step, failure to meet the requirements of section 3(d) (which prohibits the grant of patents on new forms of known drugs), and insufficient or unclear description of the invention in the specification.[172] The pre-grant opposition system has become an invaluable tool utilized by local generic companies in India to challenge pharmaceutical patent applications submitted by multinational pharmaceutical companies.[173] In addition, because any person can file a pre-grant opposition, Non-Governmental Organizations (NGOs) and healthcare advocacy groups can rely on section 25(1) to file pre-grant oppositions to the grant of patents on essential medicines.[174]

The post-grant opposition system is provided for in section 25(2) of the Indian Patents Act and it permits the filing of an opposition to the grant of a patent within one year after the patent was granted.[175] The grounds for filing a post-grant opposition are virtually the same as the grounds for filing a pre-grant opposition.[176] The

[172] See, section 25(1)(a)–(k) of the Indian Patents Act.

[173] For instance, Cipla Ltd. and others brought a successful pre-grant opposition against the application of Abbott Laboratories Ltd. for the grant of patents on ritonavir and lopinavir, two drugs used in the treatment of HIV. See, *In the matter of the application for Patent 339/MUMNP/2006 and In the matter of representation by way of opposition u/s 25(1) to the grant of patent thereon by I-MAK, Cipla Ltd, Okasa Pvt. Ltd. and Matrix Lab Ltd.*, decision of the Deputy Controller of Patents and Designs (30 December 2010) (upholding the pre-grant opposition on the grounds, *inter alia*, of lack of novelty and inventive step).

[174] For instance, the Indian Network for People Living with HIV/AIDS and the Positive Women's Network India brought a successful pre-grant opposition against the application of Boehringer Ingelheim Pharmaceuticals, Inc. for the grant of a patent on nevirapine, a drug used in the treatment of HIV. See, *In the matter of an application for patent having no. 2485/DEL/1998 made by Boehringer Ingelheim Pharmaceuticals, Inc. and In the matter of representation of an opposition thereto by Indian Network for People Living with HIV/AIDS and Positive Women's Network India and In the Matter of opposition u/s 25(1) of the Patents Act, 1970 and rule 55 of the Patent Rules, 2003*, decision of the Assistant Controller of Patents and Designs (11 June 2008) (upholding the pre-grant opposition on the grounds, *inter alia*, of lack of inventive step).

[175] Section 25(2) of the Indian Patents Act provides that, '[a]t any time after the grant of patent but before the expiry of a period of one year from the date of publication of grant of a patent, any person interested may give notice of opposition . . .'. The Indian post-grant opposition system is similar to the American inter partes review system introduced via the Leahy-Smith America Invents Act of 2011 and whose constitutional validity was recently upheld by the US Supreme Court in *Oil States Energy Services, LLC v. Greene's Energy Group, LLC et al*, 138 S. Ct. 1365 (2018) (decided 24 April 2018). See also Jonathan Darrow, Reed Beall, and Aaron Kesselheim, 'The Generic Drug Industry Embraces a Faster, Cheaper Pathway for Challenging Patents' (2018) 17 *Applied Health Economics and Health Policy* 47, who noted that 'In the pharmaceutical market, the inter partes review process can meaningfully contribute to ensuring that invalid patents do not block timely availability of generic drugs.'

[176] See section 25(2)(a)–(k) of the Indian Patents Act.

post-grant opposition procedure has also been used to good effect to revoke the grant of a pharmaceutical patent to a multinational pharmaceutical company in India. The post-grant opposition mechanism was successfully used by an Indian NGO, Sankalp Rehabilitation Trust, to revoke Roche's patent on Pegasys, a drug used in the treatment of Hepatitis C.[177]

The crucial importance of the pre-grant opposition system in India with regard to facilitating civic participation in the process leading to the grant of patents, fostering access to affordable medicines, and preventing the grant of patents on trivial inventions is demonstrated by the decision of the Indian Supreme Court in the case of *Novartis* v. *Union of India*.[178] In that case, the Indian Supreme Court upheld the decision of the Assistant Controller of Patents who, pursuant to the provisions of section 3(d) of the Indian Patents Act, had denied Novartis' application for a patent on its drug, Glivec, because it was a new form of a known drug. It is noteworthy that the process that eventually culminated in the denial of the patent on Glivec was commenced by five separate pre-grant oppositions filed by an NGO and four generic drug manufacturing companies.[179] The *Novartis* case thus demonstrates the importance of civic participation in the patent system as it empowers members of society to scrutinize the process leading to the grant of patents and ensure that only deserving inventions are granted patent rights. The pre-grant opposition and post-grant opposition mechanisms can be utilized by NGOs and generic drug manufacturers to prevent powerful multinational pharmaceutical companies from capturing the process for the grant of patents on pharmaceutical products and processes.

The *model of market failure*, according to Ghosh, 'is a well-understood rationale for regulation and a particularly well-acknowledged justification for intellectual property'.[180] Market failure, as it relates to intellectual property, corresponds with the utilitarian framework discussed in Section 2.4. In economic terms, intellectual property is seen as an instrument that is useful in solving the problem of market failure that arises from the public goods characteristics exhibited by intellectual

[177] See *Sankalp Rehabilitation Trust* v. *Hoffman-La Roche*, Order (No. 250/2012), decision of the Indian Intellectual Property Appellate Board (2 November 2012) (revoking the patent on the ground of lack of inventive steps).

[178] See *Novartis AG* v. *Union of India & Ors*, Civil Appeal Nos. 2706–2716 of 2013 (Supreme Court of India, 1 April 2013).

[179] Ibid., para 13, which noted that the pre-grant oppositions to the patent on Glivec were filed by Cancer Patients Aid Association (an NGO), Natco Pharma Ltd., Cipla Ltd., Ranbaxy Laboratories, and Hetero Drugs Ltd.

[180] Ghosh, 'When Property Is Something Else', 116. In this regard Ghosh builds on the works of Peter Strauss, Ian Ayres and John Braithwaite. See Peter Strauss, *An Introduction to Administrative Justice in the United States* (Carolina Academic Press, 1989). Ian Ayres and John Braithwaite, *Responsive Regulation: Transcending the Deregulation Debate* (Oxford University Press, 1992).

products.[181] A public good is one that cannot be exhausted once it is produced and it is also difficult to prevent free-riders from using such goods.[182] Due to the public goods characteristics exhibited by intellectual goods such as inventions, such goods will normally be under-produced if left to the private market.[183] Once an invention or a book is disclosed to the public, they can be used by several consumers without exhausting the supply, and many people can simultaneously use the new invention or reproduce the book without physically depriving others from using the invention or the book.[184] With regard to inventions, patent law helps to cure this market failure by granting exclusive rights to inventors over their inventions, which enables them to exclude free-riders from using their patented inventions without the payment of a fee. In this way, patent law helps to 'create markets for information and new knowledge that is embodied in products'.[185]

Utilizing intellectual property to cure the problem of market failure arising from the public goods characteristics of intellectual products can, however, also cause problems. This is because the fees demanded by the owners of intellectual property rights may make it difficult for some people in society to gain access to such intellectual products.[186] When this occurs, as Gordon notes, 'the market cannot be relied on to mediate public interests in dissemination and private interests in remuneration' and, in extreme cases, it may become imperative to correct this problem through the imposition of a 'regulatory solution such as a compulsory licensing scheme'.[187] Ghosh also points out that, while 'the model of market failure squarely recognises the use of patents to create markets', it equally recognizes 'the need to limit the patent right if the market is being harmed or compromised'.[188]

[181] Wendy Gordon, 'Fair Use as Market Failure: A Structural and Economic Analysis of the *Betamax* Case and Its Predecessors' (1982) 82 *Columbia Law Review* 1600, 1610. See also Dan Burk, 'Law and Economics of Intellectual Property: In Search of First Principles' (2012) 8 *Annual Review of Law and Social Science* 397, 400.

[182] Gordon, 'Fair Use as Market Failure', 1611; Samuelson, 'The Pure Theory of Public Expenditure', 387–9.

[183] Gordon, 'Fair Use as Market Failure', 1611.

[184] Ibid., 1611.

[185] Ghosh, 'When Property Is Something Else', 116.

[186] As Burk points out, 'the social costs of such exclusion may be high. Allowing the creator to artificially raise the price and restrict the output of the creation may price certain consumers out of the market. Consumers who might have enjoyed the product for free, or at a very low marginal cost, will be unwilling or unable to pay the new higher price. They may not value the good that much, or they may simply lack the funds to pay the higher price. Economists refer to the dissipation of such consumer surplus as the deadweight loss of gains that go unrealized either to the producer or the consumer' (Burk, 'Law and Economics of Intellectual Property', 402).

[187] Gordon, 'Fair Use as Market Failure', 1613.

[188] Ghosh, 'When Property Is Something Else', 119. See also Burk, 'Law and Economics of Intellectual Property', 402, who noted that 'None of the exclusive rights associated with intellectual property is absolute; all are subject to a host of exceptions, limitations, and user privileges.'

An example of a limitation imposed on the rights of patent owners (to solve the problem caused by the use of patents to cure market failure) is the use of compulsory licences by governments of developing countries to facilitate access to affordable medicines for poor patients in their countries. As noted in the discussion of the *model of expertise*, India (through its tribunals) has utilized the grant of a compulsory licence in the case of *Bayer* v. *India* to facilitate cheaper access to Bayer's anti-cancer drug, Nexavar. One of the grounds for the grant of the compulsory licence was the failure of Bayer to sell the drug in India at a price that was reasonably affordable. In addition, in 2007, after unsuccessful negotiations[189] with Merck for price reductions on the anti-retroviral drug called efavirenz, the Brazilian government issued a compulsory licence on the drug and began importation of the generic version of the drug from India.[190] Prior to the issuance of the compulsory licence, the price of the drug was reportedly US$580 per patient per year, but the generic version of the same drug was reportedly imported from India at the cost of US$190 per patient per year.[191]

It should, however, be noted that the *model of market failure*, which is constructed on the public goods characteristics of intellectual goods, is also plagued by the criticisms levelled against the utilitarian framework. For instance, it seems to ignore the fact that certain intellectual goods may still be produced even in the absence of exclusive rights.[192] As Burk points out, '[t]he public goods rationale for intellectual property is contested and certainly does not offer a clear-cut explanation for implementing systems of exclusive rights'.[193] Burk further notes that, using intellectual property rights to cure the problem of market failure may not be worth it if 'the justification for granting exclusive rights in intangible works is to allow a return on investment but it is unclear that the benefits of doing so exceed the social costs'.[194] Nevertheless, if the *model of market failure* is combined with any of the other models in the regulatory theory of intellectual property,[195] it may attenuate some of the social costs that can result from relying solely on the *model of market failure*.

The *model of management*, according to Ghosh, 'follows from the existence of resources that need to be collectively managed in order to maximise the social value

189 According to Amy Nunn, '... since 2001, Brazil has engaged in price negotiations for five patented ARVs [antiretroviral drugs] consuming the largest share of treatment costs ... Price negotiations for patented drugs resulted in a total of $1.2 billion in cost savings over the period of 2001–2005.' Amy Nunn, *The Politics and History of AIDS Treatment in Brazil* (Springer, 2009) 153.

190 Gabriela Chaves, Marcela Vieira, and Renata Reis, 'Access to Medicines and Intellectual Property in Brazil: Reflections and Strategies of Civil Society' (2008) 8 *Sur – International Journal on Human Rights* 163, 171.

191 Ibid., 171.

192 Burk, 'Law and Economics of Intellectual Property', 403.

193 Ibid., 404.

194 Ibid.

195 Ghosh points out that an intellectual property system may have elements of each model or it may be informed by only one model. See Ghosh, 'When Property Is Something Else', 114.

from the resources'.[196] Ghosh refers to natural habitats, parklands, and coastal properties as examples of resources that demand collective management.[197] Ghosh contends that the domain of intellectual property may also constitute part of the resources that require collective management.[198] The *model of management*, according to Ghosh, can 'help in recognising the obligations of intellectual property owners to manage their creations for the general public'[199] and it would also 'call for limitations on the private right to exclude granted by the patent'.[200]

Thus, in line with the *model of management*, some countries impose certain limitations on patent rights in order to maximize the social value from patented inventions. Such limitations include compulsory licensing,[201] adoption of the principle of international exhaustion of patent rights (thus permitting parallel importation of patented inventions),[202] research exception,[203] and regulatory review exemptions for generic drug manufacturers.[204] These limitations help to ensure that patent rights are not exercised in a way that prevents the country from deriving social value from patented inventions. Furthermore, these limitations can also help to ensure that patent rights on pharmaceutical products are not exercised in a manner that is detrimental to the public health interests of the country.

A fifth model, the *model of human rights* can be added to the list of normative implications that flow from conceptualizing intellectual property through the lens of regulatory justice.[205] The *model of human rights* demands that any regulatory instrument implemented by a state must not constitute a breach of its international

[196] Ibid., 116. In this regard Ghosh builds on the work of James Wilson. See James Wilson, *Bureaucracy: What Government Agencies Do and Why They Do It* (Basic Books, 1989).

[197] Ghosh, 'When Property Is Something Else', 116–17.

[198] Ibid., 117.

[199] Ibid.

[200] Ibid., 119.

[201] See section 84 of the Indian Patents Act; section 56 of the South African Patents Act; and section 72 of the Kenyan Industrial Property Act.

[202] See section 107A(b) of the Indian Patents Act; section 15C of the South African Medicines and Related Substances Control Amendment Act of 1997; and section 58(2) of the Kenyan Industrial Property Law. In relation to the South African provision, it should be noted that it is limited only to medicines and the law only empowers the Health Minister to allow parallel imports in certain circumstances. See Carlos Correa, *Intellectual Property Rights, the WTO and Developing Countries: The TRIPS Agreement and Policy Options* (Zed Books Ltd and Third World Network, 2000), 87–8.

[203] See section 47(3) of the Indian Patents Act and section 58(1) of the Kenyan Industrial Property Act.

[204] See section 107A(a) of the Indian Patents Act and section 69A(1) of the South African Patents Act.

[205] Though Ghosh only discusses four models, he does not appear to have considered these four models as the only possible normative implications of his regulatory theory. According to him, 'There are several possible normative implications for what I have called regulatory justice.' See Ghosh, 'When Property Is Something Else', 114. Thus, it is not out of place to insert a *model of human rights* into the list of the possible normative implications of Ghosh's regulatory theory of intellectual property.

human rights obligations. In this regard, this implies that the design, implementation, interpretation, and enforcement of intellectual property laws at the national level must not be done in a manner that impinges on any of the rights contained in any treaty on human rights to which a state is a party. This applies to the executive, legislative, and judicial arms of government. As Shelton points out, '[h]uman rights obligations fall on all State actors, irrespective of the level or branch of government in which they serve ... Whenever a State organ, official, or public entity violates a guaranteed right, this constitutes a failure of the State's obligation'.[206]

The *model of human rights* is relevant in the context of intellectual property rights because intellectual property rights do have an impact on the enjoyment of a number of human rights. For instance, copyright law impacts the enjoyment of the right to education,[207] while trademark law and the right of publicity both impact the enjoyment of the right to freedom of expression.[208] More importantly for the purposes of this chapter, patent law impacts the enjoyment of the right to health (which includes the right to have access to medicines). Patent rights have a direct impact on the right to health, especially in developing countries where pharmaceutical products are priced beyond the reach of poor patients. Patents confer exclusive rights on patent owners, and this can lead to the inflation of prices of patented products and, as Joseph notes, this can be 'problematic as goods that are essential for the enjoyment of human rights, such as new medicines, can be priced out of the reach of poor people'.[209] As noted in Chapter 1, it is impossible to resolve the tension between patent rights and access to medicines by relying only on the internal principles contained in intellectual property law.[210] Therefore, the best way to resolve the tension between patent rights and access to medicines is by using external norms contained in the human rights system, and this can be done by incorporating a *model of human rights* into the patent system.[211]

[206] D. L. Shelton, *Advanced Introduction to International Human Rights Law* (Edward Elgar, 2014), 191.

[207] See generally, Susan Isiko Štrba, *International Copyright Law and Access to Education in Developing Countries: Exploring Multilateral Legal and Quasi-Legal Solutions* (Martinus Nijhoff, 2012).

[208] See generally, Eugene Volokh, 'Freedom of Speech and Intellectual Property: Some Thoughts after Eldred, 44 Liquormart, and Bartnicki' (2003) 40 *Houston Law Review* 697, 698, who noted that, 'most intellectual property rules – copyright law, trademark law, right of publicity law, and trade secret law – are speech restrictions: They keep people from publishing, producing, and performing the speech that they want to publish, produce, and perform. The laws may be well motivated and often beneficial, but they are speech restrictions.'

[209] Sarah Joseph, 'Trade and the Right to Health', in Andrew Clapham and Mary Robinson (eds.), *Realizing the Right to Health*, Swiss Human Rights Book Series, Vol. 3 (Ruffer & Rub, 2009), 360.

[210] See generally, Amanda Barratt, 'The Curious Absence of Human Rights: Can the WIPO Development Agenda Transform Intellectual Property Negotiation?' (2010) 14 *Law, Democracy & Development* 14, 24.

[211] As Amanda Barratt points out, human right norms 'provide specific limitations on what is negotiable, while identifying precise minimum conditions that are beyond negotiation' (ibid., 32). As Yamin notes, 'Human rights law not only offers an alternative paradigm for

Article 12 of the International Covenant on Economic, Social, and Cultural Rights (ICESCR) mandates all the state parties to the Covenant to recognize the right of everyone to the enjoyment of the highest attainable standard of physical and mental health. In its elaboration on Article 12 of the ICESCR, the United Nations Committee on Economic, Social and Cultural Rights (CESCR) in its General Comment No.14 states that the provision of essential drugs is one of the core obligations of state parties with regard to the right to heath.[212] Furthermore, the CESCR notes that the adoption of laws or policies that interfere with the enjoyment of any of the components of the right to health constitutes a violation of a state's obligation to respect the right to health.[213] The failure of a state to take into account its legal obligations regarding the right to health when entering into bilateral or multilateral agreements with other states, international organizations and other entities, such as multinational corporations, is also viewed as a violation of the obligation to respect the right to health.[214]

It is contended that the incorporation of a *model of human rights* into a country's national patent system may not be in conflict with its obligations under the TRIPS Agreement in light of paragraph 4 of the Doha Declaration on the TRIPS Agreement and Public Health (Doha Declaration).[215] Paragraph 4 of the Doha Declaration provides that '... the TRIPS Agreement ... can and should be interpreted and implemented in a manner supportive of WTO members' right to protect public health and, in particular, to promote access to medicines for all'. Thus, the use of flexibilities such as the exclusion of new forms of known drugs from patent protection, compulsory licences, parallel importation, and regulatory review exception, pursuant to a *model of human rights* is compatible with the text of the TRIPS Agreement in the context of the Doha Declaration.

Thus, it is imperative for states to secure the right to health of their citizens by ensuring that a *model of human rights* is incorporated into the design, implementation, interpretation, and enforcement of their patent laws. In simple terms, the

understanding issues relating to the availability and distribution of medications, it also provides a workable framework for influencing the way in which adjudicative and legislative bodies, as well as other actors, make decisions that affect access to medications ... [T]reaties and statutes relating to trade, competition, intellectual property, or other factors bearing on access to medications can often be ambiguous; in such cases, a human rights framework imposes an obligation to interpret such treaties and legislation in the manner that most fully advances the public's health interests ... Further, human rights provides a set of principles according to which laws, policies and programs can be evaluated and reformed.' Alicia E. Yamin, 'Not Just a Tragedy: Access to Medications as a Right under International Law' (2003) 21 *Boston University International Law Journal* 325, 327–9.

[212] UN Committee on Economic, Social and Cultural Rights (CESCR), 'General Comment No. 14', E/C.12/2000/4 (2000), para 43(d).

[213] Ibid., para 50.

[214] Ibid.

[215] See WTO Ministerial Conference, 'Declaration on the TRIPS Agreement and Public Health', adopted on 14 November 2001, WT/MIN(01)/DEC/2 (20 November 2001).

model of human rights, in the context of intellectual property rights, demands that fundamental human rights such as the right to health should not be subordinated or trumped by intellectual property rights such as patent rights.[216] In subsequent chapters, examples of countries such as India, Kenya, and South Africa that have incorporated a *model of human rights* into their national patent laws will be examined.

According to Ghosh's regulatory theory, all the models are distinct, though they are not mutually exclusive.[217] Ghosh points out that an intellectual property system may have elements of each model or it may be informed by only one model.[218] A society is also free, within Ghosh's regulatory theory, to choose one or more of these models through its democratic institutions and design an intellectual property system that reflects its normative choices.[219] Thus, a society that is interested in securing access to medicines for its citizens ought to, at least, elect to incorporate the *model of human rights* into its patent law system.

2.6 CONCLUSION

A socio-centric approach to the design of patent law and policy is essential for any developing country that seeks to ensure that its national patent law does not impede access to medicines. The adoption of a socio-centric approach in the design and enforcement of a country's patent law helps to incorporate 'the interests and rights of users'[220] and helps to prevent a situation where the primary focus of a country's patent law is on the interests and rights of inventors. As Ghosh points out, a user-centred approach to intellectual property law (including patent law) 'has implications for how intellectual property law would operate in practice through public debate and through judicial and administrative enforcement'.[221]

The adoption of a socio-centric approach can also assist a country to preserve its patent policy space. For instance, in deciding whether to provide patent protection for new forms of known drugs, a country that adopts a creator-centric approach may choose to recognize new forms of known drugs as patentable subject matter while

[216] As stated by the UK Commission on Intellectual Property Rights in its report published in 2002, 'We therefore consider that an IP right is best viewed as one of the means by which nations and societies can help to promote the fulfilment of human economic and social rights. In particular, there are no circumstances in which the most fundamental human rights should be subordinated to the requirements of IP protection. IP rights are granted by states for limited times (at least in the case of patents and copyrights) whereas human rights are inalienable and universal.' See Commission on Intellectual Property Rights, *Integrating Intellectual Property Rights and Development Policy: Report of the Commission on Intellectual Property Rights* (London, September 2002), 6.

[217] Ghosh, 'When Property Is Something Else', 114.

[218] Ibid.

[219] Ibid.

[220] Ghosh, 'Managing the Intellectual Property Sprawl', 982.

[221] Ibid.

providing for some exceptions. But a country that adopts a socio-centric approach may, as Ghosh notes, 'ask us to question whether property rights should be recognized in the first instance and provide grounds for recognizing limitations in the scope of any right that is recognized'.[222] Thus, a country like India, that has refused to recognize new forms of known drugs as patentable subject matter, is following a socio-centric approach because its patent law is designed to prevent the grant of patents on trivial inventions and to also facilitate access to cheaper generic drugs.[223] By refusing to merely focus on the interests of inventors, section 3(d) of the Indian Patents Act, which prohibits the patenting of new forms of known drugs, helps to preserve India's patent policy space. Section 3(d) of the Indian Patents Act incorporates the interests and rights of other users in society, such as local pharmaceutical companies engaged in the production of cheaper generic drugs and poor patients who require access to cheaper generic drugs.

Of all the theoretical justifications examined in this chapter, the regulatory theory of intellectual property is the only theory that adopts a broad socio-centric approach. Therefore, any developing country that seeks to preserve its patent policy space and secure access to medicines for its citizens should treat intellectual property as an instrument that regulates the exclusive rights granted to creators and incorporate (at least) the *model of human rights* into the design, implementation, interpretation, and enforcement of its national patent law. This will ensure that the right to health of its citizens is not violated. Chapter 3 will proceed to examine the nature of the relationship between patent rights and the right to health under international human rights law.

[222] Ibid., 985.

[223] See section 3(d) of the Indian Patents Act. See also *Novartis AG* v. *Union of India & Ors*, Civil Appeal Nos. 2706–2716 of 2013 (Supreme Court of India, 1 April 2013).

3

The Interface between Patent Rights and the Right to Health under International Human Rights Law

3.1 INTRODUCTION

Building on the discussion in Chapter 2, this chapter seeks to answer two key questions that are integral to the issues addressed in this book. First, are patent rights human rights? Second, is the incorporation of a *model of human rights* compatible with the TRIPS Agreement? The answers to these two key questions will determine whether or not developing countries can successfully incorporate a *model of human rights* into the design, implementation, interpretation, and enforcement of their national patent laws.

This chapter is structured into three main sections. Section 3.2 examines the human right to health under international law and highlights the obligations of states with regard to the right to health.[1] Section 3.3 provides an analysis of the

[1] The discussion of the right to health in this chapter focuses mainly on highlighting the right-to-health obligations of state actors as contained in the International Covenant on Economic, Social, and Cultural Rights, and as elaborated upon by the UN Committee on Economic, Social, and Cultural Rights in its General Comment No. 14. See UN Committee on Economic, Social and Cultural Rights (CESCR), 'General Comment No. 14, The Right to the Highest Attainable Standard of Health (Article 12)' E/C.12/2000/4 (2000) [hereinafter, CESCR, 'General Comment No. 14']. Hence, this chapter does not discuss the historical development of the right to health. For a discussion of the historical development of the right to health, see John Tobin, *The Right to Health in International Law* (Oxford University Press, 2012) 14–43. In addition, while recognizing the debate surrounding the conceptual foundations of the right to health, an exhaustive examination of the arguments in this debate is beyond the scope of this thesis. For arguments against the right to health in particular and economic and social rights in general, see William Easterly, 'Human Rights Are the Wrong Basis for Healthcare' *The Financial Times* (12 October 2009), available from www.ft.com/intl/cms/s/0/89bbbda2-b763-11de-9812-00144feab49a.html#axzz3S2G4KnFs (last accessed 27 September 2021); James Griffin, *On Human Rights* (Oxford University Press, 2008), 208–9; Aryeh Neier, 'Social and Economic Rights: A Critique' (2006) 13 *Human Rights Brief* 1–3; Onora O'Neill, 'The Dark Side of Human Rights' (2005) 81 *International Affairs* 427; Maurice Cranston, 'Are There Any Human Rights?' (1983) 112 *Daedalus* 1. For arguments in support of the right to health, see Tobin, *Right to Health*, 44–74; Jonathan Wolff, *The Human Right to Health*

nature of the relationship between patent rights and the right to health under international human rights law and provides an answer to the first key question that is being addressed in this chapter. Section 3.4 examines the extent to which the TRIPS Agreement permits developing countries to fulfil their right to health obligations and provides an answer to the second key question that is being addressed in this chapter. The chapter concludes with the view that patent rights ought not to be considered as human rights under international human rights law and that the *model of human rights* is compatible with the TRIPS Agreement. Thus, there is nothing that prohibits a developing country from insisting on the primacy of human rights obligations when attempting to resolve the tension between patent rights and the right to health at the national level.

3.2 THE HUMAN RIGHT TO HEALTH UNDER INTERNATIONAL LAW

The human right to health is recognized in several international legal instruments and in the constitutions of a number of countries across the world.[2] The recognition of this right in legal instruments, however, is not a guarantee that it is being enjoyed on an equal basis universally. The enjoyment of this right is further curtailed by the present global structure for the protection of intellectual property rights, especially patent rights. Patent rights have a direct impact on the right to health, especially in developing countries where pharmaceutical products are priced beyond the reach of poor patients.

One of the international agreements that provides for the right to health is the International Covenant on Economic, Social, and Cultural Rights (ICESCR). Article 12(1) of the ICESCR mandates the state parties to the Covenant to 'recognize the right of everyone to the enjoyment of the highest attainable standard of physical and mental health'. In 2000, the UN Committee on Economic, Social, and Cultural Rights (CESCR) adopted General Comment No. 14 in an attempt to provide further definition for Article 12 of the ICESCR.[3] Paragraph 12 of General Comment No. 14 is very relevant to the question of access to medicines. It enumerates four essential, interrelated components of the right to health: availability,

(W. W. Norton & Co., 2012), 13–38; J. P. Ruger, *Health and Social Justice* (Oxford University Press, 2010), 118; J. P. Ruger, 'Towards a Theory of a Right to Health: Capability and Incompletely Theorized Agreements' (2006) 18 *Yale Journal of Law and the Humanities* 273.

[2] See The Constitution of the WHO, 1946; Article 25 of the Universal Declaration of Human Rights, G.A. Res. 217A (III) (1948); Article 12 of the International Covenant on Economic, Social and Cultural Rights, G.A. Res. 2200A (XXI) (1966). See also Section 27 of the South African Constitution, 1996; Article 43(1)(a) of the Kenyan Constitution, 2010; and Article 196 of the Brazilian Constitution, 1988. There is also judicial recognition of the right to health as an integral component of the constitutional right to life in India. See, for instance, *Consumer Education & Research Centre & Ors.* v. *Union of India & Ors.*, 1995 SCC (3) 42 (decided on 27 January 1995).

[3] See CESCR, 'General Comment No. 14'.

accessibility, acceptability, and quality. In particular, it provides that essential drugs (as defined by the World Health Organization Action Programme on Essential Drugs) must be available in a country.[4]

According to the World Health Organization (WHO), essential drugs are drugs that 'satisfy the priority health care needs of the population' and 'are intended to be available within the context of functioning health systems at all times in adequate amounts ... and at a price the individual and the community can afford.'[5] In addition, General Comment No. 14 states that health care services must be economically accessible to everyone, suggesting that the prices of essential drugs should not be so expensive as to be unaffordable for poor patients.[6] This makes access to essential medicines an integral component of the right to health.[7] Furthermore, states are obliged to take steps 'to control the marketing of medical equipment and medicines by third parties'.[8] It has been suggested that this implies that 'states should intervene where marketing of drugs by pharmaceutical companies is detrimental to the right to health'.[9]

States have an obligation to respect, protect, and fulfil the right to health.[10] The obligation to *respect* the right to health demands that states should not interfere directly or indirectly with the enjoyment of the right to health.[11] Essentially, the obligation to respect the right to health requires that states should, *inter alia*, 'refrain from denying or limiting equal access for all persons ... to preventive, curative and palliative health services'.[12] The obligation to *protect* the right to health requires states to, *inter alia*, 'adopt legislation or to take other measures ensuring equal access to health care and health-related services provided by third parties'.[13] The obligation to *fulfil* the right to health demands that states should, *inter alia* 'give sufficient recognition to the right to health in the national political and legal systems, preferably by way of legislative implementation, and to adopt a national health policy with a detailed plan for realizing the right to health'.[14]

4 Ibid., para 12(a).
5 See WHO, 'Essential Medicines', available from www.who.int/topics/essential_medicines/en/ (last accessed 27 September 2021).
6 CESCR, 'General Comment No. 14', para 12(b).
7 See Mirela Hristova, 'Are Intellectual Property Rights Human Rights? Patent Protection and the Right to Health' (2011) 93 *Journal of the Patent & Trademark Office Society* 339, 356. See also UN Human Rights Council, 'Access to Medicines in the Context of the Right of Everyone to the Enjoyment of the Highest Attainable Standard of Physical and Mental Health,' A/HRC/RES/23/14 (2013).
8 CESCR, 'General Comment No. 14', para 35.
9 Stephen Marks, 'Access to Essential Medicines as a Component of the Right to Health', in A. Clapham and M. Robinson (eds.), *Realizing the Right to Health*, Swiss Human Rights Book Series, vol 3 (Ruffer & Rub, 2009), 90.
10 CESCR, 'General Comment No. 14', para 33.
11 Ibid., para 33.
12 Ibid., para 34.
13 Ibid., para 35.
14 Ibid., para 36.

It is contended here that the obligation of states to respect, protect, and fulfil the right to health has implications for the design, implementation, interpretation, and enforcement of their national patent laws. The obligation to fulfil the right to health demands that, when designing or amending their national patent laws, states should recognize the possible implications of such legislative proposals for the enjoyment of the right to health.[15] In order to effectively protect the right to health, patent rights owned by third parties such as pharmaceutical companies should not be exercised and enforced in a manner that makes it more difficult for poorer citizens to have access to affordable generic drugs.[16] Furthermore, the obligation to respect the right to health requires that, when designing, implementing, or interpreting patent laws, the various arms and organs of government (including the courts) should not adopt an approach that impedes the enjoyment of the right to health.[17] States equally have core obligations with regard to the right to health.[18] One of the core obligations of states is to 'provide essential drugs, as from time to time defined under the WHO Action Programme on Essential Drugs'.[19] It must be stressed that a core obligation is one from which no derogation is permissible.[20]

3.3 ARE PATENT RIGHTS HUMAN RIGHTS?

3.3.1 *The Three Broad Approaches*

There are divergent views on how the relationship between intellectual property rights (including patent rights) and human rights should be conceptualized.[21] In his

[15] Ibid., para 52, which states that 'Violations of the obligation to fulfil occur through the failure of States parties to take all necessary steps to ensure the realization of the right to health.'

[16] Ibid., para 51, which states that 'Violations of the obligation to protect follow from the failure of a State to take all necessary measures to safeguard persons within their jurisdiction from infringements of the right to health by third parties. This category includes such omissions as the failure to regulate the activities of individuals, groups or corporations so as to prevent them from violating the right to health of others.'

[17] Ibid., para 50, which staties that 'Violations of the obligation to respect are those State actions, policies or laws that contravene the standards set out in article 12 of the Covenant and are likely to result in bodily harm, unnecessary morbidity and preventable mortality. Examples include ... the suspension of legislation or the adoption of laws or policies that interfere with the enjoyment of any of the components of the right to health; and the failure of the State to take into account its legal obligations regarding the right to health when entering into bilateral or multilateral agreements with other States, international organizations and other entities, such as multinational corporations.'

[18] Ibid., para 43.

[19] Ibid., para 43(d).

[20] Ibid., para 47, which notes that 'It should be stressed, however, that a State party cannot, under any circumstances whatsoever, justify its non-compliance with the core obligations set out in paragraph 43 above, which are non-derogable.'

[21] See generally, Peter Drahos, 'Intellectual Property and Human Rights' (1999) 3 *Intellectual Property Quarterly* 349; Laurence Helfer, 'Human Rights and Intellectual Property: Conflict or Coexistence?' (2003) 5 *Minnesota Intellectual Property Review* 47; Peter Yu,

review of the literature, Gold identifies three broad approaches to the conceptualization of the relationship between patent rights and human rights:

1. The 'subjugation approach', which states that, when patent rights and human rights conflict, human rights considerations should trump patent rights;
2. The 'integrated approach', which views patents as a human right; and
3. The 'coexistence approach', which asserts that patent law and human rights law are distinct but share a basic concern in defining the optimal amount of patent protection required to incentivize and practice socially useful innovation.[22]

In his description of the 'subjugation approach', Helfer notes that this approach 'views human rights and intellectual property as being in fundamental conflict' and it considers 'strong intellectual property protection as undermining – and therefore as incompatible with – a broad spectrum of human rights obligations, especially in the area of economic, social, and cultural rights'.[23] Helfer further notes that the 'prescription that proponents of this approach advocate for resolving this conflict is to recognize the normative primacy of human rights law over intellectual property law in areas where specific treaty obligations conflict'.[24] Plomer suggests that this

'Reconceptualizing Intellectual Property Interests in a Human Rights Framework' (2007) 40 *U. C. Davis Law Review* 1039; Peter Yu, 'Ten Common Questions about Intellectual Property and Human Rights' (2007) 23 *Georgia State University Law Review* 709; Willem Grosheide (ed.), *Intellectual Property and Human Rights: A Paradox* (Edward Elgar, 2010); Paul Torremans (ed.), *Intellectual Property and Human Rights* (Kluwer Law International, 2008); Laurence Helfer and Graeme Austin, *Human Rights and Intellectual Property: Mapping the Global Interface* (Cambridge University Press, 2011); E. R. Gold, 'Patents and Human Rights: A Heterodox Analysis' (2013) 41 *The Journal of Law, Medicine & Ethics* 185; Aurora Plomer, 'The Human Rights Paradox: Intellectual Property Rights and Rights of Access to Science' (2013) 35 *Human Rights Quarterly* 143.

22 Gold, 'Patents and Human Rights', 186–7.

23 Helfer, 'Human Rights and Intellectual Property', 48. See also Gold, 'Patents and Human Rights', 186, who notes that the 'subjugation approach' 'views patents and human rights as mutually exclusive spheres of law that are sometimes at odds with one another. Where a conflict between patent and human rights law arises, this approach requires that human rights considerations trump patent rights.' For statements in support of the 'subjugation approach', see Peter Drahos with John Braithwaite, *Information Feudalism: Who Owns the Knowledge Economy?* (Earthscan, 2002), 200, who note that 'In any principled national legal system, basic human rights to health, education and indigenous rights to their cultures take precedence over (trump) utilitarian considerations'; Drahos, 'Intellectual Property and Human Rights', 367, who states that 'rights created through the enactment of intellectual property laws are instrumental rights. Ideally, under conditions of democratic sovereignty, such rights should serve the interests and needs that citizens identify through the language of human rights as being fundamental. On this view, human rights would guide the development of intellectual property rights; intellectual property rights would be pressed into service on behalf of human rights.'

24 Helfer, 'Human Rights and Intellectual Property', 48.

approach 'might arguably be more accurately described as the "primacy of human rights" view'.[25]

Gold describes the 'integrated approach' as an approach that assimilates 'patent rights into human rights analyses' instead of 'introducing human rights considerations into patent policy as advocated by some adherents of the subjugation approach'.[26] The 'integrated approach' does not consider patents and human rights as distinct, rather it views 'patents as part of human rights law'.[27] However, advocates of the 'integrated approach' typically misconstrue the provisions of international human rights instruments such as Article 15(1)(c) of the ICESCR which provides for the protection of the moral and material interests of authors and inventors.[28] They build their arguments on the incorrect premise that provisions such as Article 15(1)(c) show that intellectual property rights (including patent rights) are human rights.[29]

Helfer provides a description of the 'coexistence approach' as an approach that sees both human rights and intellectual property rights 'as concerned with the same fundamental question: defining the appropriate scope of private monopoly power that gives authors and inventors a sufficient incentive to create and innovate, while ensuring that the consuming public has adequate access to the fruit of their efforts'.[30] Helfer further notes that this approach 'views human rights law and intellectual property law as essentially compatible, although often disagreeing over where to strike the balance between incentives on the one hand and access on the other'.[31]

Before identifying the correct one among the three approaches, it is essential to first determine the status of intellectual property rights (including patent rights) under international human rights law. Article 15(1)(c) of the ICESCR recognizes the right of everyone to 'benefit from the protection of the moral and material interests resulting from any scientific, literary or artistic production of which he is the author'. A similar provision is also contained in Article 27(2) of the Universal Declaration of Human Rights (UDHR). Article 27(2) of the UDHR provides that 'Everyone has the

25 See Plomer, 'The Human Rights Paradox', 151.
26 Gold, 'Patents and Human Rights', 187–8.
27 Ibid., 188.
28 See, for instance, Marks, 'Access to Essential Medicines', 87; see also J. Millum, 'Are Pharmaceutical Patents Protected by Human Rights?' (2008) 34 *Journal of Medical Ethics* e25.
29 Gold, 'Patents and Human Rights', 188.
30 Helfer, 'Human Rights and Intellectual Property', 48. In her own description of the 'coexistence approach', Plomer notes that 'The "co-existence" view claims that the paradox and conflict between IP rights and human rights, is only apparent. Some argue that the conflict is illusory because IP rights, or some aspects of them, are fundamental human rights too, albeit of "weaker" weight than other rights. Others suggest that the normative content of the obligations prescribed by human rights instruments are so open-ended and general as to say very little on the impact of IP rights on the realization of other rights.' See Plomer, 'The Human Rights Paradox', 151. See also Gold, 'Patents and Human Rights', 187.
31 Helfer, 'Human Rights and Intellectual Property', 48–9.

right to the protection of the moral and material interests resulting from any scientific, literary or artistic production of which he is the author'. At first reading, these two provisions appear to equate intellectual property rights with other types of human rights, and this has led some authors to conclude that they provide a human rights basis for patent rights and other forms of intellectual property rights.[32]

However, the CESCR, in its General Comment No. 17, has made it clear that human rights and intellectual property rights are not on the same level, and it will be erroneous to rely on Article 15(1)(c) to equate intellectual property rights with human rights.[33] The CESCR adopted the view that Article 15(1)(c) solely 'safeguards the personal link between authors and their creations ... as well as their basic material interests which are necessary to enable authors to enjoy an adequate standard of living' while 'intellectual property regimes primarily protect business and corporate interests and investments'.[34] In essence, the human right contained in Article 15(1)(c) is not coterminous with intellectual property rights. The approach adopted by the CESCR is equally supported by the drafting history of both Article 27 (2) of the UDHR and Article 15(1)(c) of the ICESCR. It has been noted that the provisions were included in both instruments after considerable debates and controversy.[35] According to Chapman, the drafting history of both the UDHR and ICESCR supports 'relatively weak claims of intellectual property as a human right'.[36]

It is contended here that, strictly speaking, the human right contained in both Article 15(1)(c) of the ICESCR and Article 27(2) of the UDHR is a right to the protection of the 'moral and material interests' of authors and inventors in their creative works.[37] This right is separate from, and should never be confused with, intellectual property rights.[38] The CESCR, in General Comment No. 17, stresses

32 Marks, 'Access to Essential Medicines', 87; see also Millum, 'Are Pharmaceutical Patents Protected by Human Rights?', e25.

33 See UN Committee on Economic, Social and Cultural Rights (CESCR), 'General Comment No. 17, The Right of Everyone to Benefit from the Protection of the Moral and Material Interests Resulting from any Scientific, Literary or Artistic Production of which He or She is the Author (Article 15, paragraph 1(c), of the Covenant)', E/C.12/GC/17 (2006) paras 1, 3. [Hereinafter, CESCR, 'General Comment No. 17'].

34 Ibid., para 2.

35 See Yu, 'Reconceptualizing Intellectual Property Interests', 1073.

36 See Audrey Chapman, 'Approaching Intellectual Property as a Human Right: Obligations Related to Article 15(1)(c)' (2001) 35 *Copyright Bulletin* 4, 13. See also Plomer, 'The Human Rights Paradox', 175.

37 CESCR, 'General Comment No. 17', para 1, which notes that 'The right of everyone to benefit from the protection of the moral and material interests resulting from any scientific, literary or artistic production of which he or she is the author is a human right, which derives from the inherent dignity and worth of all persons. This fact distinguishes article 15, paragraph 1(c), and other human rights from most legal entitlements recognized in intellectual property systems.'

38 Ibid., para 1, which notes that 'Human rights are fundamental as they are inherent to the human person as such, whereas intellectual property rights are first and foremost means by which States seek to provide incentives for inventiveness and creativity, encourage the

the point that the protection of the moral and material interests of authors and inventors does not necessarily coincide with what is currently regarded as intellectual property rights in national laws and international agreements.[39] While the right to the protection of the moral interests and material interests of authors and inventors in their creative works is a fundamental entitlement, intellectual property rights are not fundamental entitlements, as they can be limited, traded, amended, or even forfeited.[40] It is, however, necessary to examine the real meaning of the expression 'moral and material interests', and this will be the focus of the analysis in Section 3.3.2.

3.3.2 *The Moral and Material Interests of Authors and Inventors*

In its analysis on the right to the protection of the *moral* interests of authors and inventors, the CESCR referred to the Report of the Working Group on the Declaration on Human Rights which was prepared in 1947 as part of the process leading to the emergence of the Universal Declaration on Human Rights (UDHR).[41] In the report of the Working Group, the text of the draft Article relating to the rights of authors and inventors provides that, 'Authors of all artistic, literary and scientific works and inventors shall retain in addition to the just remuneration of their labour, a moral right on their work and/or discovery, which shall not disappear, even after such work shall have become the common property of mankind.'[42] Thus, the Working Group intended that authors and inventors should be entitled to a perpetual moral right in their creative works, and this moral right was to subsist even after such works had passed into the public domain. According to the CESCR, the

dissemination of creative and innovative productions, as well as the development of cultural identities, and preserve the integrity of scientific, literary and artistic productions for the benefit of society as a whole.'

39 Ibid., para 2, which notes that 'the human right to benefit from the protection of the moral and material interests resulting from one's scientific, literary and artistic productions safeguards the personal link between authors and their creations and between peoples, communities, or other groups and their collective cultural heritage, as well as their basic material interests which are necessary to enable authors to enjoy an adequate standard of living, intellectual property regimes primarily protect business and corporate interests and investments. Moreover, the scope of protection of the moral and material interests of the author provided for by article 15, paragraph 1(c), does not necessarily coincide with what is referred to as intellectual property rights under national legislation or international agreements.'

40 Ibid., para 2, which notes that 'In contrast to human rights, intellectual property rights are generally of a temporary nature, and can be revoked, licensed or assigned to someone else. While under most intellectual property systems, intellectual property rights, often with the exception of moral rights, may be allocated, limited in time and scope, traded, amended and even forfeited, human rights are timeless expressions of fundamental entitlements of the human person.'

41 Ibid., para 12. See also UN ESCOR, Commission on Human Rights, 'Report of the Working Group on the Declaration on Human Rights,' 2nd Sess., E/CN.4/57 (10 December 1947).

42 UN ESCOR, Commission on Human Rights, 'Report of the Working Group on the Declaration on Human Rights,' 2nd Sess., E/CN.4/57 (10 December 1947) 15.

intention of the drafters of Article 27(2) of the UDHR was 'to proclaim the intrinsically personal character of every creation of the human mind and the ensuing durable link between creators and their creations'.[43]

With regard to the scope of the right to the protection of the *moral* interests of authors and inventors in their works, the CESCR notes that it includes 'the right of authors to be recognized as the creators of their scientific, literary and artistic productions and to object to any distortion, mutilation or other modification of, or other derogatory action in relation to, such productions, which would be prejudicial to their honour and reputation'.[44] In other words, the right to the protection of the *moral* interests of authors and inventors is akin to the protection of moral rights contained in the copyright laws of countries such as Germany and France.[45] The moral rights of authors should, however, not be confused with copyright.[46] One can thus infer from this that moral rights (as distinct from copyright) enjoy the status of human rights.

The CESCR's analysis on the right to the protection of the *material* interests of authors and inventors is, however, not as straightforward as its analysis on the protection of the *moral* interests of authors and inventors. In its analysis of the meaning of the right to the protection of *material* interests, the CESCR highlighted the connection between the right to the protection of *material* interests of authors and inventors and three other rights viz., the right to own property (as recognized in Article 17 of the UDHR), the right of a worker to adequate remuneration (as recognized in Article 7(a) of the ICESCR), and the right of everyone to an adequate standard of living (as recognized in Article 11(1) of the ICESCR).[47]

[43] CESCR, 'General Comment No. 17', para 12.

[44] Ibid., para 13.

[45] See Yu, 'Reconceptualizing Intellectual Property Interests', 1081–2. See also, Article 6*bis* of the Berne Convention for the Protection of Literary and Artistic Works.

[46] As Peter Drahos points out, 'The term "copyright" . . . refers to those common law systems that characterize the exclusive rights of authors in essentially economic terms (the rights to reproduce the work, to publish it and to adapt it are examples). Within civil law systems, the rights of authors are seen, at base, as being about the protection of the authorial personality (the right to be acknowledged as the author of the work and the right to control alterations to the work are the core rights). These systems are not referred to as copyright but rather as authors' rights.' See Peter Drahos, 'The Universality of Intellectual Property Rights: Origins and Development' in *Intellectual Property and Human Rights* (Proceedings of a Panel Discussion held by the World Intellectual Property Organization in collaboration with the Office of the UN High Commissioner for Human Rights, 9 November 1998), 13–14.

[47] CESCR, 'General Comment No. 17', para 15, which notes that 'The protection of "material interests" of authors in article 15, paragraph 1(c), reflects the close linkage of this provision with the right to own property, as recognized in article 17 of the Universal Declaration of Human Rights and in regional human rights instruments, as well as with the right of any worker to adequate remuneration (art. 7(a)). Unlike other human rights, the material interests of authors are not directly linked to the personality of the creator, but contribute to the enjoyment of the right to an adequate standard of living (art. 11, para. 1).'

In order to understand the scope of the right to the protection of the *material* interests of authors and inventors as contained in Article 15(1)(c) of the ICESCR, one has to examine the drafting history of the earlier Article 27(2) of the UDHR as Article 15(1)(c) of the ICESCR is a near-verbatim reproduction of the provisions of Article 27(2) of the UDHR. However, even the drafting history of Article 27(2) of the UDHR does not completely remove the difficulty surrounding the determination of the nature and exact scope of the right to the protection of the *material* interests of authors and inventors due to the ambiguity surrounding the intention of the delegates who adopted Article 27(2) of the UDHR.

The origins of the text of Article 27(2) of the UDHR is traceable to the draft text proposed by the French delegate, Rene Cassin, during the Second Session of the Drafting Committee of the Commission on Human Rights in May 1948. Cassin had proposed that the following paragraph should be included in the draft Article 30 of the draft Declaration: 'Authors of creative works and inventors shall retain, apart from financial rights, a moral right over their work or discovery, which shall remain extant after the financial rights have expired.'[48] Prior to the introduction of Cassin's proposed text, Article 30 contained only one paragraph dealing with the right to participate in the community's cultural life and to share in the benefits of scientific discoveries.[49] As Plomer points out, Cassin had played a crucial role in the international debates on both the Berne Convention and the American Declaration of the Rights and Duties of Man (which were going on around the same time as the negotiations on the UDHR) where similar demands had been made for the recognition of the moral rights of authors and scientists in their works.[50] Thus, it appears that Cassin's main objective in introducing the above paragraph into the text of the draft Declaration was to ensure that the Declaration recognized the moral rights of authors and inventors in their works.

The introduction of the phrase 'material interests' into the proposed text is traceable to Mexico's proposal in April 1948 when the draft Declaration was still being considered by the Commission on Human Rights. Mexico had successfully pressed for the inclusion of Article XIII in the American Declaration of the Rights and Duties of Man. Article XIII of the American Declaration provides for the right to the protection of the moral and material interests of authors and inventors.[51] Mexico

48 See UN ESCOR, Commission on Human Rights, 'Report of the Drafting Committee to the Commission on Human Rights', 2nd Sess., U.N. Doc. E/CN.4/95 (1948) 13.

49 UN ESCOR, Commission on Human Rights, 'Report of the Drafting Committee to the Commission on Human Rights', 2nd Sess., U.N. Doc. E/CN.4/95 (1948) 13. According to draft Article 30, 'Every one has the right to participate in the cultural life of the community, to enjoy the arts and to share in the benefits that result from scientific discoveries.' This draft provision is now Article 27(1) of the UDHR.

50 Plomer, 'The Human Rights Paradox', 167–8.

51 Ibid., 169. Article XIII of the American Declaration of the Rights and Duties of Man provides that: 'Every person has the right to take part in the cultural life of the community, to enjoy the arts, and to participate in the benefits that result from intellectual progress, especially scientific

therefore wanted to achieve a similar objective during the negotiations on the UDHR and thus it tabled a proposal for the inclusion of the right to the protection of the moral and material interests of authors and inventors.[52] Mexico proposed that the following text should be added to the draft Article 30: 'Everyone is likewise entitled to just protection, compatible with the progress of mankind, for his moral and material interests in any inventions or literary, scientific or artistic works of which he is author.'

By the time the draft Declaration arrived at the UN General Assembly for final consideration in November 1948, France, Mexico, and Cuba made a joint submission to add a second paragraph to what had now become draft Article 25 (the present Article 27 of the UDHR) to the effect that: 'Everyone has, likewise, the right to the protection of his moral and material interests in any inventions or literary, scientific or artistic works of which he is the author.'[53] Thus, the initial proposal by France, which emphasized the moral rights of authors and inventors, had now been expanded to include 'material interests'. This is when the ambiguity surrounding Article 27(2) began to crystallize. As Plomer points out, the 'uncertainty about the aims and purpose' of this second paragraph (which is now Article 27(2) of the UDHR) 'is further reflected in the absence of clarity and unity of purpose in the speeches of the delegates' who voted in favour of the joint submission made by France, Mexico, and Cuba.[54]

It would appear that the objective of the French delegation was still to secure the protection of the moral rights of authors and inventors. In his speech on behalf of France before the General Assembly, Cassin noted that, while it could be argued that royalties and patents were sufficient to protect those who produce intellectual works, he did not think so and his proposal 'not only took into account the material aspect of the question, but was also designed to protect the moral interests of artists and inventors'.[55] This was because 'many scientists attached great importance to the spiritual side of their work than to the profits that they could gain from it; they only

discoveries . . . He likewise has the right to the protection of his moral and material interests as regards his inventions or any literary, scientific or artistic works of which he is the author.'

52 UN ESCOR, Commission on Human Rights, 'Comments from Governments on the Draft International Declaration on Human Rights, Draft International Covenant on Human Rights and the Question of Implementation: Communication from Mexico (Ministry of Foreign Affairs)', 3rd Sess., U.N. Doc. E/CN.4/82/Add.1 (1948) 5. See also Plomer, 'The Human Rights Paradox', 169.

53 See UN GAOR, Commission on Human Rights, 'Cuba, France, Mexico: Joint Amendment to Article 25 of the Draft Declaration (E/800), Draft International Declaration of Human Rights', 3rd Sess., U.N. Doc. A/C.3/360 (1948).

54 Plomer, 'The Human Rights Paradox', 171. Eighteen countries voted in favour of the joint submission, thirteen voted against it, while ten countries abstained from voting. See UN GAOR, Commission on Human Rights, 'Draft International Declaration on Human Rights, Hundred and Fifty-Second Meeting', 3rd Sess., U.N. Doc. A/C.3/SR.152 (1948) 635.

55 UN GAOR, 'Draft International Declaration on Human Rights, Hundred and Fiftieth Meeting', 3rd Sess., U.N. Doc. A/C.3/SR.150 (1948) 620.

asked that their work should be recognized by future generations. That recognition, which they claimed, should be granted to them, lest injustice should be done in the future.'[56] Thus, while the French delegation supported the inclusion of the protection of both the *moral* and *material* interests of authors and inventors in the Declaration, the French delegation apparently attached more significance to the *moral* interests of authors and inventors.

The speech by the Mexican delegate, Campos Ortiz, before the General Assembly, probably provides a better clue as to the real meaning of the phrase 'material interests'. In sharp contrast to Cassin's approach, Ortiz focused more on the pecuniary interests of authors and inventors, and his speech suggests that the objective of the Mexican delegation was to secure the right of authors and inventors to earn income from their intellectual works. In his speech, Ortiz compared the pecuniary interests of intellectual workers with that of other wage earners who were engaged in other types of work. For Ortiz, the focus and emphasis were on the right of the individual as an 'intellectual worker'. According to Ortiz,

> The Committee had already recognized the rights of the wage earner, the family, the mother and the child; if it did not wish there to be a serious omission in the text it was drawing up it must now proclaim the rights of the individual as an intellectual worker, scientist, or writer; in other words, the rights of all those who contributed to the progress and well-being of humanity . . . No article in the draft declaration dealt specifically with the rights of the intellectual worker. The same omission had existed in the original version of the draft American declaration of the rights and duties of man [adopted at Bogota]. The Mexican delegation had had the honour, at Bogota, of proposing the article on the protection of intellectual and artistic work which had been unanimously adopted, and [it] was [now] submitting to the . . . Committee an amendment . . . based on the text adopted at Bogota . . . It might be argued, for instance, that the Mexican amendment dealt with the rights of one particular category of persons only; but was that not also true of property rights or the rights of the wage-earner? It might be said, further, that the general provisions concerning labour adequately protected intellectual workers; that, however, would only be true of a small number of salaried intellectual workers, and was certainly not true of all men of learning, writers, or artists, pursuing independent research. It might be said that national legislation, or international legislation itself by a system of conventions of which everyone was aware, safeguarded the rights of authors and inventors' patents: but the effectiveness of such protection, particularly in the international field, was at best relative and often non-existent.[57]

[56] Ibid., 620. Cassin further noted that 'Similarly, it often happened that a literary or artistic work was reproduced in a distorted and travestied form although it suffered no financial loss. In those cases too the artist or the author should be afforded the right to protect his work, for it was in the interest of humanity as a whole to prevent works which ennobled the human race from becoming a mockery' (ibid., 620).

[57] UN GAOR, 'Draft International Declaration on Human Rights, Hundred and Fiftieth Meeting,' 3rd Sess., U.N. Doc. A/C.3/SR.150 (1948) 617.

Since the phrase 'material interests' was introduced by the Mexican delegation, the appropriate place to uncover the true meaning of the phrase is the speech of the Mexican delegate quoted above. From this speech, it appears that the main objective of the Mexican delegation was to secure the right of 'intellectual workers' to earn a living[58] from their intellectual works. As Plomer also points out, 'Mexico's support for the inclusion of a second paragraph on the protection of the rights of authors thus appeared to be primarily based on the assimilation of an individual's intellectual creations as a form of "work" or labor to physical work or labor'.[59] Essentially, the Mexican delegation was more concerned with securing the labour rights of the 'intellectual worker' as opposed to the intellectual property rights of the 'intellectual worker'.

In his speech on the proposed second paragraph, the Cuban delegate merely stated that Cuba's amendments were in the same spirit as the ones proposed by France and Mexico.[60] However, it appears that the views of the Cuban delegation on the second paragraph aligned more with the Mexican approach than with the French approach. According to the Cuban delegate, who supported the remarks made by Mr Ortiz, 'the Cuban delegation was proposing a text of which the Mexican delegation could justly claim to be the originators, as the Mexican Government had been the first at Bogota to raise the question of the protection of the rights of the intellectual worker, artist and scientist'.[61]

The inclusion of the second paragraph on the protection of the *moral* and *material* interests of authors and inventors was opposed by a number of countries. The Ecuadorian delegation considered the proposed provision to be a confused and contradictory provision and it noted that the question of literary or scientific property should be dealt with under the general chapter on property rights.[62] The Australian delegate was of the view that the rights of the intellectual worker could not appear beside fundamental rights of a more general nature such as freedom of thought or

58 On the right to earn a living from work, see Article 23(1) of the UDHR which states that, 'Everyone has the right to work, to free choice of employment, to just and favourable conditions of work and to protection against unemployment.' See also Article 6(1) of the ICESCR which provides that 'The States Parties to the present Covenant recognize the right to work, which includes the right of everyone to the opportunity to gain his living by work which he freely chooses or accepts, and will take appropriate steps to safeguard this right.'

59 Plomer, 'The Human Rights Paradox', 172.

60 UN GAOR, 'Draft International Declaration on Human Rights, Hundred and Fiftieth Meeting', 3rd Sess., U.N. Doc. A/C.3/SR.150 (1948) 618.

61 Ibid.

62 See ibid., 618–9. The Ecuadorian delegate thought that 'article 25, as worded in the draft declaration, was one of the most confused and contradictory that the Committee had so far had to examine.' He further noted that 'the Mexican, Cuban and French amendments introduced a new element concerning literary property and the rights of the inventor . . . [and he] did not think it right, in a general declaration of human rights, to make special mention of the rights of writers and inventors, who formed only a small proportion of society. The question of literary or scientific property belonged under the general chapter on property rights.'

the right to work.[63] The United States thought that the provisions of the proposed second paragraph dealt with a specific aspect of the rights of property.[64] Nevertheless, the joint amendment submitted by France, Mexico, and Cuba was successfully included in the UDHR after it gained the vote of eighteen delegations.[65]

With regard to the drafting history of Article 15(1)(c) of the ICESCR,[66] it is noteworthy that it was UNESCO that initially submitted a draft article on the protection of the *moral* and *material* interests of authors and inventors to the Commission on Human Rights when it was discussing the provision on cultural

63 See, UN GAOR, Commission on Human Rights, 'Hundred and Fifty-First Meeting', 3rd Sess., U.N. Doc. A/C.3/SR.151 (1948) 630. According to the Australian delegate, 'The rights of artists and scientists must certainly be protected, but the problem was to discover how and by whom. That would seem to be primarily the concern of national legislation complemented by international conventions. In a declaration such as that which the Committee was called upon to draft, the indisputable rights of the intellectual worker could not appear beside fundamental rights of a more general nature, such as freedom of thought, religious freedom or the right to work.' See also the statement by the Chilean delegate noting that 'For the same reasons as those given by the representative of Australia, [Chile] would also be unable to accept the joint amendment of Cuba, France and Mexico. To what extent would it be possible in a country where there existed no law protecting authors' copyright and patents, to speak of the infringement of fundamental human rights in the case of a man of letters whose works were reproduced without his consent? The concept of the protection of intellectual work conflicted to a certain extent with that of freedom of access to all literary, artistic or scientific output. Since the joint amendment referred not to one of the fundamental human rights, but to rights affecting a special category of persons, the Chilean delegation considered that it should not be included in the declaration' (ibid., 632).

64 See UN GAOR, 'Draft International Declaration on Human Rights, Hundred and Fiftieth Meeting', 3rd Sess., U.N. Doc. A/C.3/SR.150 (1948) 621. According to the American delegate, 'With regard to the amendments submitted by the French, Cuban and Mexican delegations . . . they reproduced almost word for word the article in the Bogota Declaration dealing with patents and copyright. While it accepted the principle which they expressed, the United States delegation thought that they would be out of place in the declaration, more especially since they dealt with a specific aspect of the rights of property already covered by article 15.' See also the statement by the delegate of the United Kingdom, noting that 'The French amendment dealing with the rights of authors proclaimed a new principle which the United Kingdom delegation could not accept. The representative of France had spoken on the one hand of the recognition due to the author of an invention – a very legitimate claim – and on the other, of protecting the right of ownership attaching to an invention. Those were very different conceptions . . . the proprietary rights attaching to an invention constituted but one aspect of the right of ownership . . . Copyright was dealt with by special legislation and in international conventions; it was not a basic human right. The declaration of human rights should be universal in nature and only recognize general principles that were valid for all men. The United Kingdom delegation would therefore not support the French amendment' (ibid., 624).

65 Eighteen countries voted in favour of the joint submission, thirteen voted against it, while ten countries abstained from voting. See UN GAOR, Commission on Human Rights, 'Draft International Declaration on Human Rights, Hundred and Fifty-Second Meeting', 3rd Sess., U.N. Doc. A/C.3/SR.152 (1948) 635.

66 See, generally, Maria Green, 'Drafting History of Article 15(1)(c) of the International Covenant on Economic, Social and Cultural Rights,' U.N. Doc. E/C.12/2000/15 (2000).

rights during the seventh session of the Commission in 1951.[67] The proposal of UNESCO in this regard was quite similar to the text of Article 27(2) of the UDHR[68] and in defending its proposal before the Commission on Human Rights, the UNESCO delegation stated that it 'considered that recognition of authors' right should find a place in the Covenant, since it had already been included in the Universal Declaration, and represented a safeguard and an encouragement for those who were constantly enriching the cultural heritage of mankind. Only by such means could international cultural exchanges be fully developed.'[69] In support of this proposal, the French delegate (Rene Cassin) noted that, 'It would be unfortunate to omit from the Covenant principles already stated in the Universal Declaration regarding the protection of the moral and material rights of authors, artists and scientists.'[70] This proposal was, however, rejected by the Commission on Human Rights, with seven countries voting in favour of the proposal, seven countries voting against the proposal, and four countries abstained from voting.[71]

During the eighth session of the Commission on Human Rights in 1952, the French delegation resubmitted the proposal to include a provision on the protection of the *moral* and *material* interests of authors and inventors.[72] Adopting a language that re-echoed the sentiments of the Mexican delegation during the negotiations on Article 27(2) of the UDHR, the French delegation contended that the proposed text was necessary because the draft covenant included provisions for the protection of the emoluments of professional workers and the covenant would thus be incomplete without the protection of the *moral* and *material* interests of authors and inventors.[73]

[67] At this stage, only a single international covenant on human rights was being prepared. See ibid., 4.

[68] In this regard, UNESCO submitted two versions of the same text. The first version provided that, 'The signatory States undertake to protect by all appropriate means the material and moral interest of every man, resulting from any literary, artistic or scientific works of which he is the author.' The second version provided that the signatory states 'recognize that it is one of their principal aims to ensure conditions which will permit every one . . . to obtain protection for his moral and material interests resulting from any scientific or artistic production of which he is the author.' See UN ESCOR, Commission on Human Rights, 'Suggestions Submitted by the Director-General of the United Nations Educational, Scientific and Cultural Organization', 7th Sess., U.N. Doc. E/CN.4/541.Rev.1 (1951) 3.

[69] See UN ESCOR, Commission on Human Rights, 'Summary Record of the Two Hundred and Twenty-Eighth Meeting', 7th Sess., U.N. Doc. E/CN.4/SR.228 (1951) 13.

[70] See UN ESCOR, Commission on Human Rights, 'Summary Record of the Two Hundred and Twenty-Ninth Meeting', 7th Sess., U.N. Doc. E/CN.4/SR.229 (1951) 12–13.

[71] See UN ESCOR, Commission on Human Rights, 'Summary Record of the Two Hundred and Thirtieth Meeting', 7th Sess., U.N. Doc. E/CN.4/SR.230 (1951) 7.

[72] At this stage, two separate international covenants on human rights were being prepared. One dealt with civil and political rights and the other dealt with economic, social and cultural rights. The discussions on what is now Article 15(1)(c) of the ICESCR took place in the context of the work on the covenant dealing with economic, social, and cultural rights. See Green, 'Drafting History of Article 15(1)(c)', 8.

[73] According to the French delegation, 'The draft covenant included provisions for the protection of the property and emoluments of professional workers and should therefore be completed by

In other words, the aspect of the proposal dealing with the 'material interests' of authors and inventors in their works, as presented by the French delegation, was essentially motivated by the need to secure the rights of intellectual workers to earn an income from their works just like other professional workers. However, this proposal was opposed by a majority of countries who contended, *inter alia*, 'that authors' rights had to be considered in the light of the claims of the community and of the world at large'.[74] In particular, the proposal was opposed by Yugoslavia,[75] the United Kingdom,[76] and the United States.[77] Invariably, the French proposal was rejected again during the eighth session of the Commission on Human Rights, with seven countries voting against the proposal, six countries voting in favour of the proposal, and four countries abstained from voting.[78] Thus, the draft text that was submitted by the Commission on Human Rights to the UN General Assembly contained no provision for the protection of the *moral* and *material* interests of authors and inventors.[79]

a provision for the protection of the moral and material interests resulting from scientific, literary or artistic production.' See UN ESCOR, Commission on Human Rights, 'Summary Record of the Two Hundred and Ninety-Second Meeting', 8th Sess., U.N. Doc. E/CN.4/SR.292 (1952) 8–9. See also Green, 'Drafting History of Article 15(1)(c)', 8.

74 See UN ESCOR, Commission on Human Rights, 'Report to the Economic and Social Council on the Eighth Session of the Commission, held in New York, from 14 April to 14 June 1952', U.N. Doc. E/2256 (1952) 19.

75 UN ESCOR, Commission on Human Rights, 'Summary Record of the Two Hundred and Ninety-Third Meeting', 8th Sess., U.N. Doc. E/CN.4/SR.293 (1952) 5. According to Yugoslavia, 'authors were entitled to protection of the moral and material rights deriving from their work but . . . there was no reason to include such a right in the covenant where it could appear only in very concise form, with consequent disadvantages. Moreover the right was limited in the sense that it concerned only a few individuals. The majority of the Commission had refused to formulate in detail so important a right as the right to social security which concerned millions of persons on the ground that it was an appropriate subject for special conventions. The same argument could apply even more forcefully in the matter of authors' rights, particularly in view of the existence of an international organization to protect those rights, The International Union for the Protection of Literary and Artistic Works, to which Yugoslavia belonged.'

76 UN ESCOR, Commission on Human Rights, 'Summary Record of the Two Hundred and Ninety-Third Meeting,' 8th Sess., U.N. Doc. E/CN.4/SR.293 (1952) 9. Agreeing with Yugoslavia, the United Kingdom noted that 'it would be a mistake to refer in the covenant to so complex a right, which, moreover, was safeguarded by many international conventions'.

77 UN ESCOR, Commission on Human Rights, 'Summary Record of the Two Hundred and Ninety-Second Meeting', 8th Sess., U.N. Doc. E/CN.4/SR.292 (1952) 8–9.

78 UN ESCOR, Commission on Human Rights, 'Summary Record of the Two Hundred and Ninety-Fourth Meeting', 8th Sess., U.N. Doc. E/CN.4/SR.294 (1952) 4.

79 See UN GAOR, 'Annotations on the Text of the Draft International Covenants on Human Rights (Prepared by the Secretary General)', Agenda Item 28 (Part II) Annexes, 10th Sess., U.N. Doc. A/2929 (1955) 115, which noted that 'A proposal for the addition of a provision for the protection of rights deriving from scientific, literary or artistic productions was opposed on the grounds that the matter could not adequately be treated in a short provision, that it was properly being dealt with by UNESCO, and more adequately, and that authors' rights had to be considered in the light of the claims of the community and of the world at large.' See also Yvonne Donders, 'The Legal Framework of the Right to Take Part in Cultural Life', in Yvonne Donders and Vladimir Volodin (eds.), *Human Rights in Education, Science and Culture: Legal*

The proposal to protect the *moral* and *material* interests of authors and inventors, however, reappeared when the draft text of the covenant on economic, social, and cultural rights came before the UN General Assembly. The re-emergence of this proposal occurred after the UN General Assembly had sent the draft text to its Third Committee for review. During the discussions in the Third Committee, the French delegation noted that it was still in favour of inserting a clause similar to that contained in Article 27(2) of the UDHR and it expressed its hope 'that the idea it had put forward in the Commission on Human Rights would be reintroduced by another delegation, so that it could vote for it'.[80]

The task (of reintroducing the proposed provision on the protection of the *moral* and *material* interests of authors and inventors) was taken up by the Uruguayan delegation, which subsequently proposed that a text similar to that of Article 27(2) of the UDHR should be introduced into the covenant.[81] However, in tabling the proposal, the Uruguayan delegate (Mr Tejera) wrongly equated and conflated the protection of the *moral* and *material* interests contained in Article 27(2) of the UDHR with 'authors' copyright'. According to Mr Tejera, '. . . a reference to authors' copyright was imperative. For lack of international protection, literary and scientific works, for example, were frequently pirated by foreign countries, which paid no royalties to the authors'.[82] Mr Tejera 'therefore proposed the addition . . . of a new sub-paragraph (c), the text of which would be based on that of article 27, paragraph 2, of the Universal Declaration of Human Rights'.[83]

However, in a subsequent statement, Mr Tejera stated that the purpose of the proposed text 'was to guarantee to every author, scientist, writer or artist the right to enjoy the fruits of his work'.[84] This latter statement closely resembles the statement made by the Mexican delegation during the negotiations on Article 27(2) of the UDHR. In other words, just as other workers enjoy the fruits of their work, intellectual workers should also be entitled to enjoy the fruits of their intellectual work. Mr Tejera further highlighted another purpose behind the proposed text when he stated that 'Respect for the right of the author would assure the public of the authenticity of the works presented to it'.[85] This particular statement suggests that the Uruguayan delegation was also seeking to protect the moral rights of authors.

Developments and Challenges (Ashgate/UNESCO Publishing, 2007), 247; Green, 'Drafting History of Article 15(1)(c)', 10.

80 See UN GAOR, 'Summary Record of the General Assembly, Third Committee Twelfth Session', U.N. Doc. A/C.3/SR.796 (1957) 174.

81 Costa Rica subsequently joined Uruguay as a co-sponsor of the proposed text. See UN GAOR, 'Summary Record of the General Assembly, Third Committee Twelfth Session', U.N. Doc. A/C.3/SR.798 (1957) 183.

82 See UN GAOR, 'Summary Record of the General Assembly, Third Committee Twelfth Session', U.N. Doc. A/C.3/SR.797 (1957) 178.

83 See ibid.

84 See UN GAOR, 'Summary Record of the General Assembly, Third Committee Twelfth Session', U.N. Doc. A/C.3/SR.798 (1957) 183.

85 See ibid.

Thus, the statements made by the Uruguayan delegate in support of the proposed text can be interpreted in three different ways. It can be interpreted to mean, firstly, that the text was aimed at protecting the copyright of authors in their works, secondly, that it was aimed at protecting the right of intellectual workers to earn an income from their intellectual works, or thirdly, that it was aimed at protecting the moral rights of authors. This ambiguity was equally reflected in the way the delegates from the various countries interpreted the proposed text. The only point of agreement among some of the countries appears to have been with regard to the fact that the proposed text was based on Article 27(2) of the UDHR.

The countries in favour of the proposed text gave reasons such as the fact that it would remedy the omission of a provision similar to Article 27(2) of the UDHR in the draft covenant,[86] ensure that people enjoy the fruits of their intellectual efforts, and also protect intellectual works from piracy.[87] The countries that opposed the proposed text also did so for a variety of reasons and in a manner that reflected the ambiguity surrounding the proposed text. The USSR opposed the proposed text because it thought that: it concerned a complicated question; it would be out of place in an instrument that was meant to apply to all mankind because it applied to a particular group (authors and inventors); and there was no need to automatically reproduce a provision contained in the UDHR.[88] The USSR pointed out that if the

86 According to Italy, the text proposed by Uruguay 'made good an omission'. The United Kingdom (which had earlier opposed a similar text proposed by France when the draft covenant was before the Commission on Human Rights) noted that the Uruguayan proposal 'undoubtedly made good an omission' and that 'it was essential to include a provision corresponding to that in article 27, paragraph 2, of the Universal Declaration of Human Rights in the Covenant'. Israel stated that it 'had always considered that the provisions of the draft Covenant should not be in any way weaker than those of the Universal Declaration of Human Rights' and that it 'would be impossible to give effective encouragement to the development of culture unless the rights of authors and scientists were protected ... The specialized agencies would later have to define in detail the steps which would have to be taken to protect literary, artistic or scientific production, as UNESCO had done in the case of the Universal Copyright Convention, to which Israel was a party'. See UN GAOR, 'Summary Record of the General Assembly, Third Committee Twelfth Session', U.N. Doc. A/C.3/SR.798 (1957) 182, 184.

87 The Dominican Republic stated that the proposed text 'should have the support of all delegations, as its essential purpose was to ensure that men and women should enjoy the fruits of their intellectual and artistic efforts and that their work should not be pirated or exploited by unprincipled editors and publishers' and it further noted that it did not have any difficulty accepting the proposed text because 'its own legislation on the subject was excellent and it was one of the signatories of the Universal Copyright Convention'. See UN GAOR, 'Summary Record of the General Assembly, Third Committee Twelfth Session', U.N. Doc. A/C.3/SR.799 (1957) 187.

88 According to the USSR, 'The question of authors' rights occupied a very important place in the law of all States, and especially in that of the Soviet Union, but it was a very complicated question and the regulations varied from country to country. That was why the Commission on Human Rights had not wanted to burden those who were to draft the Covenants with the extremely difficult task of drawing up a clause which would be valid for all States. A clause of a general nature would be of no value because everyone could interpret it as he pleased. But if it

proposed text concerned 'relations between States in regard to copyright and patents' then 'such relations should be governed by special agreements outside the scope of the covenants on human rights'.[89] Other countries that opposed the proposed text such as India and Czechoslovakia thought that the proposed text dealt with copyright, which was already being competently addressed by UNESCO,[90] and was equally the subject of international instruments such as the Universal Copyright Convention of 1952.[91] The Federation of Malaya considered the proposed text to be superfluous, since most countries had already enacted laws to protect the rights of authors.[92]

The proposed text was adopted by a vote of thirty-nine countries against nine opposing countries, while twenty-four countries abstained from voting on the text.[93]

were desired to go into greater detail, one meeting would not be enough in view of the intricate character of the question. Furthermore, if a clause of that kind were inserted, the balance of the Covenant would be upset. An examination of the nature of the rights set forth in that instrument would reveal that they were rights which concerned all mankind, but the clause that it was proposed to add ... concerned a particular group. The fact that a principle was enunciated in the Universal Declaration of Human Rights did not mean that it should be repeated automatically in the Covenant. The great difficulties which that principle would create should also be borne in mind.' See UN GAOR, 'Summary Record of the General Assembly, Third Committee Twelfth Session', U.N. Doc. A/C.3/SR.798 (1957) 182.

89 See UN GAOR, 'Summary Record of the General Assembly, Third Committee Twelfth Session', U.N. Doc. A/C.3/SR.798 (1957) 184.

90 According to India, the proposed text 'conformed to the corresponding article of the Universal Declaration of Human Rights on every point, but it was unadvisable to introduce foreign elements into the Covenant. Moreover, UNESCO and other agencies were already dealing with ... copyright quite competently.' See UN GAOR, 'Summary Record of the General Assembly, Third Committee Twelfth Session', U.N. Doc. A/C.3/SR.798 (1957) 183.

91 According to Czechoslovakia, 'The question of copyright was extremely complex and had been dealt with in many different international agreements since the Berne Conference of 1886; Czechoslovakia had signed the latest international instrument on the subject, the Universal Copyright Convention of 1952. States would find it difficult to adhere both to the existing international instruments concerning copyright and to [the text proposed] by Costa Rica and Uruguay. Article I of the Universal Copyright Convention provided for the adequate and effective protection of the rights of authors and other copyright proprietors and articles IV, V and VII dealt with the practical aspects of such protection. That Convention and the other international agreements on the subject took into account the special conditions in the different countries. If all such agreements were to be superseded by the provision proposed by Costa Rica and Uruguay, the position would be far from clear ... If [Costa Rica and Uruguay] found the existing international agreements on the subject unsatisfactory, it was difficult to see why they had not insisted on a full debate on what was a very delicate and complicated question, instead of trying to push through a hastily drafted and unsatisfactory text, which might well be misinterpreted.' See UN GAOR, 'Summary Record of the General Assembly, Third Committee Twelfth Session', U.N. Doc. A/C.3/SR.799 (1957) 188.

92 See UN GAOR, 'Summary Record of the General Assembly, Third Committee Twelfth Session', U.N. Doc. A/C.3/SR.798 (1957) 184–5. The Federation of Malaya stated that, 'as most States had enacted laws to protect the rights of authors and as artists and writers had merely to comply with the requirement of deposit to obtain proper protection, [Malaya] considered the amendment proposed by Costa Rica and Uruguay ... to be superfluous.'

93 See UN GAOR, 'Summary Record of the General Assembly, Third Committee Twelfth Session', U.N. Doc. A/C.3/SR.799 (1957) 190.

Thus, Article 15(1)(c) was adopted as part of the ICESCR.[94] However, since Article 15(1)(c) of the ICESCR is based on Article 27(2) of the UDHR, the drafting history of Article 27(2) of the UDHR provides a better explanation for the expression 'moral and material interests'. And, as pointed out above, what the Mexican delegation had in mind when it introduced the expression 'material interests' was the labour rights (and not the intellectual property rights) of intellectual workers.

Thus, as Plomer rightly points out, 'the underlying rationale for Article 27(2) provides little support for the view that IP rights are fundamental human rights, although the modalities of national and international IP and patent laws may certainly, and indeed, should be deployed to the service of human rights'.[95] In other words, while the right to the protection of the 'moral and material interests' of creators as recognized in both Article 27(2) of the UHDR and Article 15(1)(c) of the ICESCR is not coterminous with intellectual property rights, states can (and already) use national intellectual property laws as instruments to protect the moral and material interests of creators. However, as further explained below, it should be noted that neither Article 27(2) of the UDHR nor Article 15(1)(c) of the ICESCR expressly require states to use intellectual property laws to protect the moral and material interests of creators.

In distinguishing between the 'moral interests' of authors and inventors and the 'material interests' of authors and inventors, the CESCR in General Comment No. 17 notes that 'Unlike other human rights, the material interests of authors are not directly linked to the personality of the creator, *but contribute to the enjoyment of the right to an adequate standard of living*.'[96] In other words, while *moral interests* protect the permanent connection between creators and their creations (similar to the moral rights that the French had in mind during the discussions on Article 27 (2)), *material interests* deals with the labour rights or workers' rights of creators (or 'intellectual workers' as the Mexican delegation referred to them during the discussions on Article 27(2)).

In an effort to distinguish between the protection of *material interests* on the one hand and the protection of intellectual property rights on the other hand, the CESCR notes that 'the purpose of enabling authors to enjoy an adequate standard of living can also be achieved through one-time payments or by vesting an author, for a limited period of time, with the exclusive right to exploit his scientific, literary or artistic production'.[97] In other words, it is not mandatory to grant patent rights or

94 The International Covenant on Economic, Social and Cultural Rights was adopted unanimously by the UN General Assembly in 1966. See UN GAOR, '1496th Plenary Meeting', 21st Sess., U.N. Doc. A/PV.1496 (1966) 6.

95 Plomer, 'The Human Rights Paradox', 175.

96 CECSR, 'General Comment No. 17', para 15 (emphasis added).

97 Ibid., para 16.

copyright in order to protect the *material interests* of intellectual workers.[98] The right of intellectual workers to an adequate standard of living, that is, their *material interests*, can equally be protected through other means such as one-time payments, prizes, or monetary awards.[99]

The CESCR admits that Article 15(1)(c) of the ICESCR does not specify the method or procedure for the protection of the *moral* and *material* interests of authors and inventors.[100] Nevertheless, the CESCR notes that the protection under Article 15(1)(c) 'need not necessarily reflect the level and means of protection found in present copyright, patent and other intellectual property regimes, as long as the protection available is suited to secure for authors the moral and material interests resulting from their productions'.[101]

One other factor that distinguishes the protection of *moral* and *material* interests from the protection of intellectual property rights is the fact that the former, being human rights, are inalienable rights unlike intellectual property rights. As the CESCR points out,

> intellectual property rights are generally of a temporary nature, and can be revoked, licensed or assigned to someone else. While under most intellectual property systems, intellectual property rights, often with the exception of moral rights, may be allocated, limited in time and scope, amended and even forfeited, human rights [such as the moral and material interests of authors and inventors] are timeless expressions of fundamental entitlements of the human person.[102]

3.3.3 *The Right to Science and Culture*

Further insight regarding how the relationship between intellectual property rights and human rights should be conceptualized can equally be gleaned by looking at

98 As Peter Yu rightly notes, 'Although it remains unclear why the delegates voted to adopt article 27(2), one can surmise that at least some delegates might have interpreted the phrase "material interests" to mean just remuneration for intellectual labor . . . Thus, the drafting history seems to suggest that the phrase "material interests" should not be interpreted broadly to cover all forms of economic rights as protected in the existing intellectual property system, but rather narrowly to cover the limited interests in obtaining just remuneration for one's intellectual labor.' Yu, 'Reconceptualizing Intellectual Property Interests', 1088.

99 Ibid., 1089, who notes that 'To satisfy article 15(1)(c) obligations, states can consider using such other alternative systems as liability rules, prize funds, or even non-property-based authorship protection . . . [T]he key criterion for satisfying the material interests obligation is not whether the offered protection meets the level of protection required by existing international intellectual property agreements or whether such protection is based on the property rights model. Rather, one has to inquire whether the existing system provides meaningful protection of material interests in the creations by authors and inventors.'

100 CECSR, 'General Comment No. 17', para 10.

101 Ibid.

102 Ibid., para 2. See also Yu, 'Ten Common Questions', 728, who notes that 'human rights are inalienable. While corporations may have obtained rights from individual authors and inventors through assignment or under a work-made-for-hire arrangement, the human-rights-based interests of these individuals are not transferable.'

the context of Article 27(2) of the UDHR. Article 27(2) is preceded by Article 27(1), which provides that: 'Everyone has the right freely to participate in the cultural life of the community, to enjoy the arts and to share in scientific advancement and its benefits.' A similar provision can be found in Article 15(1)(a) and (b) of the ICESCR, which mandates the state parties to the ICESCR to 'recognize the right of everyone: (a) to take part in cultural life; (b) to enjoy the benefits of scientific progress and its applications.' The right recognized in Article 27(1) of the UDHR and Article 15(1)(a) and (b) of the ICESCR is typically referred to as the right to science and culture.[103] As noted in Section 3.3.2, what is now referred to as Article 27(1) of the UDHR was originally the only provision in Article 27 prior to the proposal to include what is now Article 27(2) in the UDHR. Also, unlike Article 27(2), the adoption of the text of Article 27(1) was largely uncontroversial.[104]

As equally noted in Section 3.3.2, the right to the protection of moral and material interests, while not the same as intellectual property rights, may be protected via national intellectual property laws. At the same time, the right to science and culture has implications for the design and implementation of intellectual property laws at the national level. Thus, taken as a single provision, Article 27 of the UDHR (and also Article 15(1)(a)–(c) of the ICESCR) can be regarded as a provision that aims to secure the interests of creators while at the same time ensuring that members of the society (including creators) are not deprived of access to the benefits of scientific and cultural advancements.[105] Therefore, while intellectual property laws may be used to secure the interests of creators, these laws should not be designed in a way that is detrimental to the interests of other members of the society in securing access to scientific and cultural advancements.

In relation to the implications of the right to science and culture for the relationship between patent rights and human rights (especially as it concerns access to

103 See, for instance, Lea Shaver, 'The Right to Science and Culture' (2010) 1 *Wisconsin Law Review* 121.

104 Ibid., 144, who notes that 'The "access" element of Article 27 was included in the earliest draft, and virtually no objections to its inclusion were ever raised during the extended process of international debate and ratification. The notion of protection for creators' interests, however, was introduced into the draft bill of rights later, initially rejected as inappropriate for inclusion in a human rights document and subject to protracted debate.'

105 Shaver defines 'access' in the context of the right to science and culture to mean access to opportunities to create and to consume. According to Shaver, 'In the context of the right to science and culture, "access" has multiple dimensions. It should be understood to include the ability to actively participate and share with others, not merely to play the passive role of consumer ... Participation, as well as consumption, is the essence of the right to science and culture. "Access" therefore should be understood in terms of access to scientific and cultural materials, tools, and information; access to opportunities to create as well as to consume; and to share in the senses of both taking and giving. Looking to the scientific aspect of the right, access must go beyond sharing in the diffuse benefits of scientific learning in its pure form. The treaty language specifies the right to enjoy the benefits "of scientific progress and its applications." Everyone is meant to enjoy access to and benefit from new technological discoveries' (ibid., 171).

medicines), the report of the former UN Special Rapporteur on patent policy and the right to science and culture provides some useful insights.[106] In her report, the Special Rapporteur notes that the right to science and culture can be promoted through the use of limitations and exceptions to patent rights:

> Patents, when properly structured, expand the options and well-being of all people by making available new possibilities. Yet, they also give patent owners the power to deny others access, thereby limiting or denying the public's right of participation to science and culture. The human rights perspective demands that patents do not extend so far as to interfere with individuals' dignity and well-being … Various exceptions and limitations on patents are required to protect the right of participation in culture, science and technology.[107]

According to the Special Rapporteur, while the implementation of limitations and exceptions to patent rights at the national level is optional from the perspective of international trade law, '[f]rom the perspective of human rights, however, they are often to be considered as obligations.'[108] According to the Special Rapporteur:

> States have a positive obligation to provide for a robust and flexible system of patent exclusions, exceptions and flexibilities based on domestic circumstances, including through the establishment of compulsory and government use licences when needed. States have a human rights obligation not to support, adopt or accept intellectual property rules, such as TRIPS-Plus provisions, that would impede them from using exclusions, exceptions and flexibilities and thus from reconciling patent protection with human rights. International agreements that do not provide sufficient flexibility should be renounced or modified.[109]

This further supports the view that states need to incorporate a *model of human rights* into the design, implementation, interpretation, and enforcement of their national patent laws. This would help to ensure that the interests of creators are not protected via patent laws to the detriment of the other members of the society. From a human rights perspective, states therefore have an obligation to make use of the flexibilities available to them under international patent law as codified in the TRIPS Agreement.

3.3.4 *Patent Rights Are Not Human Rights under International Human Rights Law: Paving the Way for the Model of Human Rights*

The analysis in Section 3.3.2 on the real meaning of the phrase 'moral and material interests' should be enough to dispel any notion that patent rights or any other forms

[106] See Report of the Special Rapporteur in the field of cultural rights, Farida Shaheed, 'Patent policy and the right to science and culture ,' A/70/279 (2015).
[107] Ibid., para 47.
[108] Ibid., para 72.
[109] Ibid., paras 103–4.

of intellectual property rights are human rights under international human rights law[110] as canvassed by proponents of the 'integrated approach'. Furthermore, in relation to the human rights status of intellectual property rights, it is also important to note the decision of the Constitutional Court of South Africa in *Re Certification of the Constitution of the Republic of South Africa, 1996*, where with regard to the objection lodged against the failure of the new text of the South African Constitution to recognize a right to intellectual property based on the grounds that it was a 'universally accepted fundamental right', the court held that the recognition of a right to intellectual property 'cannot be characterised as a trend which is universally accepted'.[111]

Moreover, the analysis in Section 3.3.3 demonstrates that, even where intellectual property laws are used to protect the moral and material interests of creators and inventors, these laws should be designed in a way that promotes access to scientific advancements (including medicines and vaccines) in line with the obligation of states to protect and promote the right to science and culture. Thus, the incorporation of a *model of human rights* into the design, implementation, and interpretation of national intellectual property laws is an integral component of protecting the moral and material interests of creators and promoting the right to science and culture.

With regard to the 'coexistence approach', which (in substance) is quite akin to the utilitarian justification for patent rights examined in Chapter 2, Gold provides a very good critique thus:

[110] It should be noted that the mere fact that intellectual property rights are not human rights under international human rights law does not imply that states cannot decide to explicitly recognize intellectual property rights as human rights at the national or regional level. The analysis in this chapter is limited to the status of intellectual property rights under international human rights law. Europe provides a good example of a region where intellectual property rights are recognized as human rights. Thus, the European Court of Human Rights has consistently ruled that intellectual property rights are protected by the right to property contained in Article 1 of Protocol 1 of the European Convention on Human Rights. See *Melnychuk* v. *Ukraine*, App. no. 28743/03 (ECtHR, 5 July 2005); *Anheuser-Busch Inc* v. *Portugal* (2007) 45 EHRR 36; *Paeffgen Gmbh* v. *Germany*, App. nos 25379/04, 21688/05, 21722/05, and 21770/05 (ECtHR, 18 September 2007); *Balan* v. *Moldova*, App. no. 19247/03 (ECtHR, 29 January 2008). Furthermore, Article 17(2) of the Charter of Fundamental Rights of the European Union provides that 'Intellectual property shall be protected'. For critical commentaries on the status of intellectual property rights within the human rights framework in Europe, see Laurence Helfer, 'The New Innovation Frontier? Intellectual Property and the European Court of Human Rights,' in Paul Torremans (ed.), *Intellectual Property and Human Rights* (Kluwer Law International, 2008), 25; Christophe Geiger, 'Intellectual Property Shall Be Protected!? Article 17(2) of the Charter of Fundamental Rights of the European Union: A Mysterious Provision with an Unclear Scope' (2009) 31(3) *European Intellectual Property Review* 113; Jonathan Griffiths and Luke McDonagh, 'Fundamental Rights and European IP Law: The Case of Art 17(2) of the EU Charter', in Christophe Geiger (ed.), *Constructing European Intellectual Property: Achievements and New Perspectives* (Edward Elgar, 2013), 75.

[111] *Certification of the Constitution of the Republic of South Africa, 1996*, Case CCT 23/96, (6 September 1996, Judgment of the Constitutional Court of South Africa), para 75.

> ... while proponents of the coexistence approach view human rights law and patent protection as essentially compatible in theory, disagreement often arises in practice over exactly where to strike the balance between incentives for innovation on the one hand and access on the other ... little exists by way of concrete examples of just how this "coexistence" plays out in practice. At best, the coexistence asserted by the proponents of this theory is more properly viewed as a *need* for coexistence, a need that recognises that neither intellectual property rights nor human rights are likely to disappear as concepts or institutions anytime soon.[112]

Thus, in practice, it is quite difficult to foresee how human rights and intellectual property rights (including patent rights) can coexist in all aspects. There are aspects of patent rights, particularly patent rights on pharmaceutical products and processes, that negatively impact on the human right to health, and, when such conflicts occur, a practical choice has to be made between patent rights or human rights. More importantly, any notion that patent rights and human rights can 'peacefully coexist' is swiftly dispelled by the recent trend of incorporating TRIPS-plus standards[113] into bilateral and plurilateral free trade agreements negotiated (or currently being negotiated) between developed and developing countries outside the multilateral framework provided by the WTO.[114] These TRIPS-plus standards further exacerbate the negative impact that patent rights have on the enjoyment of the right to health in developing countries.[115]

For instance, the United States has concluded a number of bilateral free trade agreements (containing TRIPS-plus standards) with some developing countries.[116]

[112] Gold, 'Patents and Human Rights', 189 (emphasis in the original).

[113] TRIPS-plus standards are standards that exceed the obligations contained in the TRIPS Agreement.

[114] See Susan Sell, 'TRIPS-Plus Free Trade Agreements and Access to Medicines' (2007) 28 *Liverpool Law Review* 41, 59, who notes that '... the US and the EU aggressively have been pursuing efforts to ratchet up TRIPS standards, to eliminate TRIPS flexibilities and close TRIPS loopholes. Playing a multi-level, multi-forum governance game, countries like the United States have been able to extract a high price from economically more vulnerable parties eager to gain access to large, affluent markets. Bilateral Investment Treaties, Bilateral Intellectual Property Agreements, and regional FTAs concluded between the European Union and developing countries invariably have been TRIPS-Plus.'

[115] See Peter Yu, 'Intellectual Property and Human Rights in the Nonmultilateral Era' (2012) 64 *Florida Law Review* 1045, 1060, who notes that 'The stakes implicated by nonmultilateral agreements and new enforcement measures are ... much higher than those implicated by the TRIPS Agreement.'

[116] The Free Trade Agreement signed in 2000 between the United States and Jordan was the first TRIPS-Plus bilateral agreement in the post-TRIPS era. See Mohammed El Said, 'The Evolution of the Jordanian TRIPS-Plus Model: Multilateralism versus Bilateralism and the Implications for the Jordanian IPRs Regime' (2006) 37 *International Review of Intellectual Property & Competition Law* 501, 514. See also Susan Sell, 'TRIPS was Never Enough: Vertical Forum Shifting, FTAs, ACTA, and TPP' (2011) 18 *Journal of Intellectual Property Law* 447, 452, who noted that 'Since signing TRIPS, the U.S. has entered into bilateral treaties that include intellectual property provisions with numerous developing countries: Australia, Bahrain, Cambodia, Central American countries, Chile, Colombia, the Dominican Republic, Jamaica, Korea, Laos, Latvia, Lithuania, Morocco, Nicaragua, Oman, Panama, Peru, Singapore, South Korea, Trinidad and Tobago, and Vietnam.'

The typical TRIPS-plus standards that are included in these bilateral and plurilateral free trade agreements include: the extension of patent terms to compensate for delays in the examination of patent applications or in obtaining marketing approval for a drug; patent linkage requirements that prevent the grant of marketing approval to producers of generic drugs when there is an existing patent on the brand name drug; the grant of patents on new forms or new uses of known drugs; periods of exclusivity for clinical test data; and border enforcement measures that permit customs authorities to seize goods suspected to have infringed patent rights.[117] These TRIPS-plus standards can limit the ability of a country to use the flexibilities in the TRIPS Agreement, delay the production of cheaper generic drugs, and consequently hinder access to affordable drugs.[118] There is, therefore, no better time than now for developing countries to insist on the primacy of human rights obligations.

The 'subjugation approach' therefore appears to be the preferable way to conceptualize the relationship between patent rights and human rights. Properly construed, the 'subjugation approach' does not suggest that patent rights should be discarded or abolished. It rather recognizes the essential distinction between the fundamental nature of human rights and the regulatory nature of patent rights. As noted in Chapter 2, the patent system is best construed as a policy instrument or set of laws meant to define and regulate the grant of exclusive rights to creators. Furthermore, as pointed out in Chapter 2, conceptualizing patents through a regulatory lens has certain normative implications, including the fact that any regulatory instrument implemented by a state must not constitute a breach of its international human rights obligations as demanded by the *model of human rights*. Thus, if patent rights are not human rights under international human rights law, there is no justifiable reason why a country should allow its patent system to trump the enjoyment of the human right to health. This does not necessarily mean that patent rights should no longer be protected, but it means that states should not permit patent rights to be exercised in ways that impede the enjoyment of the human right to health. In addition, patent rights should be made to serve the interests protected by human rights.[119]

3.4 THE TRIPS AGREEMENT AND THE RIGHT TO HEALTH

3.4.1 *On the Necessity of a Model of Human Rights in the Implementation of the TRIPS Agreement at the National Level*

The TRIPS Agreement gives member states some leeway with regard to ensuring that the protection of intellectual property rights does not impede public health

[117] See Carlos Correa and Duncan Matthews, *The Doha Declaration Ten Years on and Its Impact on Access to Medicines and the Right to Health* (United Nations Development Programme, 2011), 21.

[118] Ibid.

[119] See Drahos, 'Intellectual Property and Human Rights', 367.

interests. For instance, in setting out the objectives of the TRIPS Agreement, Article 7 provides that the protection and enforcement of intellectual property rights should be done in a manner conducive to social and economic welfare. Article 8.1 of the TRIPS Agreement further permits states to adopt measures necessary to protect public health and nutrition as long as such measures are consistent with the provisions of the Agreement. Thus, there seems to be an intrinsic recognition within the TRIPS Agreement that states should protect intellectual property rights in a manner that is calibrated to advance social and economic welfare.[120]

Apart from compulsory licenses,[121] the TRIPS Agreement also offers certain flexibilities that states can use to address public health challenges in their territories. Such flexibilities include the freedom to exclude new forms of known drugs from patent protection,[122] freedom to adopt the principle of international exhaustion of patent rights to facilitate the parallel importation of drugs,[123] regulatory review exemption for producers of generic drugs,[124] and delinking the grant of marketing approval for generic drugs from the patent status of branded drugs.[125] The use of flexibilities was further reinforced and reaffirmed by the Doha Declaration on the TRIPS Agreement and Public Health of 2001.[126] According to the Doha

[120] UNCTAD-ICTSD, *Resource Book on TRIPS and Development* (Cambridge University Press, 2005), 126; Carlos Correa, *Trade Related Aspects of Intellectual Property Rights: A Commentary on the TRIPS Agreement* (Oxford University Press, 2007), 103.

[121] See Article 31 of the TRIPS Agreement.

[122] Article 27.1 of the TRIPS Agreement provides, *inter alia*, that 'patents shall be available for any inventions, whether products or processes, in all fields of technology, provided that they are new, involve an inventive step and are capable of industrial application.' However, since the TRIPS Agreement fails to define the meaning of terms such as 'invention', 'new', 'inventive step', and 'industrial application', states are free to define the meaning of these terms under their national patent laws. States are therefore free to define what does and does not constitute an invention under their national patent laws and this can include excluding new forms of known drugs from patent protection. See, for instance, Section 3(d) of the Indian Patents Act which prohibits the patenting of new forms of known substances and new uses of known substances. It may be argued that provisions such as Section 3(d) of the Indian Patents Act violate the non-discrimination principle in Article 27.1 of the TRIPS Agreement as it appears to be specifically aimed at the pharmaceutical industry. However, even if one assumes that Section 3(d) is aimed at the pharmaceutical industry, Article 27.1 of the TRIPS Agreement does not prohibit the justified imposition of differential treatment. See WTO, *Canada – Patent Protection of Pharmaceutical Products*, Panel Report, WT/DS114/R (17 March 2000) para 7.47. See also Swaraj P. Barooah, 'India's Pharmaceutical Innovation Policy: Developing Strategies for Developing Country Needs' (2013) 5 *Trade, Law and Development* 150, 181–2.

[123] See Article 6 of the TRIPS Agreement.

[124] See Article 30 of the TRIPS Agreement. See also, WTO, *Canada – Patent Protection of Pharmaceutical Products*, Panel Report, WT/DS114/R (17 March 2000). In this case, a WTO dispute settlement panel held that the regulatory review exemption under Canadian patent law is compatible with Article 30 of the TRIPS Agreement.

[125] This is not addressed by the TRIPS Agreement and, thus, states are not required to implement a patent linkage system.

[126] WTO Ministerial Conference, 'Declaration on the TRIPS Agreement and Public Health', adopted on 14 November 2001, WT/MIN(01)/DEC/2 (20 November 2001).

Declaration, the TRIPS Agreement 'does not and should not prevent members from taking measures to protect public health' and the Agreement 'can and should be interpreted and implemented in a manner supportive of WTO members' right to protect public health and, in particular to promote access to medicines for all'.[127] However, in practice, a number of developing countries are unable to make any beneficial use of these flexibilities because of political pressure from industrialized countries.[128]

The nature of the pressure faced by developing countries that attempt to utilize the flexibilities contained in the TRIPS Agreement is exemplified by the experience of India. India has been confronted with enormous pressure from its trading partners and multinational pharmaceutical corporations as a result of the flexibilities contained in the Indian patent law. In addition, multinational pharmaceutical companies have equally been urging the United States government to impose tougher measures on India because of its patent law.[129] This pressure from multinational pharmaceutical companies is one of the factors that contributed to the inclusion of India on the priority watch list in the 2014 edition of the Special 301 Report[130] compiled annually by the Office of the United States Trade Representative (USTR).[131]

[127] Ibid., para 4.

[128] Rachel Hermann, 'Developing Countries Are Not Making the Most of TRIPS Flexibilities because of Political Pressure' (2011) 343 *British Medical Journal* d7706.

[129] See Sumeet Chatterjee and Ben Hirschler, 'Big Pharma Pushes for U.S. Action against India over Patent Worries', *Reuters* (6 February 2014), available from www.reuters.com/article/india-usa-pharma/big-pharma-pushes-for-u-s-action-against-india-over-patent-worries-idUKL3N0LB18N20140206?edition-redirect=uk (last accessed 27 September 2021). There are also indications of resistance to India's patent law within India. For instance, the Bangalore based Association of Biotechnology-Led Enterprises which represents the Indian biotech sector has argued that, while the association believes that 'drugs will have to be affordable … revoking patents or slapping compulsory licensing is not the way to go about this.' See Killugudi Jayaraman, 'India Flouts Patent for Blockbuster Biologic' (2013) 31 *Nature Biotechnology* 9.

[130] This report is described by the USTR as an 'annual review of the global state of IPR protection and enforcement'. See USTR, 'USTR Releases Annual Special 301 Report on Intellectual Property Rights', Office of the USTR (April 2014), available from https://ustr.gov/about-us/policy-offices/press-office/press-releases/2014/April/USTR-Releases-Annual-Special-301-Report-on-Intellectual-Property-Rights (last accessed 27 September 2021). The review is conducted pursuant to American law contained in Section 182 of the Trade Act of 1974, as amended by the Omnibus Trade and Competitiveness Act of 1988 and the Uruguay Round Agreements Act of 1994. The Special 301 Report, which was first issued in 1989 before the emergence of the WTO, provides a list of countries with weak levels of IPR protection and enforcement. The report classifies countries into three groups according to the level of perceived weakness in the protection of IPRs. The 'bad offenders' are placed on the 'Watch List', 'worse offenders' are placed on the 'Priority Watch List', and the 'worst offenders' are designated as 'Priority Foreign Countries'.

[131] See USTR, '2014 Special 301 Report', Office of the USTR (April 2014), available from www.ustr.gov/sites/default/files/USTR%202014%20Special%20301%20Report%20to%20Congress%20FINAL.pdf (last accessed 27 September 2021). See also, Pharmaceutical Research and Manufacturers of America (PhRMA), 'Special 301 Submission 2014' (PhRMA, 2014), available

Among the concerns raised by the USTR is the use of two key flexibilities contained in India's Patents Act, that is, the exclusion of new forms of known drugs from patent protection (section 3(d)) and local working requirements (section 84(1)(c)). In the report, the USTR suggested that the exclusion of new forms of known drugs is not compatible with the TRIPS Agreement[132] and that it may have the effect of limiting the patentability of potentially beneficial innovations.[133] In addition, the USTR was concerned that the recent grant of a compulsory licence on the grounds, *inter alia*, that the patentee failed to satisfy the local working requirements contained in India's patent law[134] 'could inappropriately pressure innovators outside of India … to manufacture in India in order to avoid being compelled to license an invention to third parties.'[135]

However, developing countries are apparently free to exclude new forms of known drugs from patent protection because the TRIPS Agreement permits members to calibrate their standards of patentability to suit their domestic needs. There is no specific provision in the TRIPS Agreement that prohibits developing countries from excluding new forms of known drugs from patent protection. This is a crucial flexibility because a number of pharmaceutical companies have perfected the art of seeking secondary patents on trivial modifications of known drugs in order to extend their period of market exclusivity. In addition, the TRIPS Agreement does not contain any provision that expressly forbids countries from incorporating local working requirements into their national patent laws to remedy the failure of a patentee to engage in the local production of patented products.[136]

from http://phrma-docs.phrma.org/sites/default/files/pdf/2014-special-301-submission.pdf. See also Catherine Saez, 'India IP Policy Misrepresented by US Trade Representative, Indian Pharma Says', Intellectual Property Watch (22 July 2014), available from www.ip-watch.org/2014/07/22/india-ip-policy-misrepresented-by-us-trade-representative-indian-pharma-says/.

132 According to the USTR, 'a patent system should encourage the development of inventions that meet the well-established international criteria of being new, involving an inventive step, and being capable of industrial application, including as provided for in the TRIPS Agreement' (USTR, '2014 Special 301 Report', 39).

133 According to the USTR, 'The United States is concerned that section 3(d), as interpreted, may have the effect of limiting the patentability of potentially beneficial innovations. Such innovations would include drugs with fewer side effects, decreased toxicity, improved delivery systems, or temperature or storage stability' (USTR, '2014 Special 301 Report', 40).

134 See *Natco* v. *Bayer*, Compulsory Licence Application No.1 of 2011, decision of the Indian Controller of Patents (9 March 2012); *Bayer* v. *Union of India & Others*, OA/35/2012/PT/MUM, decision of the Indian Intellectual Property Appellate Board (4 March 2013).

135 USTR, '2014 Special 301 Report', 41.

136 Article 27.1 of the TRIPS Agreement, which provides in part that 'patents shall be available and patent rights enjoyable without discrimination as to … whether products are imported or locally produced', appears to prohibit the use of local working requirements. However, as Mercurio and Tyagi contend, interpreting Article 27 of the TRIPS Agreement under the various elements of Article 31 of the Vienna Convention on the Law of Treaties (1969) reveals that the imposition of local working requirements do not violate Article 27 of the TRIPS Agreement. See Bryan Mercurio and Mitali Tyagi, 'Treaty Interpretation in WTO Dispute

The experience of India in this regard thus demonstrates that the current international patent law regime may not be of great assistance to developing countries that intend to secure the right to health of their citizens. The experience of India also mirrors the earlier experiences of countries like Brazil and South Africa with regard to relying on the flexibilities contained in the TRIPS Agreement. In 1997 South Africa created a special regime for the parallel importation of medicines into the country. This was done by amending the Medicines and Related Substances Control Act of 1965 (hereinafter Medicines Act) via the Medicines and Related Substances Control Amendment Act of 1997 which introduced section 15C into the principal Act.[137] This special regime for the parallel importation of medicines was challenged in court by pharmaceutical companies.[138] In 1998, thirty-nine pharmaceutical companies lodged a complaint at the Pretoria High Court in South Africa alleging that the 1997 amendment to the Medicines Act was, *inter alia*, incompatible with the TRIPS Agreement.[139] In response to the 1997 amendment, the US government also tentatively withheld preferential treatment for several South African exports.[140] However, after significant public outcry by NGOs, 'the legal action turned into a public relations disaster for the drug companies, and the suit was finally withdrawn in April 2001'.[141] In addition, in 2000, the United States initiated dispute settlement proceedings in the WTO against Brazil because of the local working requirements contained in article 68(1)(I) of the Brazilian Industrial Property Law.[142] The dispute was, however, not resolved by the WTO as both countries reached a settlement and the United States withdrew its claim in 2001.[143]

Settlement: The Outstanding Question of the Legality of Local Working Requirements' (2010) 19 *Minnesota Journal of International Law* 275, 313, 326.

[137] According to Heinz Klug, 'the new government [of Nelson Mandela] published a national drug policy in January 1996. As a way of attacking the comparatively high cost of drugs in the South African market, the new policy promoted the use of generic drugs and suggested several ways to reduce unacceptably high retail prices, including allowing the state to facilitate the availability of affordable drugs in the private sector. It was that policy imperative that led to the passage of the Medicines and Related Substances Control Amendment Act in December 1997... with the aim of bringing down the cost of medicines.' Heinz Klug, 'Access to Medicines and the Transformation of the South African State: Exploring the Interactions of Legal and Policy Changes in Health, Intellectual Property, Trade, and Competition Law in the Context of South Africa's HIV/AIDS Pandemic' (2012) 37 *Law & Social Inquiry* 297, 312.

[138] See *Pharmaceutical Manufacturers' Association and Others* v. *President of the Republic of South Africa and Others*, case no. 4183/98, High Court of South Africa (Transvaal Provincial Division).

[139] See Haochen Sun, 'The Road to Doha and Beyond: Some Reflections on the TRIPS Agreement and Public Health' (2004)15 *European Journal of International Law* 123, 131.

[140] Ibid.

[141] Ibid.

[142] See *Brazil – Measures Affecting Patent Protection – Request for Consultations by the United States*, WT/DS199/1, G/L/385, IP/D/23 (8 June 2000).

[143] See *Brazil – Measures Affecting Patent Protection – Notification of Mutually Agreed Solution*, WT/DS199/4, G/L/454, IP/D/23/Add.1 (19 July 2001).

The experiences of these developing countries demonstrate that the use of the flexibilities contained in the TRIPS Agreement for the purposes of facilitating access to medicines in developing countries is a highly contested issue. However, since access to medicines is an integral component of the right to health, developing countries can rely on the stronger normative framework established under international human rights law with regard to the right to health to justify their use of the flexibilities contained in the TRIPS Agreement. In other words, developing countries seeking to exploit the flexibilities contained in the TRIPS Agreement to provide access to affordable medicines for poor patients in their countries can assert that they have a responsibility to respect, protect, and fulfil the human right to health of their citizens.

As pointed out in Section 3.2, the provision of essential drugs is one of the core obligations of states with regard to the right to health[144] and a core obligation is one from which no derogation is permissible.[145] Furthermore, the CESCR notes in General Comment No. 14 that the adoption of laws or policies that interfere with the enjoyment of any of the components of the right to health constitutes a violation of a state's obligation to respect the right to health.[146] The failure of a state to take into account its legal obligations regarding the right to health when entering into bilateral or multilateral agreements with other states, international organizations, and other entities, such as multinational corporations, is also viewed as a violation of the obligation to respect the right to health.[147]

States that are seeking to respect, protect, and fulfil the right to health of their citizens can therefore, as suggested in Chapter 2, incorporate a *model of human rights* into the design, implementation, interpretation, and enforcement of their national patent laws. Furthermore, as pointed out in Chapter 1, paragraph 4 of the Doha Declaration (which states that the TRIPS Agreement 'should be interpreted and implemented in a manner supportive of WTO Members' right to protect public

[144] CESCR, 'General Comment No. 14', para 43(d). It is true that the ICESCR provides for the progressive realization of the obligations contained in the Covenant, as stated in Article 2(1) of the ICESCR. However, as the UN CESCR points out in its General Comment No. 3, 'while the Covenant provides for progressive realization and acknowledges the constraints due to the limits of available resources, it also imposes various obligations which are of immediate effect'. See UN Committee on Economic, Social and Cultural Rights (CESCR), 'General Comment No. 3, The Nature of States Parties' Obligations (Art. 2, Para. 1, of the Covenant)' E/1991/23 (14 December 1990) para 1. Furthermore, in paragraph 10 of General Comment No. 3, the CESCR states that, 'the Committee is of the view that a minimum core obligation to ensure the satisfaction of, at the very least, minimum essential levels of each of the rights is incumbent upon every State party. Thus, for example, a State party in which any significant number of individuals is deprived of essential foodstuffs, of essential primary health care, of basic shelter and housing, or of the most basic forms of education is, prima facie, failing to discharge its obligations under the Covenant. If the Covenant were to be read in such a way as not to establish such a minimum core obligation, it would be largely deprived of its raison d'être.'

[145] See CESCR, 'General Comment No. 14', para 47.

[146] Ibid., para 50.

[147] Ibid.

health and, in particular, to promote access to medicines for all')[148] provides a linchpin that developing countries can use to preserve their patent policy space as it sanctions the incorporation of a right to health perspective into the design, implementation, interpretation, and enforcement of their national patent laws. This is because access to essential medicines is an integral component of the right to health, and the promotion and provision of access to essential medicines is a non-derogable obligation for countries that are parties to the ICESCR.

3.4.2 *Is the Model of Human Rights Compatible with Obligations under the TRIPS Agreement?*

Is the *model of human rights* proposed in this book compatible with the obligations of states under the TRIPS Agreement? In response to this question, it should be noted that the *model of human rights* being proposed here merely demands in this context that, as part of their duty to respect, protect, and fulfil the right to health, states should make use of the existing flexibilities in the TRIPS Agreement to facilitate access to medicines. Crucially, the use of flexibilities such as the exclusion of new forms of known drugs from patent protection, compulsory licences, parallel importation, and regulatory review exemption, pursuant to a *model of human rights*, is compatible with the text of the TRIPS Agreement. In other words, none of these flexibilities are actually prohibited by the text of the TRIPS Agreement. Simply stated, the argument being made here is that the incorporation of a *model of human rights* into a country's patent system provides a stronger normative basis for the utilization of the flexibilities in the TRIPS Agreement by a country that is willing to facilitate access to medicines and protect the right to health of its citizens.[149]

In the event that a state's implementation of any of these flexibilities (especially the more controversial ones such as local working requirements or the exclusion of new forms of known drugs from patent protection) is challenged as incompatible with the TRIPS Agreement by another state before a WTO dispute settlement panel, can the former state rely on its human rights obligations as a defence to such a challenge? In other words, to what extent can a state rely on its right to health obligations under the ICESCR as a defence in a dispute involving the TRIPS Agreement before a WTO panel? This question touches on the debate concerning the role of non-WTO law (such as human rights law) in WTO disputes.[150]

[148] See WTO Ministerial Conference, 'Declaration on the TRIPS Agreement and Public Health', para 4.

[149] See also Yu, 'Intellectual Property and Human Rights', 1092, who notes that 'To some extent, greater utilization of the human rights system may help less developed countries uphold the flexibilities in the TRIPS Agreement.'

[150] In this regard, see generally, Joost Pauwelyn, 'The Role of Public International Law in the WTO: How Far Can We Go?' (2001) 95 *American Journal of International Law* 535; Gabrielle Marceau, 'WTO Dispute Settlement and Human Rights' (2002) 13(4) *European Journal of*

A dispute in 2010 between India and the European Union over the seizures by Dutch Customs Authorities of generic drugs in transit from India to developing countries in Africa and Latin America could have provided an opportunity to determine the extent to which a WTO dispute settlement panel would be willing to interpret the TRIPS Agreement in light of the right to health as enshrined in Article 12(1) of the ICESCR. Pursuant to Article 4 of the WTO's Dispute Settlement Understanding, India had filed a request for consultations challenging the seizure of the generic drugs. In its request for consultations, India had argued, *inter alia*, that, 'the provisions of the TRIPS Agreement ... must be interpreted and implemented in light of the objectives and principles set forth in Articles 7 and 8 of the TRIPS Agreement, the Doha Ministerial Declaration on the TRIPS Agreement and Public Health adopted on 14 November 2001 and in the light of Article 12(1) of the International Covenant on Economic, Social and Cultural Rights, which recognizes the right of all persons to the enjoyment of the highest attainable standard of physical and mental health'.[151]

If this case had proceeded to the dispute settlement stage before a WTO panel, it would have revealed the weight which the WTO panel would attach to the right to health vis-à-vis the protection of patent rights when interpreting the provisions of the TRIPS Agreement.[152] However, in July 2011, India announced that it had reached an understanding with the European Union with regard to the dispute,[153] though (as at

International Law 573; Joost Pauwelyn, *Conflict of Norms in Public International Law. How WTO Relates to Other Rules of International Law* (Cambridge University Press, 2003); Holger Hestermeyer, 'Economic, Social, and Cultural Rights in the World Trade Organization: Legal Aspects and Practice', in Eibe Riedel, Gilles Giacca, and Christophe Golay (eds.), *Economic, Social, and Cultural Rights in International Law: Contemporary Issues and Challenges* (Oxford University Press, 2014), 260; Holger Hestermeyer, 'International Human Rights Law and Dispute Settlement in the World Trade Organization', in Martin Scheinin (ed.), *Human Rights Norms in 'Other' International Courts* (Cambridge University Press, 2019), 199.

151 See *European Union and a Member State – Seizure of Generic Drugs in Transit: Request for Consultations by India*, WT/DS408/1, G/L/921, IP/D/28 (19 May 2010) 3.

152 See Lisa Forman, 'An Elementary Consideration of Humanity? Linking Trade-Related Intellectual Property Rights to the Human Right to Health in International Law' (2011) 14 *The Journal of World Intellectual Property* 155, 168, who notes that, if the case should proceed to the WTO dispute settlement panel, it 'will provide an important testing ground for the interpretation of TRIPS provisions in the context of the agreement as a whole, and in relation to article 12 of the International Covenant on Economic, Social and Cultural Rights. Moreover, the outcomes of these complaints may illustrate the extent to which the WTO dispute settlement process could provide protection to developing countries to access affordable medicines [within] the framework of TRIPS and subsequent amendments and agreements.'

153 See Government of India, Ministry of Commerce and Industry, 'India EU Reach an Understanding on Issue of Seizure of Indian Generic Drugs in Transit' (28 July 2011) http://pib.nic.in/newsite/erelease.aspx?relid=73554 (website no longer active, an alternative version is available from https://taxguru.in/finance/india-eu-reach-understanding-issue-seizure-indian-generic-drugs-transit.html, last accessed 30 September 2021). See also B. K. Baker, 'Settlement of India/EU WTO Dispute re Seizures of In-Transit Medicines: Why the Proposed EU Border Regulations Isn't Good Enough', PIJIP Research Paper No. 2012-02 (2012).

the time of writing) the dispute has not been formally withdrawn and the WTO has not been notified of a mutually agreed solution.

Nevertheless, the decisions of both the panel and the Appellate Body in the *Australia – Plain Packaging* case provides some insights regarding the potential role that non-WTO law can play in WTO disputes.[154] In this case, Australia's obligations under the WHO's Framework Convention on Tobacco Control (FCTC) was treated as factual evidence by the panel.[155] This was upheld on appeal by the Appellate Body.[156] This therefore suggests that, at the very least, the obligations of states under human rights treaties such as the ICESCR could be used as evidence in disputes involving the TRIPS Agreement before a WTO panel.[157]

[154] WTO, *Australia – Certain Measures Concerning Trademarks, Geographical Indications and Other Plain Packaging Requirements Applicable to Tobacco Products and Packaging*, Panel Report, WT/DS435/R, WT/DS441/R WT/DS458/R, WT/DS467/R (28 June 2018) [hereinafter, *Australia – Plain Packaging*]; WTO, *Australia – Certain Measures Concerning Trademarks, Geographical Indications and Other Plain Packaging Requirements Applicable to Tobacco Products and Packaging*, Appellate Body Report, WT/DS435/AB/R, WT/DS441/AB/R (9 June 2020) [hereinafter, *Australia – Plain Packaging*, AB Report].

[155] See Lukasz Gruszczynski and Margherita Melillo, 'The FCTC and Its Role in WTO Law: Some Remarks on the WTO Plain Packaging Report' (2018) 9(3) *European Journal of Risk Regulation* 564, 572, who observed that 'The panel referred to several provisions of the FCTC and its guidelines to support, confirm, or corroborate its findings on: the purpose of the TPP measures (paras. 7.243, 7.250, 7.2589); the outcomes of the TPP measures (para. 7.555); the effectiveness of regulation of packaging and health warnings (paras. 7.664–7.665, 7.798; 7.800; 7.803–7.804; 7.807); the health consequences of tobacco use and exposure (para. 7.1309); the need for a comprehensive approach to tobacco (paras. 7.1388–7.1389, 7.1457, 7.1527, 7.1614, 7.1728); the effectiveness of other tobacco control measures (paras. 7.1442, 7.1457, 7.1509, 7.1594, 7.1660); as well as the fundamental rationale of the TPP measures (paras. 7.1670, 7.2595–7.2596, 7.2604).'

[156] *Australia – Plain Packaging*, AB Report, para 6.702, which states that, 'The Panel noted that Australia and certain complainants referred to the FCTC and its Guidelines as "evidence in support of specific arguments". The Panel saw no reason to assume that the FCTC and its Guidelines "could not inform, together with other relevant evidence", the Panel's understanding of relevant aspects of the matters at issue, such as "tobacco control measures ... to reduce ... the prevalence of tobacco use". These preliminary observations about the FCTC and its Guidelines suggest that the Panel intended to use them, where relevant, "as evidence" rather than as an interpretative tool'; and para 6.707, which states that '... we do not agree with Honduras that the Panel attributed undue legal weight to Articles 11 and 13 of the FCTC Guidelines in its analysis by relying on those provisions to justify Australia's imposition of the TPP measures. In our view, the Panel referred to Articles 11 and 13 of the FCTC Guidelines as additional factual support to its previous conclusion that the complainants failed to establish that Australia acted inconsistently with Article 20 of the TRIPS Agreement.'

[157] As Diane Desierto contends: 'The ICESCR does not have to be viewed as being in frontal conflict with WTO obligations. Where a WTO Member is a State Party to the ICESCR, its duties to respect, protect, and fulfill ICESCR rights can substantively inform how it exercises the regulatory freedoms recognized under the provisions of WTO law ... The WTO Member's social protection commitments and status of protection afforded under such commitments as a State Party to the ICESCR provide WTO tribunals with information that may be useful in their assessments of the "reasonableness" of challenged measures that had been issued to vindicate public policy values as reflected in the ICESCR ... Depending on the scope and effect of

3.5 CONCLUSION

Two key questions have been answered in this chapter. First, patent rights ought not to be regarded as human rights and there is therefore no justification for countries to permit patent rights to be exercised and enforced in a manner that impedes the enjoyment of the right to health. Second, the *model of human rights* is compatible with the TRIPS Agreement. Therefore, the TRIPS Agreement does not prohibit countries from incorporating a *model of human rights* into their national patent laws. Thus, countries can incorporate a right to health perspective into the design, implementation, interpretation, and enforcement of their national patent laws. Invariably, there is nothing that prohibits a developing country from insisting on the primacy of human rights obligations when attempting to resolve the tension between patent rights and the right to health at the national level. Chapters 4–6 will examine how three developing countries (Kenya, South Africa, and India) have incorporated a *model of human rights* into their national patent systems.

regulatory freedom recognized in the WTO provision invoked, the WTO Member who is also a State Party to the ICESCR can marshal information on its ICESCR compliance for various evidentiary purposes when seeking to establish independent defenses (e.g. GATT Article XX/ GATS Article XIV), obtain flexibility in trade commitments or negotiating technical assistance (e.g. S&D treatment), or trigger interpretive principles (e.g. Article 8.1, TRIPS Agreement) based on the State's public policy objectives, such as respecting, protecting and fulfilling ICESCR rights.' Diane Desierto, *Public Policy in International Economic Law: The ICESCR in Trade, Finance, and Investment* (Oxford University Press, 2015) 230.

4

Incorporating a Model of Human Rights into the Adjudication of Pharmaceutical Patent Cases (Part One)

Kenya as a Case Study

4.1 INTRODUCTION

This chapter is structured into three main sections. Section 4.2 gives a brief overview of the legal framework on pharmaceutical patent law in Kenya. Section 4.3 deals with the key issue in this chapter, that is, the incorporation of a *model of human rights* into the adjudication of disputes involving pharmaceutical patent rights by courts in Kenya. In this regard, it is worth noting that the right to health was only introduced into the Kenyan Constitution in 2010.[1] Section 4.4 examines whether, in the light of Article 40(5) of the Kenyan Constitution, which provides that the state 'shall support, promote and protect the intellectual property rights of the people of Kenya', intellectual property rights can be considered as a human right in Kenya. The chapter concludes with the view that it is essential for courts seeking to protect the right of poor patients to have access to affordable medicines to incorporate a *model of human rights* when they adjudicate disputes involving pharmaceutical patent rights.

4.2 PHARMACEUTICAL PATENT LAW IN KENYA

Before 1989, the only route for registering patents locally in Kenya was via the Patents Registration Act of 1933.[2] Under this regime, only patents which had been granted in the United Kingdom could be registered in Kenya.[3] In a bid to establish an independent patent system, the Industrial Property Act of 1989 was enacted to

[1] See Article 43(1)(a) of the Kenyan Constitution of 2010, which provides that everyone has the right to 'the highest attainable standard of health, which includes the right to heath care services, including reproductive health care'.

[2] See James Odek, 'The Kenya Patent Law: Promoting Local Inventiveness or Protecting Foreign Patentees?' (1994) 38 *Journal of African Law* 79.

[3] See ibid., 79, who notes that 'To obtain patent protection in Kenya [prior to 1989], an applicant was required to present a certified copy of letters patent from the U.K. Patents Office. The U.K.

replace the Patents Registration Act.[4] Kenya was a founding member of the World Trade Organization in 1995 and a party to the TRIPS Agreement.[5] In compliance with the requirements of the TRIPS Agreement, the Industrial Property Act of 1989 was reviewed to bring it in line with the TRIPS Agreement.[6] This process led to the enactment of the Kenyan Industrial Property Act of 2001.[7] The Kenyan Industrial Property Act was subsequently amended in 2002, 2007, and 2017.[8]

Section 22 of the Kenyan Industrial Property Act of 2001 (as amended) provides that '[a]n invention is patentable if it is new, involves an inventive step and, is industrially applicable'. Section 21(3) of the same Act excludes the following, *inter alia*, from patent protection: discoveries, methods for doing business, methods for the treatment of humans or animals, diagnostic methods, mere presentation of information, and 'public health related methods of use or uses of any molecule or other substance whatsoever used for the prevention or treatment of any disease which the Minister responsible for matters relating to Health may designate as a serious health hazard or as a life threatening disease.'

The Kenyan patent law equally contains key flexibilities that can be used to facilitate access to affordable medicines. These key flexibilities include: compulsory licensing,[9] adoption of the principle of international exhaustion of patent rights (thus permitting parallel importation of patented inventions),[10] and research exception.[11] Mey has observed that, unlike compulsory licensing, Kenya has made good use of the flexibility permitting parallel importation of patented inventions.[12]

patent was subsequently re-registered in Kenya without further examination. Accordingly, the patents granted in Kenya were dependent upon patent grant in the U.K and the rights conferred to the Kenyan patentee were rights existing in the U.K. patent law. Two essential features of this were, first, that only patents granted in the U.K. could be registered in Kenya, and, secondly, that the duration of patent protection was determined by the U.K. term.' See also Brenda Pamela Mey, 'Unfettered Consumer Access to Affordable Therapies in the Post-TRIPS Era: A Dead-End Journey for Patients? Kenya and India Case Studies' (2010) 13 *The Journal of World Intellectual Property* 403, 406–7.

4 See Patricia Kameri-Mbote, 'Intellectual Property Protection in Africa: An Assessment of the Status of Laws, Research and Policy Analysis on Intellectual Property Rights in Kenya', International Environmental Law Research Centre Working Paper 2005-2 (2005) 6.

5 See Moni Wekesa, 'An Overview of the Intellectual Property Rights (IPRS) Regime in Kenya', in Moni Wekesa and Ben Sihanya (eds.), *Intellectual Property Rights in Kenya* (Konrad Adenauer Stiftung & SportsLink Ltd., 2009), 6–7.

6 Ibid.

7 Ibid.

8 See Act No. 2 of 2002; Act No. 7 of 2007; Act No. 11 of 2017. It should also be noted that Kenya is currently planning to codify and combine all its intellectual property laws into a single legislation via the Intellectual Property Bill of 2020 (which, as at the time of writing has not yet been passed into law).

9 See sections 72–8 of the Kenyan Industrial Property Act.

10 See section 58(2) of the Kenyan Industrial Property Act.

11 See section 58(1) of the Kenyan Industrial Property Act.

12 Mey, 'Unfettered Consumer Access', 426. According to Mey, 'The first use of the parallel import mechanism in Kenya occurred in 2002 shortly after the enactment of [the Industrial

The analysis in Section 4.3 will demonstrate how the incorporation of a *model of human rights* into the process of adjudicating disputes involving patent rights can assist a court to properly construe and apply important flexibilities that are contained in a country's patent law.

4.3 INCORPORATING A MODEL OF HUMAN RIGHTS INTO THE ADJUDICATION OF DISPUTES INVOLVING PHARMACEUTICAL PATENTS IN KENYA

In 2012, a Kenyan High Court made landmark pronouncements on the relationship between the right to health and intellectual property rights.[13] Prior to this case, however, it appears that the courts in Kenya had never considered the potential impact that the enforcement of patent rights can have on the right to health. This is illustrated by the decision of the Kenyan Industrial Property Tribunal in an earlier dispute between a foreign multinational pharmaceutical company and a local pharmaceutical company in Kenya.[14]

4.3.1 Pfizer *v.* Cosmos: *Failure to Incorporate a Model of Human Rights*

In the 2008 case of *Pfizer Inc.* v. *Cosmos Limited*, Pfizer alleged that Cosmos had infringed its patent on a medicinal product known as 'azithromycin dihydrate'.[15] Cosmos, however, contended that the patent was not in force between 2003 and 2006 (when the alleged infringement occurred) due to the failure of Pfizer to pay the renewal fees on the patent. The tribunal, however, held that there was no evidence that the patent had lapsed or that it had been removed from the patent register at any time.[16] The patent in question was registered by the African Regional Intellectual Property Organization (ARIPO), of which Kenya is a member, and Kenya was among the designated states for the patent. Section 59 of the Kenyan Industrial Property Act of 2001 provides, *inter alia*, that 'a patent, in respect of which Kenya is a

Property Act 2001], when [Medecins Sans Frontieres] and Action Aid ... imported anti-retroviral drugs for the treatment of HIV/AIDS and other opportunistic infections and for use in providing free treatment. This was rapidly followed by an order for generic drugs from India by the Mission for Essential Drugs and Supplies (MEDS) to be distributed at no cost through the mission hospitals run by the organization ... [T]he increased use of parallel imports has not only brought the prices of pharmaceutical products under control but has also, by allowing multiple independent distributors to operate in the market, ensured the regular supply of the much-needed medicines to different patient groups in Kenya' (426–7).

13 See *PA Ochieng, M Atieno, and J Munyo* v. *Attorney General* (Petition No. 409 of 2009, Judgment of the Kenyan High Court, 20 April 2012) [hereinafter, *Ochieng*].

14 See *Pfizer Inc.* v. *Cosmos Limited* (Case No. 49 of 2006, Judgment of the Industrial Property Tribunal at Nairobi, 25 April 2008) [hereinafter, *Pfizer*].

15 Ibid., 1.

16 Ibid., 7.

designated state, granted by ARIPO by virtue of the ARIPO Protocol shall have the same effect in Kenya as a patent granted under this Act'.

Cosmos raised an alternative defence that it was entitled to import, manufacture, sell, and export the patented product without the authority of Pfizer by virtue of section 58(2) of the Industrial Property Act, which allows parallel importation. Section 58(2) provides that 'the rights under the patent shall not extend to acts in respect of articles which have been put on the market in Kenya or in any other country or imported into Kenya by the owner of the patent or with his express consent.' Cosmos presented evidence to the tribunal establishing that the medicines containing the patented product were available in Kenya having been imported from India, Bangladesh, and China.[17] In other words, the patent rights of Pfizer, with respect to those products which were readily available in Kenya, had been exhausted. Cosmos was trying to rely on the principle of international exhaustion of patent rights, as reflected in section 58(2), and though this principle might not give Cosmos the right to manufacture the patented product, it would entitle Cosmos to buy those products from India, Bangladesh, and China, and to resell them in Kenya.[18]

However, in a rather curious and confusing manner, the tribunal conflated parallel importation with compulsory licenses and voluntary licenses. According to the tribunal, 'parallel importation ... is applicable for instance where the government has allowed a third party to exploit the patent, and that party imports the product from other countries where it is legitimately put on the market ... This could also be with the authority of the patent holder by way of a contractual or voluntary license'.[19] The tribunal could not comprehend a situation where a third party could engage in the parallel importation of a patented product without the authorization of the patentee or the government and its definition of parallel importation clearly contradicts what is contained in section 58(2). Section 58(2) does not require a person or a company to obtain government authorization or a compulsory/voluntary license before engaging in parallel importation.[20]

Cosmos equally argued that the patented product was used for the treatment of opportunistic infections in HIV/AIDS patients and that the WHO listed the product as an essential medicine for the treatment of genital chlamydia trachomatis and trachoma.[21] By raising this argument, Cosmos highlighted a tension between the enforcement of Pfizer's patent rights on one hand and the need to facilitate access to

17 Ibid., 3, 4.

18 Rajnish K. Rai and Srinath Jagannathan, 'Parallel Imports and Unparallel Laws: An Examination of the Exhaustion Doctrine through the Lens of Pharmaceutical Products' (2012) 21 *Information & Communications Technology Law* 53

19 *Pfizer*, 13.

20 See also Linda M. Opati, 'Intellectual Property Rights in Health – Impact on Access to Drugs', in Moni Wekesa and Ben Sihanya (eds.), *Intellectual Property Rights in Kenya* (Konrad Adenauer Stiftung & SportsLink Ltd., 2009), 27.

21 *Pfizer*, 16.

this essential medicine for Kenyan patients on the other hand. The resolution of this tension therefore required a proper appreciation of the fact that patent rights ought to serve the needs and interests of the beneficiaries of human rights such as the right to have access to affordable medicines.[22] If the tension had been approached from this dimension, it would have enabled the tribunal to interpret the patent law with the objective of ensuring that it does not impede access to medicines. However, in this particular case, the Kenyan tribunal took the view that the product was not a first-line treatment for HIV/AIDS patients and that, even if this were the case, it would not entitle the respondents to exploit the patent without authorization.[23]

By interpreting the provisions of section 58(2) in this manner and ignoring the impact this approach could have on access to medicines in Kenya, the tribunal overlooked the rationale behind the introduction of parallel importation into the Kenyan Industrial Property Act of 2001 via the provisions of section 58(2). During the parliamentary debates on the 2001 Act, it was stated that the provision on parallel importation was specifically introduced to permit the importation into Kenya of 'medicines which are required for human life, especially [for the treatment of] HIV/AIDS and [other] opportunistic diseases, as well as malaria'.[24]

The tribunal thus failed to appreciate the essential distinction between the regulatory nature of patent rights and the fundamental nature of the right to have access to essential medicines. It could be argued that the tribunal failed to appreciate this essential distinction because Article 43(1)(a), which made the right to health a justiciable right in Kenya, was only introduced into the Kenyan Constitution in 2010, that is, two years after the tribunal's judgment. However, even without invoking a constitutional right to health, a court that is mindful of the fundamental importance of securing access to medicines would have examined the rationale behind the inclusion of section 58(2) in the Kenyan patent law. As noted above, section 58(2) was introduced in order to facilitate the importation of medicines for the treatment of HIV/AIDS and opportunistic ailments. A court that is mindful of the fundamental importance of facilitating access to affordable medicines would have construed section 58(2) in accordance with the objective of ensuring that the enforcement of a patent right does not defeat the aims of the drafters of the patent law.

A classic example of a case where the court recognized this essential distinction, even in the absence of a constitutional right to health, is the English case of

[22] See Peter Drahos, 'Intellectual Property and Human Rights' (1999) 3 *Intellectual Property Quarterly* 349, 367, who states that 'rights created through the enactment of intellectual property laws are instrumental rights. Ideally, under conditions of democratic sovereignty, such rights should serve the interests and needs that citizens identify through the language of human rights as being fundamental.'

[23] *Pfizer*, 17.

[24] Statement by the Kenyan Minister for Trade and Industry during the parliamentary debates on the Industrial Property Act. See Kenyan National Assembly Official Record (Hansard), 12 June 2001, p. 1043.

Roussel-Uclaf v. *G. D. Searle & Co.*[25] In that case, the plaintiffs (who held a license under a patent to exclusively sell certain drugs) sought to restrain the defendants from selling one of those drugs in the United Kingdom. However, the court refused to grant an injunction restraining the defendants from selling the drug because it was a unique, life-saving drug with no precise equivalent in the market, as the plaintiffs were not yet selling the drug in the United Kingdom. Thus, the English court was clearly concerned about preserving access to this life-saving drug for patients in the United Kingdom and it prioritized this over the patent rights of the plaintiffs.

A court that is mindful of the fundamental importance of securing access to medicines ought not to permit the enforcement of patent rights in a manner that impedes access to medicines. In *Pfizer* v. *Cosmos*, the approach adopted by the Kenyan tribunal essentially elevated the rights of patentees above the right to health of patients in need of essential medicines. The tribunal lost sight of the fundamental importance of securing access to essential medicines while it was adjudicating the patent dispute between the parties.

4.3.2 Ochieng *v.* Attorney General: *The Facts and Arguments of the Parties*

In the more recent case of *Patricia Asero Ochieng et al.* v. *Attorney General*, the Kenyan High Court had an opportunity to consider the relationship between intellectual property rights and the right to health. In that case, the petitioners were HIV/AIDS patients, and they alleged that certain sections of the Kenyan Anti-Counterfeit Act of 2008[26] threatened their access to essential drugs, thereby infringing their right to life, dignity, and health.[27] The petitioners argued that the government failed to specifically exempt generic drugs from the definition of counterfeit goods in the Act.[28] Specifically, section 2 of the Act defines counterfeiting in relation to medicine to mean 'the deliberate and fraudulent mislabelling of medicine with respect to identity or source, whether or not such products have correct ingredients, wrong ingredients, have sufficient active ingredients or have fake packaging'. The respondents, however, argued that the Anti-Counterfeit Act was enacted to prohibit trade in counterfeit goods in Kenya and was not intended to prohibit generic drugs.[29] The respondents argued that the Act was intended to 'protect the public from the harm of using counterfeit goods and that extra care

[25] *Roussel-Uclaf* v. *G. D. Searle & Co. Ltd & Another* [1977] F.S.R. 125 (Judgment of the English High Court of Justice – Chancery Division).

[26] The Kenyan Anti-Counterfeit Act has been amended a number of times and the most recent amendment occurred in 2018 via Act No.18 of 2018.

[27] *Ochieng*, para 1.

[28] Ibid., para 14.

[29] Ibid., para 39.

needs to be taken to ensure that the medicine in the market meets the required standard'.[30]

Contrary to the arguments of the respondents in this case, it appears that the real intent behind the Kenyan Anti-Counterfeit Act is not really the protection of the public from harm but the Act was designed to secure, among other things, the intellectual property rights of pharmaceutical companies. Von Braun and Munyi point out that, because the two bills preceding the enactment of the Anti-Counterfeit Act were not backed by any public policy decision, it is 'difficult to discern the real motive or motivations behind the enactment of the legislation' but 'during the legislative process, there was a lot of public debate, at least as demonstrated by numerous media reports on the effect counterfeiting has had on the local manufacturing sector' and the 'Kenya Association of Manufacturers ... was leading in the lobbying towards legislation on anti-counterfeiting'.[31] Harrington and O'Hare equally note that the Kenya Association of Manufacturers played a key role in securing the passage of the Act.[32] According to Harrington and O'Hare, the Kenya Association of Manufacturers 'represents over 700 members, both domestic and foreign-owned firms, among whom are major pharmaceutical concerns marketing and manufacturing their products in Kenya'.[33] They note that the Association established an Anti-Counterfeit Committee and 'engaged closely in the legislative process itself' while also 'frequently briefing key parliamentary committees'.[34]

A former UN Special Rapporteur on the right to health, Anand Grover, filed an *amicus* brief in the *Ochieng* case. According to the former Special Rapporteur, 'the definition of "counterfeiting" within the Act effectively conflates generic medicines with medicines which are produced in violation of private intellectual property rights, and this conflation of legitimately produced generic medicines with those that possibly violate intellectual property rights is likely to have a serious adverse impact on the availability, affordability and accessibility of low-cost, high-quality medicines'.[35] Grover agreed with the contention of the petitioners that the Act could endanger the right to health because it does not exclude generic drugs.[36] Grover also provided a definition of generic medicines (which was quoted in the court's judgment) as drugs that 'have the same composition and contain the same

30 Ibid., para 42.

31 Johanna Von Braun and Peter Munyi, 'New Enforcement Mechanisms Challenge the Legality of Generics in the Name of Public Health: The Emergence of Anti-Counterfeiting Legislation in East Africa' (2010) 18 *African Journal of International and Comparative Law* 238, 243.

32 John Harrington and Alasdair O'Hare, 'Framing the National Interest: Debating Intellectual Property and Access to Essential Medicines in Kenya' (2014) 17 *The Journal of World Intellectual Property* 16, 22.

33 Ibid.

34 Ibid.

35 *Ochieng*, para 35.

36 Ibid., para 34.

substances as patented formulations of the same drugs, and are essentially identical copies [that] can be used for the same purposes as their non-generic counterparts'.[37]

4.3.3 Ochieng *v.* Attorney General: *The Decision of the Kenyan High Court: Incorporating a Model of Human Rights*

In its analysis of the meaning and implication of the right to health, the High Court referred to Article 43(1)(a) of the Kenyan Constitution which guarantees the right to health, Article 12 of the International Covenant on Economic, Social and Cultural Rights (ICESCR), and the UN Committee on Economic, Social, and Cultural Rights (CESCR) General Comment No. 14 on the Right to Health.[38] The High Court proceeded to delineate the nature of the state's obligation with regard to the right to health. The court held that the state's obligation entails both a positive and a negative duty. The state has a positive duty to ensure that its citizens have access to health care services and medicines; it equally has a negative duty to refrain from taking actions that would affect access to these health care services and medicines.[39] Thus, any legislative enactment that would make medicines too expensive for citizens would be in violation of the state's obligation.[40]

The court equally highlighted the danger inherent in conflating the definition of counterfeit drugs and generic drugs by referring to cases where generic drugs in transit were seized on the basis of being counterfeit.[41] Though the court did not mention any particular country, it is reasonable to assume that the court was referring to instances like the seizure by Dutch Customs authorities in 2008 and 2009 of multiple shipments of drugs that were in-transit from India to developing countries in Africa and Latin America.[42] The court agreed with the petitioners and the Special Rapporteur that the 'definition of "counterfeit" in section 2 of the Act is likely to be read as including generic medication' and quoting from the Special Rapporteur's *amicus* brief, it stated that 'this would affect the availability of generic drugs and pose a real threat to the petitioners' right to life, dignity and health'.[43] The court disagreed with the respondent's argument that the Act was primarily intended

[37] Ibid., para 76.

[38] See UN Committee on Economic, Social and Cultural Rights (CESCR), 'General Comment No. 14: The Right to the Highest Attainable Standard of Health (Art. 12)' E/C.12/2000/4 (2000).

[39] *Ochieng*, para 66.

[40] Ibid.

[41] Ibid., para 75.

[42] See Anna G. Micara, 'TRIPS-plus Border Measures and Access to Medicines' (2012) 15 *The Journal of World Intellectual Property* 73; Brook K. Baker, 'ACTA – Risks of Third-Party Enforcement for Access to Medicines' (2012) 26 *American University International Law Review* 579, 581–2.

[43] *Ochieng*, para 78.

to protect consumers from counterfeit medicines. According to the court, 'the tenor and object of the Act is to protect the intellectual property rights of individuals'.[44]

The court was of the view that the rights to life, dignity, and health must take priority over intellectual property rights. The court noted that if the Act is implemented as originally written, 'the danger that it poses to the right of the petitioners to access essential medicine . . . is far greater and more critical than the protection of the intellectual property rights that the Act seeks to protect. The right to life, dignity and health of the petitioners must take precedence over the intellectual property rights of patent holders'.[45] The court thus adopted and applied the 'subjugation approach' by upholding the primacy of human rights over intellectual property rights.

The court further held that, '[i]t is incumbent on the state to reconsider the provisions of section 2 of the Anti-Counterfeit Act alongside its constitutional obligation to ensure that its citizens have access to the highest attainable standard of health and make appropriate amendments to ensure that the rights of petitioners and others dependent on generic medicines are not put in jeopardy.'[46] However, despite the fact that the Anti-Counterfeit Act has been amended a number of times, the Kenyan government has not yet amended section 2 of the Act to incorporate the ruling of the court in this case. It is therefore hoped that the ruling of the High Court in this case will be taken into consideration in future attempts to amend the Kenyan Anti-Counterfeit Act.

Thus, unlike the approach adopted by the tribunal in the *Pfizer* v. *Cosmos* case, the decision of the Kenyan High Court in this case demonstrates the court's recognition of the tension between the enforcement of intellectual property rights and the protection of the right to health. The court refused to be misguided into overlooking the fact that the Anti-Counterfeit Act was enacted to enhance the protection of intellectual property rights in Kenya. With the recognition that there was a tension to be resolved, the court equally demonstrated an implicit understanding of the essential distinction between the fundamental nature of the right to health and the regulatory nature of intellectual property rights. This can be seen from the court's statement that the danger posed by the Anti-Counterfeit Act to the petitioner's right to access essential medicines was far greater and more critical than the protection of intellectual property rights. It is therefore not surprising that the court, while not disparaging intellectual property rights, held that the right to health must take priority over intellectual property rights.

From the High Court's decision, a two-stage process is discernible in the incorporation of a *model of human rights* into the adjudication of patent law disputes. The first stage involves the *recognition* of the tension between patent rights and the right to health. The second stage involves the *resolution* of this tension by distinguishing between the fundamental nature of the right to health and the regulatory nature of patent rights.

44 Ibid., para 82.
45 Ibid., para 85.
46 Ibid., para 88.

The court's decision in the *Ochieng* case also demonstrates that the incorporation of a *model of human rights* into pharmaceutical patent cases enables a court to properly construe and apply the flexibilities already contained in the domestic patent law such as provisions on compulsory licenses and parallel importation. For instance, the tribunal in the *Pfizer* case failed to recognize the tension between patent rights and access to medicines; it is therefore not surprising that it also failed to properly construe and apply the provisions on parallel importation in the Kenyan patent law. However, in its decision in the *Ochieng* case, the Kenyan High Court incorporated a *model of human rights* into its decision and properly construed the provision on parallel importation. The Kenyan High Court noted that:

> ... [U]ntil the passage of the Industrial Property Act in 2001 ... it was not possible for poor people infected with HIV/AIDS to access anti-retroviral medication as the only ones available were expensive branded medicines. Generic anti-retroviral drugs were not available in Kenya as the existing legislation did not allow parallel importation of generic drugs and medicines. Section 58(2) [of the 2001 Act] ... allowed the parallel importation of generic drugs. It is on the basis of this legislation that availability and access to anti-retroviral drugs has increased and greatly enhanced the life and health of persons such as the petitioners who have been living with HIV/AIDS.[47]

The incorporation of a *model of human rights* can therefore also assist a court in construing patent laws and flexibilities in a manner that serves the fundamental and critical need of securing access to medicines.

These two cases from Kenya illustrate the important role that courts can play in enhancing access to medicines in developing countries. In a situation where most courts adopt the approach of the tribunal in the *Pfizer* case, there is no doubt that patent rights will almost always trump the right to health. However, if courts adopt the more robust approach that was applied by the Kenyan High Court in the *Ochieng* case, it will lead to two things: first, states will be careful in implementing legislation (especially legislation on patent rights) that can significantly impede access to medicines; and, second, pharmaceutical companies that own patents on pharmaceutical products will ensure that they do not exercise their patent rights in ways that negatively affect the enjoyment of the right to health.

4.4 ARE INTELLECTUAL PROPERTY RIGHTS HUMAN RIGHTS IN KENYA?

It is necessary and pertinent to highlight the fact that the Kenyan Constitution of 2010 appears to elevate intellectual property rights to the status of human rights. Article 11(2)(c) of the Constitution imposes an obligation on the Kenyan State to

[47] Ibid., para 51.

'promote the intellectual property rights of the people of Kenya'. More importantly, Article 40 of the Kenyan Constitution, which deals with the protection of the right to property, contains a provision (Article 40(5)) which provides that the state 'shall support, promote and protect the intellectual property rights of the people of Kenya'. This provision, located in the fourth chapter of the Kenyan Constitution, that is, the chapter that contains the Bill of Rights, appears to suggest that intellectual property rights share the same status as other human rights within the Kenyan Constitution.

If this is the correct interpretation of Article 40(5), then it has implications for the incorporation of a *model of human rights* in the interpretation and enforcement of patent rights in Kenya. It implies that the Kenyan courts will have to find a way to strike a balance between human rights such as the right to health and intellectual property rights. Interestingly, Article 40(5) was neither referred to nor discussed by either the parties or the court in the *Ochieng* case. It needs to be noted that certain owners of intellectual property rights in Kenya have attempted to rely on Article 40 (5) to argue that intellectual property rights should be treated as human rights in Kenya. However, Kenyan courts have adopted the view that Article 40(5) does not mean that intellectual property rights should be treated as human rights.

In the case of *Sanitam Services Ltd.* v. *Tamia Ltd. and Others*,[48] the petitioner (Sanitam), the owner of a patent on an invention for a foot operated litter/sanitary disposal, was seeking, *inter alia*, a declaration against the respondents for violating and/or infringing its intellectual property rights contrary to, *inter alia*, Articles 11(2) (c) and 40(5) of the Kenyan Constitution.[49] Sanitam argued that the said provisions impose an obligation on the government to protect and promote intellectual property rights and (in an attempt to equate intellectual property rights with other human rights) it invoked the jurisdiction of the court to grant an injunction to restrain the breach of fundamental rights.[50] The respondents, however, countered this argument by stating, *inter alia*, that 'any issue of patent infringement would be handled by the Industrial Property Tribunal established by the Industrial Property Act' and that 'there was no cause of action established in the petition as against the respondents as no breach of rights of fundamental freedoms had been alleged' against the respondents.[51]

In its decision, the High Court noted that the tenor and purport of Articles 11(2)(c) and 40(5) is to place an obligation on the state to support, promote, and protect the intellectual property rights of Kenyans.[52] The court did not, however, consider the said provisions as provisions that granted human rights but as 'constitutional

[48] *Sanitam Services (EA) Ltd.* v. *Tamia Ltd. and others* (Petition 305 of 2012, Decision of the Kenyan High Court, 5 December 2012) [hereinafter, *Sanitam*].

[49] Ibid., paras 1, 3.

[50] Ibid., para 5. Article 23(3)(b) of the Kenyan Constitution permits a court to grant an injunction in any proceedings for the enforcement of any right contained in the Bill of Rights.

[51] *Sanitam*, para 6.

[52] Ibid., para 8.

objectives' that the state is meant to achieve through 'legal, policy or other measures'.[53] According to the court, the said provisions 'are not self enforcing, they require the state to take steps and the state has done so by enacting and establishing an intellectual property law regime which any intellectual property holder can take advantage of to protect its property rights acquired under the law'.[54] The court ruled that, 'any breach of ... intellectual property rights ... can be enforced through the legal mechanisms provided by statute or common law, where applicable, hence it is unnecessary to invoke the provisions of Article 22 [which provides for the enforcement of the Bill of Rights][55] to enforce what are *ordinary rights*'.[56] The petition was ultimately struck out by the court.[57]

Thus, in the *Sanitam* case, the Kenyan High Court took the view that, despite the provisions of Article 40(5), intellectual property rights are still *ordinary rights* and not *human rights* in Kenya. This implies that a patent owner cannot rely on the provisions of Article 40(5) to argue that an infringement of its patent rights is an infringement of its human rights. Article 40(5) places an obligation on the state to protect intellectual property rights (which the state has already fulfilled by enacting laws such as the Industrial Property Act), but it does not translate intellectual property rights into human rights for citizens of the state. The attempt by Sanitam to conflate the infringement of its patent rights with the infringement of human rights was therefore based on an incorrect interpretation of the provisions of Article 40(5).

In the case of *Royal Media Services Ltd. and Others* v. *Attorney General and Others*,[58] the Kenyan High Court confirmed its earlier approach in the *Sanitam* case. In this case, which involved questions relating to copyright in the petitioner's broadcasts, the High Court ruled that 'a violation of intellectual property rights is not a matter to be addressed by a petition to enforce fundamental rights and freedoms because there is a specific legal regime established by law to address intellectual property rights'.[59] However, when the case went on appeal to the Kenyan Court of Appeal, the Appellate Court appeared to prefer a different approach. At the Appellate Court, the majority (two out of three Appellate Judges) appeared to take the view that matters relating to intellectual property rights could be treated as falling under the rubric of the Bill of Rights.[60] One of the judges in the majority, Maraga

[53] Ibid., para 9.

[54] Ibid.

[55] Article 22(1) of the Kenyan Constitution provides that 'Every person has the right to institute court proceedings claiming that a right or fundamental freedom in the Bill of Rights has been denied, violated or infringed, or is threatened.'

[56] *Sanitam*, para 10 (emphasis added).

[57] Ibid., para 14.

[58] *Royal Media Services Ltd. and others* v. *Attorney General and others* (Petition No 557 of 2013, Decision of the Kenyan High Court, 23 December 2013).

[59] Ibid., para 134.

[60] See *Royal Media Services Ltd. and others* v. *Attorney General and others* (Civil Appeal No. 4 of 2014, Decision of the Kenyan Court of Appeal, 28 March 2014). According to Nambuye J. A.,

J. A., was of the view that even though 'there is a corpus of laws for [the] enforcement of IPR[s], in this case the appellants did not need to file two cases, one, a constitutional petition ... and another case to enforce their IPRs'.[61] But in his judgment, Musinga J. A. agreed with the High Court and he stated that, 'a violation of intellectual property rights is not a matter to be addressed by a petition to enforce fundamental rights and freedoms when there is a specific legal regime established by an Act of Parliament to address such complaints'.[62]

Upon further appeal to the Kenyan Supreme Court, Musinga J. A.'s approach was endorsed and the Supreme Court gave its imprimatur to the approach adopted by the High Court in the *Sanitam* case. The Supreme Court noted that the Copyright Act provides an avenue for redressing infringements[63] and it held that the claims 'regarding infringement of intellectual property rights, was a plain copyright-infringement claim, and it was not properly laid before [the High Court] as a constitutional issue'.[64]

The implication of these cases is that Article 40(5) cannot provide succour to any patentee seeking to argue that an infringement of its patent rights is an infringement of human rights. Thus, Kenyan courts are free to adopt the 'subjugation approach' (as discussed in Chapter 3) when seeking to incorporate a *model of human rights* whenever they are adjudicating disputes involving the exercise or enforcement of patent rights. However, as pointed out in Chapter 3, the adoption of the 'subjugation approach' does not necessarily mean that patent rights should no longer be protected, but it means that states should not permit patent rights to be exercised in ways that impede the enjoyment of the human right to health.

'The appellants took issue with that directive because it required them to relinquish their contents to others for airing without their consent. The letter gave them no choice but to comply. To them, this was an infringement of their intellectual property rights ... As indicated in Article 40(5), the State has a duty to protect that property ... The moment it becomes personal property, then it falls into the protective bracket provided in Article 40(1) of the Constitution ... I find merit in the appellants' contention that their intellectual property rights had been violated and there was a real threat of continued violation if no restraint order was forthcoming from the Court' (ibid., 31–2). Later on in her judgment, Nambuye J. A. stated that 'there was sufficient material to link the appellants claim to Constitutional issues capable of being adjudicated upon by the High Court ... There is no set number of issues required to be met before one can access a Constitutional Court ... Herein there were several constitutional issues which called for a merit determination by the learned Judge ... The proper forum mandated by the Constitution to adjudicate over issues touching on the Bill of Rights is the High Court' (ibid., 39).

61 See *Royal Media Services Ltd. and others* v. *Attorney General and others* (Civil Appeal No. 4 of 2014, Decision of the Kenyan Court of Appeal, 28 March 2014), 79.

62 Ibid., 113.

63 See *Communications Commission of Kenya and others* v. *Royal Media Services Ltd.* (Petition Nos. 14, 14A, 14B & 14C of 2014 (consolidated), Decision of the Supreme Court of Kenya, 29 September 2014), para 255.

64 Ibid., para 258.

4.5 CONCLUSION

It is essential for courts seeking to protect the right of poor patients to obtain access to affordable medicines to incorporate *a model of human rights* when they adjudicate disputes involving pharmaceutical patent rights. As the impact of non-communicable diseases such as cancer continues to increase in developing countries, it is reasonable to assume that more patients will require access to expensive but essential drugs in order to sustain a healthy lifestyle. The incorporation of a *model of human rights* will therefore ensure that courts are mindful of the importance of the availability of cheaper generic drugs in the market. The Kenyan High Court in the *Ochieng* case was mindful of the need to ensure that generic antiretroviral drugs remained affordable and accessible. The court noted that '[m]any of those who are infected with the virus are, like the petitioners, unemployed and therefore financially incapable of procuring for themselves the anti-retroviral branded medication that they need to remain healthy. They are therefore dependent on generic anti-retroviral medication which is much cheaper and therefore more accessible to them'.[65]

Chapter 5 will continue with the theme of incorporating *a model of human rights* into the adjudication of disputes involving pharmaceutical patent rights in national courts. In Chapter 5, there will be an examination of the extent to which South African courts incorporate *a model of human rights* into their decisions in disputes involving patent rights on pharmaceutical products.

[65] *Ochieng*, para 50.

5

Incorporating a Model of Human Rights into the Adjudication of Pharmaceutical Patent Cases (Part Two)

South Africa as a Case Study

5.1 INTRODUCTION

This chapter, like Chapter 4 on Kenya, will critically examine how the *model of human rights* has been incorporated into the adjudication of disputes involving pharmaceutical patent rights by courts in South Africa. The chapter is divided into three sections. Section 5.2 provides a brief overview of the legal framework on pharmaceutical patent law in South Africa while Section 5.3 examines the jurisprudence on the right to health in South Africa. Section 5.4 deals with the incorporation of *a model of human rights* into the adjudication of disputes involving pharmaceutical patent rights by courts in South Africa. The chapter concludes with the view that the incorporation of *a model of human rights* does not necessarily translate to the abrogation of patent rights, it only means that the courts should not permit patent rights on pharmaceutical products to be exercised and enforced in a manner that impedes the enjoyment of the human right to health.

5.2 PHARMACEUTICAL PATENT LAW IN SOUTH AFRICA

The current legislative framework for patent rights in South Africa is contained in the Patents Act, 1978 (as amended).[1] The requirements for patentability in South Africa are similar to that of other member states of the World Trade Organization (WTO) that have signed the TRIPS Agreement, despite the fact that the South

[1] The South African Patents Act 57 of 1978 has been subject to several amendments. Since its enactment, it has been amended in 1979, 1983, 1986, 1988, 1996, 1997, 2001, 2002, 2005, and 2008. See Patents Amendment Act 14 of 1979; Patents Amendment Act 67 of 1983; Patents Amendment Act 44 of 1986; Patents Amendment Act 76 of 1988; General Law Amendment Act 49 of 1996; Intellectual Property Laws Amendment Act 38 of 1997; Patents Amendment Act 10 of 2001; Patents Amendment Act 58 of 2002; Patents Amendment Act 20 of 2005; Companies Act 71 of 2008.

African Patents Act predates the TRIPS Agreement.[2] An invention will be accorded patent protection if it is new, involves an inventive step, and it is capable of being used or applied in trade or industry or agriculture.[3] The Patents Act also provides a list of what does not constitute an invention for purposes of the law.[4] Furthermore, the South African patent law contains key flexibilities that can be utilized to facilitate access to affordable medicines. These key flexibilities include compulsory licensing,[5] permitting the parallel importation of patented pharmaceutical products,[6] and regulatory review exemptions for generic drug manufacturers.[7]

In 2013, South Africa's Department of Trade and Industry released a draft national intellectual property policy.[8] The draft intellectual property policy addresses, *inter alia*, a crucial lacuna in the current patent system in South Africa, that is, the failure to conduct substantive examination of patent applications. Currently, South Africa employs a registration system for patent applications in which patent applications are merely registered without any examination as to compliance with the substantive requirements of the patent law.[9] As expected, this results in a proliferation of weak patents in South Africa. It has been reported that in 2008 alone, South Africa registered 2,442 pharmaceutical patents, whereas in Brazil only 278 pharmaceutical patents were granted between 2003 and 2008.[10] In India, between 2005 and 2008, 2,347 pharmaceutical patents were granted, and this figure is not up to the number of pharmaceutical patents registered in South Africa in 2008 alone.[11]

[2] See Alexandra Bhattacharya, 'The Use of Paragraph 6 of the Doha Declaration on the TRIPS Agreement and Public Health (2001): A Review of Implementation Experiences in the Developing Countries' (2012) 13 *The Journal of World Investment and Trade* 186, 201, who notes that '[t]hough South Africa, as a developing country did not have to be TRIPS compliant until 2005, it had already established an advanced regulatory framework … prior to that deadline'. See also Chenxi Jiao, 'The Negative Effect of Pharmaceutical Patents on South African Industry' (2007) 5 *Cardozo Public Law, Policy, and Ethics Journal* 655, 564, who notes that '[p]rior to the passage of TRIPS … South Africa gave relatively strong protection to intellectual property rights, compared to other developing nations'.

[3] See section 25(1) of the South African Patents Act.

[4] Section 25(2) of the South African Patents Act excludes the following from being patented in South Africa: a discovery; a scientific theory; a mathematical method; a literary, dramatic, musical, or artistic work, or any other aesthetic creation; a scheme, rule, or method for performing a mental act, playing a game, or doing business; a program for a computer; or the presentation of information.

[5] See section 56 of the South African Patents Act.

[6] See section 15C of the South African Medicines and Related Substances Control Amendment Act of 1997.

[7] See section 69A(1) of the South African Patents Act.

[8] See Department of Trade and Industry, 'Draft National Policy on Intellectual Property (IP) of South Africa: A Policy Framework' (Notice 918 of 2013, Government Gazette, 4 September 2013).

[9] Carlos Correa, 'Pharmaceutical Innovation, Incremental Patenting and Compulsory Licensing', Research Paper No. 41, South Centre (2011) 7.

[10] Ibid.

[11] Ibid.

It is quite risky for a country not to have a mechanism in place to filter pharmaceutical patent applications. In the absence of any substantive examination of patent applications, patent applicants can obtain patents on inventions that are not deserving of patent protection and they can equally exploit the patent system to extend their monopoly by obtaining patent rights on minor modifications of known drugs. This lacuna in the examination of patent applications in the South African patent system is recognized in the draft national policy on intellectual property.[12] In order to remedy this situation, the draft policy recommends that South Africa 'should consider adopting the Search and Examination of Patents to co-exist with the current registration' of patents.[13] The draft policy also recommends that the search and examination of patent applications should be complemented with the pre-grant and post-grant opposition procedures.[14]

In 2018, the Department of Trade and Industry released the 'Intellectual Property Policy of the Republic of South Africa Phase I'[15] which, *inter alia*, appears to suggest that the recommendations relating to substantive search and examinations of patent applications and the oppositions procedures contained in the 2013 draft policy would be implemented gradually in a phased manner. In relation to substantive search and examination of patent applications, while acknowledging that this would be 'of great benefit to holders and users of IP, in that it provides a robust framework for the awarding and management of IP', the 2018 policy notes that implementing this recommendation requires a 'phased, strategic approach' due to 'capacity constraints'.[16]

Concerning pre-grant and post-grant opposition procedures, the 2018 policy document notes that these opposition procedures 'afford an opportunity for public intervention in the patent application process, and it is recommended that participation in the process be made open in order to maximally benefit the state and South African industry and society.'[17] While recommending that these procedures be eventually enacted into law, the 2018 policy goes on to state that, 'owing to capacity constraints, it is recommended that patent law recognises a third-party

[12] See Department of Trade and Industry, 'Draft National Policy on Intellectual Property (IP) of South Africa: A Policy Framework' (Notice 918 of 2013, Government Gazette, 4 September 2013), 10–11, which notes that 'South Africa uses a registration system that is not *per se* able to scientifically critique "newness", "obviousness", "novelty" and "usefulness in trade or agriculture". Due to this, weaker patents are granted. Coupled with the fact that the South African Patent Act does not have "pre-opposition" and "post-opposition" procedures . . . the registration [system] is allowing "weaker" patents that are pliable to frustrate access to public health. Similar economies such as Brazil, India and Egypt are granting fewer patents due to the fact that they use the Substantive Search and Examination of Patents.'

[13] Ibid., 11.

[14] Ibid.

[15] Department of Trade and Industry, 'Intellectual Property Policy of The Republic of South Africa Phase I' (2018).

[16] Ibid., 17.

[17] Ibid., 19.

submission system or "observation" to stand in for the pre-grant opposition process and for existing provisions in administrative law to be used in lieu of post-grant oppositions."[18] It is therefore unclear if and when any of these recommendations will be implemented in South Africa.

5.3 THE RIGHT TO HEALTH IN SOUTH AFRICA

Section 27(1)(a) of the South African Constitution of 1996 provides that everyone has the right to have access to 'health care services, including reproductive health care'. Section 27(2) further mandates the South African government to take 'reasonable legislative and other measures, within its available resources, to achieve the progressive realisation of each of these rights'. Section 27(3) provides that no one may be refused emergency medical treatment. The South African Constitutional Court has, in a line of cases, made pronouncements on the meaning and effect of these provisions on the right to health.

In *Soobramoney* v. *Minister of Health*,[19] the appellant was a patient suffering from chronic renal failure but whose life could be prolonged by regular renal dialysis. The appellant sought treatment from the renal unit of a state hospital in Durban but the hospital could only provide dialysis treatment to a limited number of patients.[20] Due to the shortage of resources, the hospital followed a policy with regard to the use of its dialysis resources.[21] According to the hospital's policy, only patients suffering from acute renal failure which could be treated and remedied by renal dialysis are given automatic access to renal dialysis at the hospital.[22] The appellant was, however, suffering from chronic renal failure which was irreversible and he could not be given automatic access to renal dialysis.[23] The hospital also had a set of guidelines for patients suffering from chronic renal failure, and such patients could only be given dialysis treatment if they were eligible for a kidney transplant.[24] However, according to the hospital's guidelines, a patient is only eligible for a kidney transplant if he or she is free from significant vascular or cardiac disease and, as the appellant was suffering from ischaemic heart disease and cerebro-vascular disease, he was thus not eligible for a kidney transplant.[25]

The appellant's argument was that section 27(3) of the South African Constitution imposed an obligation on the government to provide treatment such as renal dialysis

18 Ibid.
19 *Soobramoney* v. *Minister of Health* (CCT32/97) [1997] ZACC 17; 1998 (1) SA 765 (CC) [hereinafter, *Soobramoney*].
20 Ibid., para 1.
21 Ibid., para 3.
22 Ibid.
23 Ibid.
24 Ibid.
25 Ibid., para 4.

to patients who suffer from terminal illnesses.[26] However, the South African Constitutional Court made it clear that section 27 does not impose an absolute obligation on the government to provide access to health care and the obligation to do so is 'dependent upon the resources available for such purposes' and the right to have access to health care is equally 'limited by reason of the lack of resources'.[27]

The court took the view that the implication of the appellant's argument would be that the treatment of terminal illnesses would take priority over other forms of medical care and this would reduce the resources available for other purposes like preventative health care and medical treatment for persons with no life threatening ailments.[28] The court noted that section 27(3) was designed to secure treatment in emergency situations, for instance, for persons who suffer sudden catastrophes which call for immediate medical attention.[29] It was held that the appellant's condition was not an emergency that called for immediate remedial treatment and that section 27(3) was inapplicable to his case.[30] It was further held that the appellant's demand to receive dialysis treatment at a state hospital must be determined in accordance with sections 27(1) & (2) which provides for access to health care services provided by the state 'within its available resources'.[31]

The court in this case adopted what Ferraz calls the 'reasonableness approach' and, as Ferraz points out, the court confined its role 'to an assessment of the rationality and good faith of the decisions taken at the political and technical branches of the state'.[32] The court was wary of crossing the boundaries set by the doctrine of separation of powers[33] and it also wanted to avoid making an order that would result in the denial of resources to other patients to whom those resources could be better devoted.[34] According to Sachs J., '[i]n all the open and democratic societies ... the rationing of access to life-prolonging resources is

26 Ibid., para 12.
27 Ibid., para 11.
28 Ibid., para 19.
29 Ibid., paras 20, 51.
30 Ibid., para 21.
31 Ibid., para 22. According to the court, 'The provincial administration which is responsible for health services in KwaZulu-Natal has to make decisions about the funding that should be made available for health care and how such funds should be spent. These choices involve difficult decisions to be taken at the political level in fixing the health budget, and at the functional level in deciding upon the priorities to be met. A court will be slow to interfere with rational decisions taken in good faith by the political organs and medical authorities whose responsibility it is to deal with such matters' (ibid., para 29).
32 Octavio L. M. Ferraz, 'Between Usurpation and Abdication? The Right to Health in the Courts of Brazil and South Africa', in Oscar Vilhena, Upendra Baxi, and Frans Viljoen (eds.), *Transformative Constitutionalism: Comparing the Apex Courts of Brazil, India and South Africa* (Pretoria University Law Press, 2013), 385.
33 Ibid.
34 *Soobramoney*, para 30.

regarded as integral to, rather than incompatible with, a human rights approach to health care'.[35]

The 'reasonableness approach' to the right to access to health care was also followed in the decision of the same court in the latter case of *Minister of Health & Ors* v. *Treatment Action Campaign & Ors (No.2)*[36] where it was held that 'section 27(1) of the Constitution does not give rise to a self-standing and independent positive right enforceable irrespective of the considerations mentioned in section 27(2). Sections 27(1) and 27(2) must be read together as defining the scope of the positive rights that everyone has and the corresponding obligations on the state to "respect, protect, promote and fulfil" such rights'.[37]

There are, however, crucial differences between the facts of *Soobramoney* and *Treatment Action Campaign (TAC)*. In the *TAC case*, TAC (an NGO involved in HIV/AIDS Advocacy) challenged the restrictions imposed by the South African government on the availability of nevirapine (a drug that can be used to prevent mother-to-child transmission of HIV) in the public health sector.[38] The government had confined the administration of the drug to research and training sites. TAC contended that these restrictions were unreasonable vis-à-vis the provisions of the Constitution.[39] According to TAC, 'the measures adopted by government to provide access to health care services to HIV-positive pregnant women were deficient in two material respects: first, because they prohibited the administration of nevirapine at public hospitals and clinics outside the research and training sites; and second, because they failed to implement a comprehensive programme for the prevention of mother-to-child transmission of HIV'.[40] One of the key issues the court had to consider was whether, in the light of provisions such as section 27 of the Constitution, the government was constitutionally obliged and was required to plan and implement an effective, comprehensive, and progressive programme for the prevention of mother-to-child transmission of HIV throughout the country.[41]

The government gave four reasons for confining the administration of nevirapine to research and training sites. The first reason relates to the efficacy of the drug in the absence of substitutes for breastfeeding, with the government expressing concern that the benefits of the drug would be counteracted by transmission of HIV through

[35] Ibid., para 52.

[36] *Minister of Health & Ors* v. *Treatment Action Campaign & Ors (No.2)*, (CCT8/02) [2002] ZACC 15; 2002 (5) SA 721 [hereinafter, *TAC*].

[37] Ibid., para 39. In this case, the court declared that, 'Sections 27(1) and (2) of the Constitution require the government to devise and implement within its available resources a comprehensive and co-ordinated programme to realise progressively the rights of pregnant women and their newborn children to have access to health services to combat mother-to-child transmission of HIV' (ibid., para 135(2)(a)).

[38] Ibid., para 4.

[39] Ibid.

[40] Ibid., para 44.

[41] Ibid., para 5.

breastfeeding.[42] The second reason relates to the concern that the administration of the drug might lead to the development of resistance to the efficacy of the drug and related anti-retroviral drugs in later years.[43] The third reason was about the safety of the drug as it was not known what hazards may attach to its use.[44] The fourth reason concerned the question of the capacity of the public health system to administer nevirapine on a comprehensive basis because of the lack of trained counsellors and counselling facilities, and also because of budgetary constraints which precluded the implementation of such a comprehensive scheme.[45]

The court, however, held that the wealth of scientific material makes plain that nevirapine remains to some extent efficacious in combating mother-to-child transmission of HIV even if the mother breastfeeds her baby.[46] With regard to the development of resistance to the drug, the court held that the prospects of the child surviving if infected are so slim, and the nature of the suffering so grave, that the risk of some resistance manifesting at some time in the future is worth running.[47] The court also stated that there is no evidence to suggest that a dose of nevirapine to both mother and child at the time of birth will result in any harm to either of them.[48] In relation to the concerns of the government about the capacity of the government to provide the drug on a comprehensive basis, the court held that, although these concerns were relevant to the ability of the government to make a full package available throughout the public health sector, they are not relevant to the question of whether nevirapine should be used to reduce mother-to-child transmission of HIV at those public hospitals and clinics outside the research sites where facilities in fact exist for testing and counselling.[49]

Based on these factors, the court, in applying its 'reasonableness approach', held that the

> policy of confining nevirapine to research and training sites fails to address the needs of mothers and their newborn children who do not have access to these sites. It fails to distinguish between the evaluation of programmes for reducing mother-to-child transmission and the need to provide access to health care required by those who do not have access to the sites.[50]

Unlike its attitude toward government's policy in *Soobramoney*, in this case, the court was willing to question the government's policy with regard to the administration of nevirapine and it held that 'the policy of government in so far as it confines

42 Ibid., para 51.
43 Ibid., para 52.
44 Ibid., para 53.
45 Ibid., para 54.
46 Ibid., para 58.
47 Ibid., para 59.
48 Ibid., para 60.
49 Ibid., para 66.
50 Ibid., para 67.

the use of nevirapine to hospitals and clinics which are research and training sites constitutes a breach of the state's obligations under section 27(2) read with section 27(1)(a) of the Constitution'.[51] The policy was held to be unreasonable. According to the court, 'a policy of waiting for a protracted period before taking a decision on the use of nevirapine beyond the research and training sites is also not reasonable within the meaning of section 27(2) of the Constitution'.[52]

The South African government tried to argue in the *TAC* case that, even if its policies fell short of what the Constitution demands, the only competent order that a court can make is to issue a declaration of rights to that effect as this is what is mandated by the doctrine of separation of powers.[53] In other words, the government contended that the court could only grant a declaratory order but not a mandatory order because, according to the doctrine of separation of powers, as the government argued, 'the making of policy is the prerogative of the executive and not the courts' and 'courts cannot make orders that have the effect of requiring the executive to pursue a particular policy'.[54] The court, however, held that the doctrine of separation of powers does not mean 'that courts cannot or should not make orders that have an impact on policy'.[55] According to the court,

> We thus reject the argument that the only power that this Court has in the present case is to issue a declaratory order. Where a breach of any right has taken place, including a socio-economic right, a court is under a duty to ensure that effective relief is granted. The nature of the right infringed and the nature of the infringement will provide guidance as to the appropriate relief in a particular case. Where necessary this may include both the issuing of a mandamus and the exercise of supervisory jurisdiction.[56]

The court thus ordered the government to, *inter alia*, remove without delay, 'the restrictions that prevent nevirapine from being made available for the purpose of reducing the risk of mother-to-child transmission of HIV at public hospitals and clinics that are not research and training sites'.[57]

The implication of the *TAC* case is that, even though the South African Constitutional Court prefers to adopt a 'reasonableness approach' in its evaluation of government policies that affect socio-economic rights, and despite the fact that the court equally respects the doctrine of separation of powers, where the government adopts a policy that is unreasonable and inconsistent with the provisions of the Constitution, the court can actually give an order that has an impact on policy making. It should also be noted that in the *TAC* case, the government's policies with

[51] Ibid., para 80.
[52] Ibid., para 81.
[53] Ibid., para 96.
[54] Ibid., para 97.
[55] Ibid., para 98.
[56] Ibid., para 106.
[57] Ibid., para 135(3)(a).

regard to the administration of nevirapine was not based on resource constraints like in the *Soobramoney* case. As Ferraz notes, the 'cost of providing the drug was virtually none, given a pledge by the pharmaceutical suppliers to give it for free'.[58] Even the court acknowledged the fact that the 'cost of nevirapine for preventing mother-to-child transmission is not an issue in the present proceedings' and that it was 'admittedly within the resources of the state'.[59] The government policies on nevirapine were based on what Ferraz calls 'dubious (not to say completely ungrounded) assertions that the drug in question (Nevirapine) was not scientifically proven to work'.[60]

Subsequently, in *Minister of Health* v. *New Clicks*,[61] the South African Constitutional Court held that the right to health also includes the right to have access to affordable medicines and that the state has an obligation to 'promote access to medicines that are affordable'.[62] According to Sachs J. in this case, 'preventing excessive profit-taking from the manufacturing, distribution and sale of medicines is more than an option for government. It is a constitutional obligation flowing from its duties under section 27(2)'.[63] In the same case, Moseneke J. stated that,

> It seems self-evident that there can be no adequate access to medicines if they are not within one's means. Prohibitive pricing of medicine . . . would in effect equate to a denial of the right of access to health care. Equally true is that the state bears the obligation to everyone to facilitate equity in the access to essential drugs which in turn affect the quality of care.[64]

A combined reading of section 27 and the decisions in *Soobramoney*, *TAC*, and *New Clicks* leads one to conclude that the right to health care in South Africa, which includes the right to have access to affordable medicines, imposes an obligation on the government to facilitate access to affordable medicines through the adoption of reasonable measures, although this obligation can only be fulfilled within the limits of available resources. Furthermore, where the government adopts a policy that is inconsistent with the Constitution and which also violates the right to health, the court can demand that the government should change its policy.

58 Ferraz, 'Between Usurpation and Abdication?', 388.

59 *TAC*, para 71.

60 Ferraz, 'Between Usurpation and Abdication?', 388.

61 *Minister of Health* v. *New Clicks* [2005] ZACC 14; 2006 (8) BCLR 872 (CC) [hereinafter, *New Clicks*]. This case concerned certain regulations made pursuant to the South African Medicines Act to give effect to the pricing system for the sale of medicines instituted by the Act. The South African Medicines Act was amended in 1997 in order to facilitate access to cheaper drugs and the amendment, among other things, established a pricing committee to make recommendations for the introduction of a pricing system for all medicines sold in South Africa. See also, Andrew L. Gray, 'Medicine Pricing Interventions – The South African Experience' (2009) 2 *Southern Med Review* 15.

62 *New Clicks*, para 514.

63 Ibid., para 659.

64 Ibid., para 706.

5.4 INCORPORATING A MODEL OF HUMAN RIGHTS INTO THE ADJUDICATION OF DISPUTES INVOLVING PHARMACEUTICAL PATENTS IN SOUTH AFRICA

Before delving into the analysis of the decisions of the South African courts in this regard, it bears noting that the South African Constitution does not contain any provision such as the one contained in Article 40(5) of the Kenyan Constitution discussed in Chapter 4.[65] Furthermore, the South African Constitutional Court has held in *Re Certification of the Constitution of the Republic of South Africa, 1996*, (in response to an objection lodged against the failure of the new text of the South African Constitution to recognize a right to intellectual property based on the grounds that it was a 'universally accepted fundamental right') that the recognition of a right to intellectual property 'cannot be characterised as a trend which is universally accepted'.[66]

5.4.1 Pfizer *v.* Cipla Medpro: *Failure to Incorporate a Model of Human Rights*

The first case that will be examined is that of *Pfizer* v. *Cipla Medpro*,[67] where Cipla Medpro had initiated revocation proceedings against Pfizer in 2004 with regard to one of Pfizer's pharmaceutical patents. Cipla contended that the alleged invention was unclear and obvious. The patent in question concerned a 'besylate salt of amlodipine, a drug used for hypertension and reduction of blood pressure'.[68] Pfizer marketed a product called Norvasc which contained the patented chemical, while Cipla had started to market its own generic version called Nortwin in South Africa before Pfizer's patent expired or was revoked.[69] In response to Cipla's application for the revocation of its patent (which was set to expire in 2007), Pfizer brought this action for an interim interdict against Cipla to prevent the infringement of its patent pending the final determination of the revocation proceedings. In granting Pfizer's application for an interim interdict, Botha J., sitting as the Commissioner of Patents, held that:

> If one looks at the broad picture: the respondents have hardly entered the market. The applicants have only two years of their patent left. In two years the respondents will be at liberty to sell Nortwin in any event. The applicant is a manufacturer that relies on patent protection to recoup the cost of research and development.

65 Article 40(5) of the Kenyan Constitution provides that the state 'shall support, promote and protect the intellectual property rights of the people of Kenya'.

66 *Re Certification of the Constitution of the Republic of South Africa, 1996*, Case CCT 23/96 (6 September 1996, Judgment of the Constitutional Court of South Africa), para 75.

67 *Pfizer Ltd.* v. *Cipla Medpro (Pty) Ltd.* (2005) BIP 1 [2005] ZACCP 1.

68 Ibid., 2.

69 Ibid.

> The respondent is a manufacturer of generic products that are manufactured without the expense of original research. For that reason it is wrong to argue, as the respondents have done endlessly, that the applicants can retain their market share by reducing their prices. The regime of an open market is only something to which they have to submit on the expiry of the patent.[70]

It is rather surprising that the only characters that featured in the court's 'broad picture' were just the applicant and the respondent – Pfizer and Cipla. This is, however, a glaring example of the problem that can ensue when reliance is placed on the utilitarian theory to justify patent rights (as noted in Chapter 2). This statement by the court reflects the utilitarian approach to patent rights and it is not surprising that the court failed to see the tension between patent rights on one hand and the need to facilitate access to medicines, which is an essential component of the right to health, on the other hand.

While it is fair for pharmaceutical companies to seek to recoup their investment in producing new drugs, the approach adopted by the court completely ignores other important characters like poor patients who might not be able to afford to pay for Norvasc, sold by Pfizer, but who might be able to afford Nortwin, sold by Cipla. It is contended here that the court should have considered the potential impact that Pfizer's patent rights could have on the enjoyment of the right to health by poor patients in South Africa. The court could have done this if it had incorporated a *model of human rights* into its analysis when it was considering the balance of convenience before granting the interim interdict.[71]

5.4.2 Aventis *v.* Cipla: *Applying a Model of Human Rights Need Not Lead to the Abrogation of Patent Rights*

In a latter case, *Aventis* v. *Cipla*,[72] the dispute involved a patent for 'New Taxoid-Based Compositions' that belonged to Aventis and which covered claims for compositions containing 'Taxane' derivatives including the Taxane derivative known as 'docetaxel'.[73] Taxane derivatives such as docetaxel are used as chemotherapy

70 Ibid., 22.

71 According to Lord Diplock, the factors to be considered when determining the balance of convenience will vary from case to case. See *American Cyanamid* v. *Ethicon Ltd.* [1975] AC 396 at 408. One of such factors can be the public interest in ensuring that patients have access to a life-saving drug as was held in the English case of *Roussel-Uclaf* v. *G. D. Searle and Co. Ltd.* [1977] FSR 125, 131–2. This approach of considering the public interest before granting injunctions is also supported by the American case of *eBay Inc.* v. *MercExchange LLC*, 126 SC 1837 (2006) and the Indian case of *Hoffman-La Roche Ltd v. Cipla*, I.A. 642/2008 in CS(OS) 89/2008 (Delhi High Court).

72 *Aventis* v. *Cipla* (Court of the Commissioner of Patents, Unreported Case No. P93/8936, Judgment delivered on 20 October 2011).

73 Ibid., para 2.

treatments for a number of cancers.[74] Aventis was seeking an interim interdict against Cipla because, in March 2011, Aventis discovered that Cipla was about to import into South Africa two products made in India, 'Cipla Docetaxel' and 'Cipla Docetaxel solvent', which when mixed with the relevant product will constitute an infringement of the patent belonging to Aventis.[75] Cipla's intention was to distribute and sell the two products in South Africa to oncologists and other healthcare professionals involved in the treatment of cancer.[76] Aventis therefore brought an application for an interdict to prohibit the respondents from mixing the Cipla products and an interdict to prohibit the respondents from selling the products to any person who will mix the products in accordance with the patent.[77]

Aventis had applied for the patent in South Africa in November 1993 and it was granted in October 1994 with the patent due to expire in 2013.[78] The application for the interim interdict was concerned with the threatened infringement of 'claim 1' of Aventis' patent.[79] The said 'claim 1' covers:

> An injectable composition comprising (a) a taxane derivative in a poly sorbate and (b) an additive, (a) and (b) being provided in ampoules, bottles or a double compartment device, the injectable composition being produced by mixing (a) and (b) to form an intermediate solution, wherein the additive prevents the formation of, or breaks, a gelled phase during the mixing of the intermediate solution with an aqueous medium.[80]

Cipla, however, challenged the validity of the patent by arguing, *inter alia*, that 'claim 1' was not clear. The court noted that Cipla presented evidence to the effect that 'claim 1' was ambiguous and could be interpreted in either of the following two ways:

1. A claim to an unmixed collection of (a) and (b) for use in the future preparation of an injectable composition; or
2. A claim to a mixed injectable composition which was previously made by mixing (a) and (b).[81]

The court also noted that Aventis presented conflicting evidence as to whether or not 'claim 1' was ambiguous. The court therefore concluded that '[i]n the light of the experts' evidence referred to there is serious doubt about the clarity of the claim which … will not be rectified at the trial'.[82] The interim interdict was therefore

[74] Ibid.
[75] Ibid., para 3.
[76] Ibid.
[77] Ibid.
[78] Ibid., para 6.
[79] Ibid.
[80] Ibid., para 3.
[81] Ibid., para 19.
[82] Ibid., para 25.

refused because the court was of the view that the applicants' prospect of success at a full trial was slender.[83]

Aventis, however, appealed to the South African Supreme Court of Appeal.[84] The Supreme Court of Appeal overruled the decision of the Commissioner of Patents and held that 'claim 1' was clear and that the invention was both new and not obvious. The appellate court held that it was wrong for the lower court to have admitted expert evidence in its determination of the clarity of a claim.[85] According to the appellate court, in determining the clarity of a claim, words with no special technical meaning are to be given their natural and ordinary meaning while expert evidence can be admitted to determine the meaning of technical terms.[86] However, in this case, the appellate court held that what was claimed by Aventis was 'clearly and unambiguously stated'.[87]

With regard to Aventis' request for an interim interdict, the appellate court agreed with the arguments of the *amicus curiae*, Treatment Action Campaign, that the public interest cannot be ignored when deciding whether or not to issue an interim interdict.[88] The NGO based its opposition to the grant of an interim interdict on the right to health guaranteed in section 27(1) of the South African Constitution and urged the appellate court to construe the Patents Act 'through the prism of the Constitution' and in a way that appropriately balances the rights of a patentee against the constitutional rights of others.[89]

The appellate court was, however, of the view that construing the Patents Act through the prism of the Constitution does not necessarily mean that Aventis should be denied the right to enforce its patent.[90] In its consideration of the balance of convenience and the public interest, the court noted that there was no suggestion that Aventis was not able to meet the demand for the patented drug nor could it be said that Cipla's version of the drug offered superior medicinal benefits.[91] The court further noted that there would be no material disruption to patients if an interdict was granted.[92] The court was not swayed by the argument that an interdict would adversely affect patients that could not afford Cipla's drug. According to the court, '[w]here the public is denied access to a generic [drug] during the lifetime of a patent, that is the ordinary consequence of patent protection and it applies as much

[83] Ibid., para 26.
[84] *Aventis* v. *Cipla* [2012] ZASCA 108 (26 July 2012).
[85] Ibid., para 21.
[86] Ibid., para 24.
[87] Ibid., para 25.
[88] Ibid., para 46. The Treatment Action Campaign (TAC) had applied to be admitted as *amicus curiae* when the matter came before the appellate court.
[89] Ibid., para 44.
[90] Ibid., para 45.
[91] Ibid., para 55.
[92] Ibid.

in all cases. To refuse an interdict only so as to frustrate the patentee's lawful monopoly seems to . . . be an abuse of the discretionary powers of a court'.[93]

What can be deduced from this approach is that, while the court was willing to consider the public interest and the rights of patients, it was equally reluctant to allow these interests and rights to trump the monopoly rights of patentees. In essence, the court was willing to hold that the denial of access to generic drugs should be considered as part of the price the society pays for securing monopoly rights through the grant of patents.

The court did not, however, attempt to consider whether the right to health could take precedence over patent rights in certain cases. This is probably because it was unnecessary to do so in this particular case. Based on the facts presented before the court, there would be no material prejudice to poor patients if an interim interdict was granted to Aventis. It was established before the court that Aventis was already marketing its own generic version of the patented drug and, more importantly, the patented drug itself was already being sold to the government at a rate which was cheaper than the price of Cipla's generic version.[94] The court therefore held that Aventis' patented drug was 'considerably more accessible' to patients dependent on public health care than Cipla's generic version and that 'there will be no prejudice at all to those patients, or to the state, if an interdict were to be granted'.[95]

The South African Supreme Court of Appeal could still have arrived at the same result if it had fully incorporated a *model of human rights* into its decision in this case. If it had done so, it could have explicitly *recognized* that there was a tension between the patent rights of Aventis and the right to health of poor patients in South Africa. Nevertheless, in *resolving* this tension, the court could have then held that since Aventis was not exercising its patent rights in a manner that impedes the enjoyment of the right to health and that it had in fact taken steps to facilitate access to the patented drug for patients dependent on the public health system, there was no need to prevent Aventis from enforcing its patent rights in this case. Thus, the ultimate resolution of the tension between patent rights and the right to health in each case may not always be the same. In some cases, the enforcement of patent rights may not necessarily impede access to medicines, and in such cases, the rights of the patentee need not be disregarded.

5.5 CONCLUSION

This chapter has provided a brief overview of pharmaceutical patent law in South Africa. It has also examined the jurisprudence on the right to health in South Africa.

[93] Ibid., para 56.

[94] Ibid., para 57. Aventis was selling the patented drug to the state at the rate of R686 for 20 mg and R2,327 for 80 mg, while Cipla's generic version was being sold for R1,000 and R3,500 for 20 mg and 80 mg, respectively (ibid.).

[95] Ibid., para 58.

The chapter further examined how the *model of human rights* has been incorporated into the adjudication of disputes involving pharmaceutical patents in South Africa. It should be noted that incorporating *a model of human rights* into the adjudicative process will ensure that, in the interpretation, and enforcement of patent rights, a state does not violate its obligations to respect, protect, and fulfil the human right to health of its citizens. It should, however, be stressed that the incorporation of *a model of human rights* does not necessarily translate to the abrogation of patent rights, it only means that the courts should not permit patent rights on pharmaceutical products to be exercised and enforced in a manner that impedes the enjoyment of the human right to health. Where there is no risk that the exercise or the enforcement of patent rights will impede the enjoyment of the right to health, there is no need to prevent a patentee from exercising or enforcing its patent rights.

Chapter 6 will continue with the theme of incorporating *a model of human rights* into the adjudication of disputes involving pharmaceutical patent rights in national courts. In Chapter 6, there will be an examination of the extent to which Indian courts incorporate *a model of human rights* into their decisions in disputes involving patent rights on pharmaceutical products.

6

Incorporating a Model of Human Rights into the Adjudication of Pharmaceutical Patent Cases (Part Three)

India as a Case Study

6.1 INTRODUCTION

After gaining independence from the United Kingdom in 1947, India began to develop an industrialization policy that focused on encouraging the growth of its local industries.[1] India adopted a policy of central planning, regulation of private enterprises, trade protection, and limitation of foreign capital and technology.[2] This approach to industrialization equally explains the approach of India's policy makers towards patent protection and it culminated in a major revision of India's patent law in 1970. It was not until the 1990s that India began to liberalize its economy and take steps to reduce barriers to foreign direct investment, and it has been suggested that these might have been prompted by an economic crisis at the time and also by the example of the newly industrialized economies of South Korea, Singapore, and Taiwan where the local industrial policies encouraged the growth of private enterprises.[3] This era of economic liberalization coincided with the time India signed the TRIPS Agreement in 1995.

Despite the fact that India has experienced some economic growth as a result of the liberalization of its economy,[4] it still faces enormous public health challenges. Thus, for India, its patent regime must necessarily take into consideration the public

[1] The general perception in India at the time was that the British government had intentionally discouraged Indian industrial growth by distorting tariff and trade rules to favour British companies. See Tanuja Garde, 'India', in Paul Goldstein and Joseph Straus (eds.), *Intellectual Property in Asia: Law, History, Economics and Politics* (Springer, 2009), 56. Garde notes that, 'when India considered which economic model to employ, capitalism equated with a form of colonialism … India looked to the models of the former Soviet Union, attributing the latter's power and success to its socialist agenda, and Japan, attributing Japan's rapid transformation from an agrarian society to a largely industrialized society to the role of the government in keeping out foreign competition.'

[2] Ibid., 81.

[3] Ibid.

[4] Garde notes that, 'from 1992–1993 to 2003–2004, the average GDP growth was 6.1% as compared with 5.6% the previous decade' (ibid.).

health challenges in the country and not focus alone on protecting the rights of patent owners such as pharmaceutical companies. This helps to explain why most (if not all) of the flexibilities allowed under the TRIPS Agreement were incorporated into the Indian Patents Act when it was amended in 2002 and 2005 in compliance with WTO requirements.

This chapter is structured into three main sections. Section 6.2 provides an overview of pharmaceutical patent law in India, while Section 6.3 critically examines the jurisprudence on the right to health in India. Section 6.4 critically examines how Indian courts have incorporated a *model of human rights* into their decisions in cases involving patent rights on pharmaceutical products. The chapter concludes with the view that the combined effect of the liberal interpretative approach adopted with regard to the constitutional right to life and the incorporation of a *model of human rights* into their decisions in patent cases has enabled Indian courts to safeguard and protect the enjoyment of the human right to health in India.

6.2 PHARMACEUTICAL PATENT LAW IN INDIA

The historical development of the Indian patent law is traceable to its colonial master (United Kingdom) and the first patent law was enacted in 1856 when India was still under colonial rule.[5] This patent law was amended several times before India's independence. However, after independence, it soon became necessary to realign the patent law with India's nationalist approach to industrialization. By 1948 it was generally agreed in India that the system of patent protection was not protective enough to promote local industrial development in the country.[6] In addition, medicines were not being produced in India but were being imported, and this made them very expensive.[7] As a result of this, the Indian government established a Patents Enquiry Committee to review the patent law.[8] The report of

[5] Tracing the historical development of patent law in India, Mukherjee notes that 'India's patent system dates back to 1856 when it was introduced by the ruling East India Company under the recommendation of the Lord Macaulay Commission. Later it gained the status of a statute when the Indian Patents and Designs Act 1911 was enacted by the British Government in India'. See Santanu Mukherjee, 'The Journey of Indian Patent Law towards TRIPS Compliance' (2004) 35 *International Review of Intellectual Property & Competition Law* 125, 126.

[6] Garde, 'India', 59.

[7] According to Mukherjee, 'although the Patent Act [of 1911] allowed product patents, it did not encourage investment in research and development, nor the transfer of technology, nor were medicines manufactured in the country. It only helped the foreign pharmaceutical companies to import drugs (both bulk drugs, active ingredients and formulation) and sell them in the local market at extremely high prices ... It must also be noted that since these expensive medicines were only available to the limited few who had enough money to afford them, health services in India were in a pathetic state and epidemics like cholera, smallpox, malaria and plague added to the miseries of people who already faced a dearth of affordable medicines'. See Mukherjee, 'The Journey of Indian Patent Law', 127.

[8] Garde, 'India', 59.

the Patents Enquiry Committee, known as the Justice Bakshi Tek Chand Report (1950), suggested the use of compulsory licences as a means of redressing abuses in the patent system.[9]

Subsequently, in 1957, the Indian government appointed Justice Ayyangar to undertake another review of the patent law.[10] Justice Ayyangar recommended that the patent system should be retained in India but that it should be improved by:

1. Defining with precision inventions which should be patentable and by rendering unpatentable certain inventions, the grant of patents, to which will retard research, or industrial progress or be detrimental to national health or well-being;
2. Expanding the scope of "anticipation" so as to comprehend not merely what is known or published in this country, but also what is known or published outside India;
3. Providing remedies for the evils which India, in common with other countries, experiences from foreign owned patents which are not worked in the country, but which are held either to block the industries of the country or to secure a monopoly of importation;
4. Providing special provisions as regards the licensing of patents for inventions relating to food and medicine;
5. Providing remedies for other forms of abuse resorted to by patentees, to secure a more extended monopoly or a monopoly for a longer duration than what the statute grants.[11]

Specifically, with regard to medicines, Justice Ayyangar recommended that, 'inventions relating to articles of food and medicine ... should not be patentable as such but that, as in the case of substances produced by chemical processes claims for the processes for their production should alone be patentable if they satisfy the other tests for patentability'.[12] Justice Ayyangar was cognizant of the fact that (as at the time of his report), except for the United States, there were few countries that did not have 'special provisions as regards the patentability of inventions in respect of articles of food and medicine or as to the licensing and working of patents in this class'.[13] At the time, most (if not all) European countries did not grant patents on medicinal products and only the processes for manufacturing medicine were patentable.[14]

9 Ibid.
10 Ibid.
11 Shri Justice NR Ayyangar, 'Report on the Revision of the Patents Law' (Government of India, 1959), para 45.
12 Ibid., para 102.
13 Ibid., para 94.
14 In his report, Justice Ayyangar referred to the patent laws in force at the time in countries such as, among others, France (Patent Law of 1844), Belgium (Patent Law of 1854), Germany (German Empire, Law of 1877; Federal Republic (West Germany), Law of 18 July 1953 as subsequently amended; Democratic Republic (East Germany) Article 1(3), Law of 6 December

Justice Ayyangar also observed that (at the time), 'even in a large number of countries in which *per se* product claims for chemical substances [were] allowed, the laws [permitted] only claims for processes so far as articles of food and medicine [were] concerned'.[15]

In his report, Justice Ayyangar recognized that 'the degree of patentability of inventions relating to articles of food and medicine has generally been more restrictive than in regard to patents for chemical inventions in general and never more extensive'[16] and '[t]he reason for this state of law is stated to be that the denial of product claims is necessary in order that such important articles of daily use as medicine or food which are vital to the health of the community should be made available to every one at reasonable prices and that no monopoly should be granted in respect of such articles'.[17] According to Justice Ayyangar '[i]t is considered that the refusal of product patents would enlarge the area of competition and thus result in the production of these articles in sufficient quantity and at the lowest possible cost to the public.'[18]

The recommendations of Justice Ayyangar were implemented in the Patents Act of 1970 (which came into force in 1972) and, pursuant to section 5 of that Act, patent protection was no longer available for inventions on products relating to food, medicine, or drugs or substances produced by chemical processes. The only form of protection available was for the processes for manufacturing these products. According to section 5 of the Indian Patents Act of 1970, 'In the case of inventions – (a) claiming substances intended for use, or capable of being used, as food or as medicine or drug, or (b) relating to substances prepared or produced by chemical processes (including alloys, optical glass, semi-conductors and inter-metallic compounds), no patent shall be granted in respect of claims for the substances themselves, but claims for the methods or processes of manufacture shall be patentable'.

In addition, a patent claiming the process of manufacturing a substance for use as food, medicine, or drug received a term of seven years from the date of filing or five years from the date of grant, whichever was shorter.[19] Section 83 of the Patents Act of 1970 also provided that patents must be worked on a commercial scale in India, failing which a compulsory licence could be granted in respect of the patent after three years from the date of grant. The 1970 Patents Act served as a huge impetus for

1950), and Switzerland (Patent Act of 1954). In all these countries (at the time of Justice Ayyangar's report) medicinal products were not patentable though processes for manufacturing medicines were patentable (ibid., para 95). Justice Ayyangar also made references to section 38A(1) of the UK Patents and Designs Amendment Act of 1919 which excluded medicines from patent protection but he noted that this restriction was removed by the UK Patents Act of 1949 (ibid., paras 97–9).

15 Ibid., para 96.

16 Ibid., para 100.

17 Ibid., para 101.

18 Ibid.

19 Section 53 of the Indian Patents Act, 1970.

the production of generic drugs in India because pharmaceutical products patented outside India could be freely copied in India.[20] Consequently, there was a reduction in the price of medicines sold in India.[21]

India became a member of the World Trade Organization (WTO) in 1995 and, as a developing country, it was given five years to amend its patent law to make it consistent with its obligations under the TRIPS Agreement.[22] It was also given ten years from 1995 to provide patent protection for pharmaceutical products.[23] However, India was obligated to immediately provide a means for the filing of applications for pharmaceutical products pending the amendment of its patent law to provide patent protection for pharmaceutical products; this was known as the mailbox application procedure.[24] The rationale behind the mailbox application procedure was to preserve the novelty and priority of applications for patents on pharmaceutical products.[25] In addition, India was meant to provide exclusive marketing rights for five years to pharmaceutical products for which a patent application had been filed (pursuant to the mailbox application procedure) if a similar application had been filed and a patent granted in another WTO country after January 1995 and the marketing of the pharmaceutical product had been approved in that other WTO country and also in India.[26]

The implementation of these obligations in India was not an easy task, especially given that the local pharmaceutical industry would be negatively affected. It was not until the United States initiated the WTO Dispute Settlement process against India and a WTO panel ruled against India that the Indian Patents Act was amended in 1999 to provide for the mailbox application procedure and exclusive marketing rights.[27] Subsequently, there were further amendments in 2002 and 2005 to bring the patent law in line with the TRIPS Agreement. For instance, in 2002, the patent law was amended to extend the patent term to twenty years from the date of filing.[28]

[20] J. M. Mueller, 'The Tiger Awakens: The Tumultuous Transformation of India's Patent System and the Rise of Indian Pharmaceutical Innovation' (2007) 68 *University of Pittsburgh Law Review* 491, 514.

[21] Ibid.

[22] See, Article 65(2) of the TRIPS Agreement.

[23] See Article 65(4) of the TRIPS Agreement.

[24] See Article 70(8) of the TRIPS Agreement.

[25] See WTO, *India – Patent Protection for Pharmaceutical and Agricultural Chemical Products*, Appellate Body Report, WT/DS50/AB/R (4 December 1997).

[26] See Article 70(9) of the TRIPS Agreement.

[27] See WTO, *India – Patent Protection for Pharmaceutical and Agricultural Chemical Products*, Panel Report, WT/DS50/R (5 September 1997). India brought an appeal against the decision of the WTO Panel to the WTO Appellate Body, but it lost the appeal. See WTO, *India – Patent Protection for Pharmaceutical and Agricultural Chemical Products*, Appellate Body Report, WT/DS50/AB/R (4 December 1997). See also Garde, 'India', 65–7.

[28] Section 27 of the Patents (Amendment) Act of 2002 provides that 'the term of every patent granted, after the commencement of the Patents (Amendment) Act, 2002, and the term of every patent which has not expired and has not ceased to have effect, on the date of such commencement, under this Act, shall be twenty years from the date of filing of the application for

In compliance with the requirements of the TRIPS Agreement, the 2005 Amendment to the Indian Patents Act deleted section 5 of the 1970 Act and restored patent protection for pharmaceutical products. However, this was only possible after strong opposition from political groups and the local pharmaceutical industry.[29] It is therefore not surprising that the 2005 Amendment contains numerous safeguards aimed at protecting the local pharmaceutical industry in India. For instance, the 2005 Amendment contains section 3(d) which is aimed at preventing a practice termed 'ever-greening' whereby pharmaceutical companies extend the patent term of a drug by filing for and obtaining a patent on trivial and minor modifications of the same drug.[30] Section 3(d) essentially prohibits the grant of patents on new forms of known substances unless they differ significantly in properties with regard to efficacy. The current Indian patent law incorporates and implements most of the flexibilities available in the TRIPS Agreement like compulsory licences,[31] research exception,[32] regulatory review exemption,[33] and parallel importation.[34]

6.3 THE RIGHT TO HEALTH IN INDIA

The Indian Constitution, which came into force in 1950, incorporates civil and political rights as fundamental rights in Part III of the Constitution, while socio-economic rights are contained in Part IV of the Constitution which deals with the Directive Principles of State Policy. In relation to health, Article 39(e), contained in Part IV of the Constitution, provides that the state shall, in particular, direct its policy towards securing 'that the health and strength of workers, men and women, and the tender age of children are not abused'. Another provision in Part IV of the Constitution that touches on health is Article 41, which provides, *inter alia*, that the state 'shall, within the limits of its economic capacity and development, make effective provision for securing the right to ... public assistance in cases of ... sickness and disablement'. Furthermore, Article 47, also contained in Part IV of the Constitution, provides, *inter alia*, that the state 'shall regard the raising of the level of nutrition and the standard of living of its people and the improvement of public health as among its primary duties'.

However, the provisions of Part IV of the Indian Constitution are non-justiciable. According to Article 37 of the Constitution, the provisions of Part IV of the

patent'. This is in compliance with Article 33 of the TRIPS Agreement which provides that '[t]he term of protection available shall not end before the expiration of a period of twenty years counted from the filing date'.

29 Garde, 'India', 67.

30 Chan Park and Leena Menghaney, 'TRIPS Flexibilities: The Scope of Patentability and Oppositions to Patents in India', in Gaelle Krikorian and Amy Kapczynski (eds.), *Access to Knowledge in the Age of Intellectual Property* (Zone Books, 2010), 426.

31 Section 84 of the Indian Patents Act.

32 Section 47(3) of the Indian Patents Act.

33 Section 107A(a) of the Indian Patents Act.

34 Section 107A(b) of the Indian Patents Act.

Constitution 'shall not be enforceable by any court' though 'the principles therein laid are nevertheless fundamental in the governance of the country' and the state has the duty 'to apply these principles in making laws'. Initially, the Indian Supreme Court adopted a strict approach towards the interpretation of this prohibition against the justiciability of the Directive Principles of State Policy.[35]

However, in subsequent years, the Indian Supreme Court began to adopt an 'expanded reading' of the justiciable provisions on civil and political rights and they 'started to pronounce upon matters of health which were by the text of the Constitution included in the [Directive Principles of State Policy]'.[36] Essentially, the court found a way of 'settling the contours of the right to health' through the adoption of an expansive reading of the fundamental right to life contained in Article 21 of the Indian Constitution.[37]

Dhanda notes that the Indian Supreme Court 'started with a very formal and legalistic interpretation' of the right to life by ruling 'that the deprivation of life and liberty was permissible provided it was done by a duly enacted parliamentary legislation'.[38] The Supreme Court moved progressively from this formal and legalistic interpretation and it started to expand the ambit of the right to life by first enhancing 'the fairness requirements of the right to life and liberty depriving procedure' and then the court later pronounced on 'the quality of life guaranteed by the Constitution'.[39] The court ruled that the right to life 'was not a right to bare physical existence but a right to a full and meaningful life. And a full and meaningful life includes the right to health within its purview'.[40] Some of the cases where the Indian Supreme Court has made pronouncements on the right to health are examined here.

In *Consumer Education & Research Centre and others* v. *Union of India and others*,[41] the Indian Supreme Court held that the 'expression "life" assured in Art. 21 of the Constitution does not connote mere animal existence or continued drudgery

[35] As Dhanda points out, 'In the early years, this prohibition of justiciability was strictly interpreted by the Supreme Court. Thus, the Court ruled that legislation was required for the implementation of the Directives. The [Directive Principles of State Policy] without more did not create a justiciable right in favour of individuals. Consequently, courts could not compel the state to carry out any of the [Directive Principles of State Policy]. Further, due to the prohibition on justiciability, no law could be declared void on the ground that it infringed the [Directive Principles of State Policy].' See Amita Dhanda, 'Realising the Right to Health through Co-operative Judicial Review: An Analysis of the Role of the Indian Supreme Court', in Oscar Vilhena, Upendra Baxi, and Frans Viljoen (eds.), *Transformative Constitutionalism: Comparing the Apex Courts of Brazil, India and South Africa* (Pretoria University Law Press, 2013), 406.

[36] Ibid.

[37] Ibid. According to Article 21 of the Indian Constitution, 'No person shall be deprived of his life or personal liberty except according to procedure established by law'.

[38] Ibid., 406.

[39] Ibid.

[40] Ibid., 406–7.

[41] *Consumer Education & Research Centre & Ors.* v. *Union of India & Ors.*, 1995 SCC (3) 42 (decided on 27 January 1995).

through life. It has a much wider meaning which includes right to livelihood, better standard of life, hygienic conditions in [the] work place and leisure'.[42] In the same case, the Supreme Court held that 'the right to health and medical care is a fundamental right under Article 21'.[43]

In *Paschim Banga Khet Samity* v. *State of West Bengal*,[44] which involved the failure of government medical hospitals to provide timely emergency medical treatment to an individual who fell off a train and who suffered serious head injuries and brain haemorrhage, the Indian Supreme Court held that,

> Article 21 imposes an obligation on the State to safeguard the right to life of every person. Preservation of human life is thus of paramount importance. The Government hospitals run by the State and the Medical Officers employed therein are duty bound to extend medical assistance for preserving human life. Failure on the part of a Government hospital to provide timely medical treatment to a person in need of such treatment results in [a] violation of his right to life guaranteed under Article 21.[45]

The court further noted that the limitation of financial resources cannot justify the failure of the state to fulfil its constitutional obligations with regard to the provision of adequate medical services.[46]

However, arguments relating to the limitation of financial resources in the context of the right to health and the provision of medical facilities by the state are not entirely foreclosed by the Indian Supreme Court. Where, due to the limitation of financial resources, the government has adopted a particular policy with regard to the provision of medical services, the Indian Supreme Court assesses the particular policy by adopting an approach akin to the 'reasonableness approach'.[47]

For instance, in *State of Punjab and others* v. *Ram Lubhaya Bagga*,[48] the Indian Supreme Court had to determine whether the State of Punjab was justified in

[42] Ibid., para 24.

[43] Ibid., para 26.

[44] *Paschim Banga Khet Samity* v. *State of West Bengal* (1996) 4 SCC 37 (decided on 6 May 1996).

[45] Ibid., para 9.

[46] According to the court, 'It is no doubt true that financial resources are needed for providing these facilities. But at the same time it cannot be ignored that it is the constitutional obligation of the State to provide adequate medical services to the people. Whatever is necessary for this purpose has to be done. In the context of the constitutional obligation to provide free legal aid to a poor accused this Court has held that the State cannot avoid its constitutional obligation in that regard on account of financial constraints ... The said observations would apply with equal, if not greater force, in the matter of [the] discharge of [the] constitutional obligation to provide medical aid to preserve human life' (ibid., para 16).

[47] This is quite similar to the approach adopted by the South African Constitutional Court in cases involving the right to health, as discussed in Chapter 5. See the South African cases of *Soobramoney* v. *Minister of Health* (CCT32/97) [1997] ZACC 17; 1998 (1) SA 765 (CC); and *Minister of Health & Ors* v. *Treatment Action Campaign & Ors (No.2)* (CCT8/02) [2002] ZACC 15; 2002 (5) SA 721.

[48] *State of Punjab* v. *Ram Lubhaya Bagga* (1998) 4 SCC 117 (decided on 26 February 1998).

adopting a policy of not reimbursing an employee for his full medical expenses if such expenses were incurred in any hospital in India that was not a government-owned hospital in Punjab. The State of Punjab argued that no right under the Constitution is absolute and a right has to be balanced with the need, equity, and the resources available.[49] According to the State of Punjab, it would not be a violation of the Constitution if a medical facility is not provided in absolute terms because of financial constraints.[50] In this case, the Supreme Court held that,

> so far as questioning the validity of governmental policy is concerned, in our view it is not normally within the domain of any court, to weigh the pros and cons of the policy or to scrutinize it and test the degree of its beneficial or equitable disposition for the purpose of varying or modifying it, based on however sound and good reasoning, *except where it is arbitrary* or violative of any constitutional, statutory or any other provision of law. When Government forms its policy, it is based on [a] number of circumstances . . . including constraints based on its resources . . . it would be dangerous if [the] court is asked to test the utility, beneficial effect of the policy or its appraisal based on facts set out on affidavits. The Court would dissuade itself from entering into this realm which belongs to the executive. It is within this matrix that it is to be seen whether the new policy violates Article 21 when it restricts reimbursement on account of . . . financial constraints.[51]

In other words, once the government has already adopted a policy with regard to the provision of a medical facility, unless the said policy is arbitrary or unreasonable or violative of any constitutional or statutory rule, the court will not interfere in accordance with the doctrine of separation of powers. This is in congruence with the approach adopted by the South African Constitutional Court in the *Soobramoney case*,[52] which was discussed in Chapter 5. The implication of this is that the government cannot rely on the argument that it has financial constraints to justify its failure to provide a medical facility. As the court held in the *Samity case*, the state cannot avoid its obligation on account of financial constraints.[53] The state has to take steps to establish a policy with regard to the provision of medical facilities and limited financial resources will not excuse the government's failure to establish a policy in this regard. But once the government has adopted a particular policy with regard to the provision of a medical facility, the court will only interfere where that policy is unreasonable or violative of the Constitution.

Thus, in the *Lubhaya Bagga* case, the court held that, 'the State can neither urge nor say that it has no obligation to provide [a] medical facility. If that were so it would be ex facie violative of Article 21'.[54] The court then noted that, under the policy adopted by the State of Punjab, 'medical facility continues to be given

49 Ibid., 3.
50 Ibid.
51 Ibid., 10 (emphasis added).
52 *Soobramoney* v. *Minister of Health* (CCT32/97) [1997] ZACC 17; 1998 (1) SA 765 (CC).
53 *Paschim Banga Khet Samity* v. *State of West Bengal* (1996) 4 SCC 37 (decided on 6 May 1996), para 16.
54 *State of Punjab* v. *Ram Lubhaya Bagga* (1998) 4 SCC 117 (decided on 26 February 1998), 11.

and ... an employee is given [the] free choice to get treatment in any private hospital in India but the amount of payment towards reimbursement is regulated'.[55] The court held that this policy was not in violation of Articles 21 or 47 of the Constitution.[56]

The approach adopted by the court in the *Lubhaya Bagga* case was followed in the latter case of *Confederation of Ex-Servicemen Associations and others* v. *Union of India and others*.[57] In that case the court had to determine whether it was unconstitutional and unreasonable to require ex-servicemen to make one time payments before benefitting from an Ex-Servicemen Contributory Health Scheme (ECHS). The court held that 'such a contributory scheme cannot be held illegal, unlawful or unconstitutional' because '[i]n the light of financial constraints and limited means available, if a policy decision is taken to extend medical facilities to ex-defence personnel by allowing them to become members of [a] contributory scheme and by requiring them to make [a] "one time payment" which is a "reasonable amount", it cannot be said that such [an] action would violate fundamental rights guaranteed by Part III of the Constitution'.[58]

In 2014, in the case of *Mohd. Ahmed (Minor)* v. *Union of India and others*,[59] the Delhi High Court made some landmark pronouncements on the right to health in

55 Ibid.

56 Ibid. According to the court, 'No State of any country can have unlimited resources to spend on any of its project. That is why it only approves its projects to the extent [to which] it is feasible. The same holds good for providing medical facilities to its citizens including its employees. Provision of facilities cannot be unlimited. It has to be to the extent finance[s] permit.'

57 *Confederation of Ex-Servicemen Associations and others* v. *Union of India and others*, Writ Petition (civil) 210 of 1999 (decided on 22 August 2006).

58 Ibid., 26–7. Adopting the 'reasonableness approach' the court held that, 'In our considered opinion, though the right to medical aid is a fundamental right of all citizens including ex-servicemen guaranteed by Article 21 of the Constitution, [the] framing of [a] scheme for ex-servicemen and asking them to pay [a] "one time contribution" neither violates Part III nor [is it] inconsistent with Part IV of the Constitution. Ex-servicemen who are getting pension have been asked to become members of ECHS by making "one time contribution" of reasonable amount ... To us, this cannot be held illegal, unlawful, arbitrary or otherwise unreasonable ... To us, the policy decision in formulating [a] Contributory Scheme for ex-servicemen is in accordance with the provisions of the Constitution and also in consonance with the law laid down by this Court ... We, therefore, hold that getting free and full medical facilities is not a part of [the] fundamental right of ex-servicemen' (ibid., 27). However, in recognition of the 'exemplary and extremely useful services rendered by [the] defence personnel' and because 'the safety, security and comfort enjoyed by the countrymen depend largely on [the] dedication and commitment of [the] soldiers, sailors and airmen', the Indian Supreme Court directed the government 'either to waive the amount of [the] contribution or to pay such amount on behalf of those ex-servicemen ... who intend to avail [of the] medical facilities and benefits under the said scheme by exercising [the] option [of] becoming members of ECHS.' Invariably, the court ruled that 'it is open to ex-defence personnel ... to become members of ECHS and to claim medical facilities and benefits under the said scheme without payment of [the] contribution amount' (ibid., 27, 29).

59 *Mohd. Ahmed (Minor)* v. *Union of India and others*, W.P.(C) 7279/2013 (Decision of the High Court of Delhi at New Delhi, 17 April 2014).

the context of access to medicines as it affects a patient suffering from a rare disease. The central issue before the court was whether a child born to poor parents and who is suffering from Gaucher's disease (a chronic and rare disease) is entitled to free medical treatment, especially when the treatment for the disease is known, the prognosis is good, and there is every likelihood that the child can lead a normal life.[60] The court observed that the cost of the drugs for this disease is exorbitant because it is a rare disease.[61]

It was argued on behalf of the child that, since the drugs needed for the treatment of the child are available in India, both the Central Government and the Government of Delhi had an obligation under Article 21 of the Constitution to provide free treatment to the child and other patients in the same situation.[62] The child's counsel argued that the government could not raise the plea of financial constraint.[63] The plea of financial constraint was however the kernel of the submissions made by the Central Government and the Government of Delhi. They contended that because of their limited resources they were unable to fund the treatment of the child as the disease is a lifelong one and the condition of the child is chronic.[64]

In particular, the Government of Delhi contended, *inter alia*, that 'the right to health in a developing country like India could not be so stretched . . . to mean [the provision of] free health facilities to a terminally ill patient while other citizens were not even provided basic health care'.[65] In addition, the Delhi Government argued that 'the State had an equal obligation towards all citizens and it had to use its limited resources so as to provide the maximum benefit to the maximum number of people' and the state's obligation to provide health care to all people is not an absolute fundamental right as it is subject to just exceptions.[66] Essentially, the Delhi Government argued that 'the State cannot concentrate all its resources on one person, while denying basic facilities to others'.[67]

Anand Grover, the former UN Special Rapporteur on the Right to Health, equally made some legal submissions in this case. Grover argued that, as India had signed and ratified the International Covenant on Economic, Social, and Cultural Rights (ICESCR), India is duty bound to fulfil its international legal obligations.[68] Grover contended that,

60 Ibid., para 1.
61 Ibid., para 4.
62 Ibid., para 11.
63 Ibid., para 14.
64 Ibid., para 27.
65 Ibid., para 22.
66 Ibid.
67 Ibid., para 24.
68 Ibid., para 34.

> States are required to adopt and implement a public health strategy and plan of action that reflects the epidemiological burden of disease that not only addresses major disease burdens but also the health concerns of the whole population. Therefore ... even if a small percentage of the population had a life-threatening condition there should be [a] public health strategy and plan to address their treatment needs. In other words, the Government can be directed to have a plan in place to make medicines available for rare diseases, like Gaucher disease etc.[69]

Grover's argument brings into focus the central problem with the government's argument in this case. Essentially, the Indian government had failed to put in place a policy or adopt a public health strategy to provide medicines to those suffering from rare diseases such as Gaucher's disease. This is a violation of the government's obligation with regard to the right to health. It is true that the government has limited resources, but as the Indian Supreme Court held in the *Samity* case, the state cannot avoid its constitutional obligation with regard to the right to health on account of financial constraints.[70] Even in the *Lubhaya Bagga* case where the Indian Supreme Court recognized the fact that the financial resources of the state are not unlimited, the court still made it clear that the failure to adopt a policy with regard to the provision of a medical facility is, *ex facie*, violative of the constitution.[71]

In this case, neither the Central Government nor the Delhi Government had adopted any policy or public health strategy for the provision of drugs to those suffering from rare diseases. As the Delhi High Court pointed out, 'Unfortunately, the Government of India does not have any policy measure in place to address rare diseases, particularly those of a chronic nature. All the Central and State schemes at the highest provide for a one-time grant for life-saving procedures and do not contemplate continuous financial assistance for a chronic disease such as [Gaucher's disease], which involves lifelong expenditure'.[72] The court, however, stated that, in accordance with the doctrine of separation of powers, it could not

69 Ibid., para 35.

70 *Paschim Banga Khet Samity* v. *State of West Bengal* (1996) 4 SCC 37 (decided on 6 May 1996), para 16.

71 In the *Lubhaya Bagga* case, the Indian Supreme Court held that, 'the State can neither urge nor say that it has no obligation to provide [a] medical facility. If that were so it would be ex facie violative of Article 21'. See *State of Punjab* v. *Ram Lubhaya Bagga* (1998) 4 SCC 117 (decided on 26 February 1998), 11.

72 *Mohd. Ahmed (Minor)* v. *Union of India and others*, W.P.(C) 7279/2013 (Decision of the High Court of Delhi at New Delhi, 17 April 2014), para 42. The court also lamented the fact that 'no incentives were in place for Indian manufacturers to develop local alternatives to orphan drugs [i.e. drugs developed for the treatment of rare diseases]'. According to the court, no promising orphan drug will be developed and the prohibitive costs of orphan drugs will not be reduced 'unless changes are made in the applicable laws to reduce the costs of developing such drugs and to provide financial incentives to develop such drugs' (ibid., paras 42–3). The court also advised the government to increase its investment in the health sector. According to the court, 'If poor patients are to enjoy [the] benefit of recent innovations in the medical field, like robotic surgery [and] genome engineering the Government must immediately think of increasing its investment in the health sector' (ibid., para 80).

direct parliament to enact a legislation on the right to public health or with regard to rare diseases or orphan drugs, even though this may be eminently desirable.[73] According to the court, as the 'formulation of a policy is within the exclusive domain of the Executive', it will refrain from issuing directives for the formulation of a policy.[74]

In its decision in this case, the Delhi High Court noted that the human right to health is recognized in numerous international instruments including Article 25 of the Universal Declaration of Human Rights and Article 12 of the ICESCR.[75] The court also referred to the UN Committee on Economic, Social, and Cultural Rights (CESCR's) General Comment No. 14 on the right to health.[76] The court quoted paragraph 12 of General Comment No. 14 which deals with the essential elements of the right to health and which states, *inter alia*, that health facilities, goods, and services must be both available and accessible.[77] In addition, the court quoted paragraph 43(d) of General Comment No. 14 which states that one of the core obligations with regard to the right to health (from which no derogation is permissible) is the provision of essential drugs.[78] Furthermore, the court quoted paragraph 52 of General Comment No. 14 which provides that a state violates its obligation to fulfil the right to health when it fails to, *inter alia*, 'adopt or implement a national health policy designed to ensure the right to health for everyone'.[79]

The court admitted that the state does not have unlimited financial resources. According to the court, 'availability of finance with the Government is a relevant factor ... No court can direct that [the] entire budget of a country should be spent on health and medical aid' and 'courts cannot direct that all [the] inhabitants of this country [should] be given free medical treatment at [the state's] expense' and if such a directive is issued, 'it would not be implementable as there would be neither infrastructure nor finance' for complying with such a directive.[80] Nevertheless, the court held that 'no Government can say that it will not treat patients with chronic and rare diseases due to financial constraint[s]'.[81] The court, apparently relying on the provisions of paragraph 43(d) of General Comment No. 14 which it had previously quoted, adopted the view that 'core obligations under the right to health are non-derogable' and that though 'this minimum core is not easy to define', it

73 Ibid., para 44.

74 Ibid., para 45.

75 Ibid., para 52.

76 Ibid., para 53. See UN Committee on Economic, Social and Cultural Rights (CESCR), 'General Comment No. 14: The Right to the Highest Attainable Standard of Health (Art. 12)', E/C.12/2000/4 (2000).

77 *Mohd. Ahmed (Minor)* v. *Union of India and others*, W.P.(C) 7279/2013 (Decision of the High Court of Delhi at New Delhi, 17 April 2014), para 53.

78 Ibid.

79 Ibid.

80 Ibid., paras 62–3.

81 Ibid., para 64.

'includes at least the minimum decencies of life consistent with human dignity'.[82] Invariably, the court came to the conclusion that the state has an obligation to provide access to medicines, including medicines for rare diseases.[83]

Thus, by failing to adopt a policy for the provision of medicines for the treatment of rare diseases such as Gaucher's disease, the government had violated its constitutional obligation with regard to the right to health.[84] Furthermore, the government has a non-derogable core obligation to provide access to essential medicines at affordable prices (irrespective of resource constraints).[85] As health is a subject matter within the jurisdiction of the state government in India, the court ordered the Government of Delhi to 'discharge its constitutional obligation and provide the petitioner with enzyme replacement therapy … free of charge as and when he requires it'.[86]

The ruling of the court with regard to the non-derogable core obligation of the state to provide access to essential medicines at affordable prices, irrespective of resource constraints, has enormous implications for the tension between patent rights and the right to health in India. Even though the court in this case did not consider the tension between patent rights and the right to health, the court has confirmed by its ruling that the Indian government has a non-derogable core obligation to facilitate access to essential medicines at affordable prices.

This ruling implies that in any case where the exercise or enforcement of patent rights on pharmaceutical products granted by the government hinders poor patients from having access to essential medicines, there is a violation of the government's obligation to provide access to essential medicines at affordable prices. If this approach is incorporated into the decisions of the Indian courts whenever they are adjudicating disputes involving the interpretation or enforcement of patent rights, it will ensure that owners of patent rights on pharmaceutical products are not allowed to exercise their patent rights in a manner that impedes the enjoyment of the right to

82 Ibid., para 67.

83 According to the court, 'Article 21 of the Constitution clearly imposes a duty on the Government to take whatever steps are necessary to ensure that everyone has access to health facilities, goods and services so that they can enjoy, as soon as possible, the highest attainable standard of physical and mental health. By virtue of Article 21 of the Constitution, the State is under a legal obligation to ensure access to life saving drugs to patients. A reasonable and equitable access to life saving medicines is critical to promoting and protecting the right to health. This means that Government must at the bare minimum ensure that individuals have access to essential medicines even for rare diseases like enzyme replacement for Gaucher disease … Government cannot cite financial crunch as a reason not to fulfil its obligation to ensure access to medicines or to adopt a plan of action to treat rare diseases … no government can wriggle out of its core obligation of ensuring the right of access to health facilities for [the] vulnerable and marginalized section of society [such as] the petitioner by stating that it cannot afford to provide treatment for rare and chronic diseases' (ibid., paras 68–9).

84 Ibid., paras 85–6.

85 Ibid., para 87.

86 Ibid., para 89.

health. Indeed, as will be demonstrated in Section 6.4, prior to the decision of the Delhi High Court in this landmark case, some Indian courts have incorporated this *model of human rights* into their decisions whenever they adjudicate on disputes involving patent rights on pharmaceutical products.

Thus, three clear principles are discernible from the decisions of the Indian courts on the right to health. One, the state cannot justify its failure to provide medical facilities by arguing that it has limited financial resources. The state is obliged to at least adopt a policy with regard to the provision of medical facilities. Two, once a policy has been adopted by the state, the court will only interfere with such a policy if it is unconstitutional or unreasonable or arbitrary. As long as the policy itself is not unreasonable, the measures contained in the policy need not be adequate. Three, the state has a core obligation to provide access to essential medicines at affordable prices. There can be no derogation from this core obligation, irrespective of financial constraints. This implies that the state has a core obligation to, at least, adopt a reasonable policy with regard to the provision of access to affordable medicines. Section 6.4 will critically examine how some courts in India have incorporated a *model of human rights* into their decisions in cases involving the interpretation and enforcement of patent rights on pharmaceutical products.

6.4 INCORPORATING A MODEL OF HUMAN RIGHTS INTO THE ADJUDICATION OF DISPUTES INVOLVING PHARMACEUTICAL PATENTS IN INDIA

6.4.1 Novartis *v.* Union of India: *Excluding New Forms of Known Drugs from Patent Protection*

In an attempt to curb the ever-greening of pharmaceutical patents, India introduced a unique provision into its Patent Act in 2005. The unique provision, section 3(d),[87] aims to prohibit the patenting of new forms of known substances and new uses of known substances.[88] The only permissible ground on which new forms of known

[87] Section 3(d) of the Indian Patents Act provides that the following are not inventions within the meaning of the Act: 'the mere discovery of a new form of a known substance which does not result in the enhancement of the known efficacy of that substance or the mere discovery of any new property or new use for a known substance or of the mere use of a known process, machine or apparatus unless such known process results in a new product or employs at least one new reactant. *Explanation*: For purposes of this clause, salts, esters, ethers, polymorphs, metabolites, pure form, particle size, isomers, mixtures of isomers, complexes, combinations and other derivatives of known substance shall be considered to be the same substance, unless they differ significantly in properties with regard to efficacy.'

[88] As Basheer and Reddy note, 'section 3(d) aims to prevent a phenomenon commonly referred to as "ever-greening" by providing that only those pharmaceutical derivatives that demonstrate significantly enhanced "efficacy" are patentable'. Shamnad Basheer and Prashant Reddy, 'The "Efficacy" of Indian Patent Law: Ironing Out the Creases in Section 3(d)' (2008) 5 *SCRIPT-ed* 232, 238.

substances can be patented is if they result in the enhancement of the known efficacy of the previously known substance.

Section 3(d) was interpreted and applied by the Indian Supreme Court to deny patent protection to Novartis' anti-cancer drug, Glivec, in *Novartis* v. *Union of India*.[89] The active ingredient in Glivec is a derivative of a drug compound called 'imatinib'. Novartis had improved upon 'imatinib' by converting it into a salt form called 'imatinib mesylate' and it was from 'imatinib mesylate' that Novartis derived the most stable version of the drug compound, a particular polymorphic form called the 'beta crystalline form of imatinib mesylate'.[90] This beta crystalline form became the active ingredient in Glivec.[91] Several generic drug companies in India, however, opposed Novartis' patent application on Glivec on the ground that it failed to comply with section 3(d). Novartis contended that Glivec could not be denied a patent based on section 3(d) because the active ingredient in Glivec is more effective than 'imatinib' as it is absorbed easily in the bloodstream and there is a 30 per cent increase in bioavailability.

In its decision, the Indian Supreme Court had to define what is meant by 'efficacy' as contained in section 3(d). The court held that 'efficacy', in the context of medicines, means 'therapeutic efficacy'.[92] The court could not, however, make up its mind as to how the test of 'therapeutic efficacy' should be applied to specific cases.[93] Two divergent views were presented to the court in this regard. The 'more rigid position' on therapeutic efficacy was presented by Anand Grover (who appeared as counsel to the Cancer Patients Aid Association, one of the parties that objected to the grant of a patent on Glivec) and he argued that an increase in bioavailability (such as the 30 per cent increase in bioavailability argued by Novartis in the present case) is not a demonstration of enhanced efficacy.[94] The 'less rigid position' on therapeutic efficacy was presented by Professor Shamnad Basheer

[89] See *Novartis AG* v. *Union of India & Ors*, Civil Appeal Nos. 2706–16 of 2013 (Supreme Court of India, 1 April 2013) [hereinafter, *Novartis* v. *India*].

[90] Basheer and Reddy, 'The "Efficacy" of Indian Patent Law', 235–6.

[91] Ibid.

[92] *Novartis* v. *India*, para 180. In the words of the court, 'Efficacy means "the ability to produce a desired or intended result". Hence ... the test of efficacy would depend upon the function, utility or the purpose of the product under consideration. Therefore, in the case of a medicine that claims to cure a disease, the test of efficacy can only be "therapeutic efficacy". The question then arises, what would be the parameter of therapeutic efficacy and what are the advantages and benefits that may be taken into account for determining the enhancement of therapeutic efficacy? ... [W]e have no doubt that the "therapeutic efficacy" of a medicine must be judged strictly and narrowly ... It may be noted that the text added to section 3(d) by the 2005 amendment lays down the condition of "enhancement of the known efficacy". Further, the explanation requires the derivative to "differ significantly in properties with regard to efficacy". What is evident, therefore, is that not all advantageous or beneficial properties are relevant, but only such properties that directly relate to efficacy, which in [the] case of medicine, as seen above, is its therapeutic efficacy' (ibid.).

[93] Ibid., paras 182–6.

[94] Ibid., paras 183–4.

(who appeared as an academic intervenor-cum-amicus in the case) and he argued that, while not all advantageous properties of a new form of a known drug such as improved processability and storage potential ought to satisfy the requirements of section 3(d), other features such as safety or significantly reduced toxicity should also be taken into consideration to determine the enhanced therapeutic efficacy of a drug under section 3(d).[95] With regard to increased bioavailability, Professor Basheer argued that '... it is theoretically possible for increased bioavailability to result in increased enhanced efficacy in some cases. However, this must be independently established, without assuming that an increase in bioavailability automatically translates to enhanced efficacy.'[96]

The Indian Supreme Court however deemed it unnecessary to make any pronouncement on these two views since the case before it could be 'effectively decided without adverting to the different points of view' presented by Mr Grover and Professor Basheer.[97] Nevertheless, the Indian Supreme Court had to decide whether the claim by Novartis, that Glivec possessed a 30 per cent increase in bioavailability, satisfied the requirements of section 3(d). In this regard, the court adopted the position of Professor Basheer, who had noted that, while Novartis '... sought to establish that when compared with the Imatinib free base, the beta crystalline form demonstrates a 30% increase in bio-availability',[98] this 'does not demonstrate any therapeutic advantage in relation to the patient' and that 'such advantage has to be independently established' and this 'has not been done in this case'.[99]

Adopting Professor Basheer's position in this regard, the Indian Supreme Court held that Novartis had failed to present evidence to show that the 'beta crystalline form of imatinib mesylate' 'will produce an enhanced or superior efficacy (therapeutic) on molecular basis than what could be achieved with Imatinib free base *in vivo* animal model'.[100] The court noted that an increase in bioavailability alone may not qualify as an enhancement of therapeutic efficacy and that 'whether or not an increase in bioavailability leads to an enhancement of therapeutic efficacy in any given case must be specifically claimed and established by research data'.[101]

Even though the Indian Supreme Court appears to have left the door open as to whether an increase in bioavailability can qualify as an enhancement of therapeutic efficacy in future cases, the Court however stated clearly in its judgment that certain physico-chemical properties of drugs cannot be taken into account for the purposes of determining therapeutic efficacy. According to the court,

[95] Ibid., para 185.

[96] See Shamnad Basheer 'Written Submissions on Behalf of the Intervenor', in *Novartis* v. *India* (Part 1) 11, available from https://docs.google.com/file/d/0Bxi2TzVXul5ZcEJRU105NXhWbGM/edit (last accessed 27 September 2021).

[97] *Novartis* v. India, para 186.

[98] Basheer 'Written Submissions on Behalf of the Intervenor', 11.

[99] Ibid., 11–12.

[100] *Novartis* v. *India*, para 189.

[101] Ibid.

> In whatever way therapeutic efficacy may be interpreted, this much is absolutely clear: that the physico-chemical properties of beta crystalline form of Imatinib Mesylate, namely (i) more beneficial flow properties, (ii) better thermodynamic stability, and (iii) lower hygroscopicity, may be otherwise beneficial but these properties cannot even be taken into account for the purpose of the test of section 3(d) of the Act, since these properties have nothing to do with therapeutic efficacy.[102]

In other words, while increased bioavailability may satisfy the requirements of section 3(d) in deserving cases (particularly where a patent applicant presents evidence to demonstrate how increased bioavailability results in enhanced therapeutic efficacy), other possibly beneficial properties of a drug such as better thermodynamic stability and lower hygroscopicity cannot satisfy the requirements of section 3(d) as these properties are unrelated to therapeutic efficacy.

The strategic importance of section 3(d) was also recognized by the Indian Supreme Court. According to the court, section 3(d) 'clearly sets up a second tier of qualifying standards for chemical substances/pharmaceutical products in order to leave the door open for true and genuine inventions but, at the same time, to check any attempt at repetitive patenting or extension of the patent term on spurious grounds'.[103]

In addition, the Indian Supreme Court stated clearly that even though it held that Novartis had failed to fulfil the requirements of section 3(d) in this particular case, 'that is not to say that Section 3(d) bars patent protection for all incremental inventions of chemical and pharmaceutical substances'.[104] Section 3(d) is designed to weed out trivial inventions and prevent ever-greening in the pharmaceutical sector. It is not aimed at preventing the patenting of beneficial incremental pharmaceutical innovations. Section 3(d), as interpreted by the Indian Supreme Court, only requires that anyone seeking to patent a new form of a known drug should present evidence to show that the new form of the known drug will produce an enhanced therapeutic efficacy beyond that offered by the previously known drug. The veracity of the Supreme Court's statement that its decision is not aimed at barring patent protection for incremental pharmaceutical innovations is confirmed by its apparent willingness to leave the door open for the granting of patent protection for new forms of known drugs that possess an increase in bioavailability, particularly where there is evidence that the increased bioavailability results in enhanced therapeutic efficacy.

Beyond all these, it also needs to be stressed that section 3(d) was introduced into the Indian Patents Act in order to secure the right of Indians to have access to affordable medicines and in fulfilment of the Indian government's obligation to protect the right to health of its citizens. When the *Novartis* case was still before the

[102] Ibid., para 187.
[103] Ibid., para 103.
[104] Ibid., para 191.

Madras High Court, the court noted that one of the objectives behind the amendment of the Indian Patents Acts in 2005 was to prevent the ever-greening of pharmaceutical patents and to enable the Indian government 'to provide easy access to the citizens of this country to life saving drugs and to discharge their Constitutional obligation of providing good health care to its citizens'.[105] Thus the Madras High Court incorporated a *model of human rights* into its decision in the *Novartis* case. Furthermore, in its ruling on the same matter, the Indian Intellectual Property Appellate Board was of the view that the grant of patent protection to Novartis in this case will have a disastrous effect on the society.[106]

In its decision in the *Novartis case*, the Indian Supreme Court was mindful of the relationship between section 3(d) and the provision of access to essential medicines at affordable prices. In its discussion of the legislative history behind section 3(d), the Indian Supreme Court noted that,

> Parliament had an absolutely unenviable task on its hands. It was required to forge, within a very limited time, an Act that would be TRIPS compliant without, in any way, compromising on public health considerations ... [T]he TRIPS Agreement had aroused grave concerns about its impact on public health. India had learnt from experience the inverse relationship between product patents and the indigenous pharmaceutical industry, and its effects on the availability of essential drugs at affordable prices ... [A]fter the patent system in India barred the grant of patents for pharmaceutical and chemical substances, the pharmaceutical industry in the country scaled great heights and became the major supplier of drugs at cheap prices to a number of developing and under developed countries. Hence, the reintroduction of product patents in the Indian patent system through the TRIPS Agreement became a cause of alarm not only in this country but also for some international agencies.[107]

The Supreme Court highlighted the fact that, while deliberating on the Bill that led to the introduction of section 3(d) into the Indian patent law in 2005, the legislature was not oblivious to the human rights implications of the proposed law. As the court pointed out,

> To anyone going through the debate on the Bill, Parliament would appear keenly alive to national interests, *human rights considerations* and the role of India as the producer and supplier of drugs to different parts of the world where impoverished humanity is critically in need of those drugs at cheap and affordable prices. Cutting across party lines, member after member from the Opposition benches highlighted

[105] *Novartis* AG v. *Union of India & Others*, 2007 A.I.R. 24759 (Madras High Court, 2007), para 19.

[106] *Novartis AG* v. *Union of India & Others*, Order (No. 100/2009), decision of the Indian Intellectual Property Appellate Board, (26 June 2009), para 10. According to the Appellate Board, '... a grant of product patent on this application can create havoc [in] the lives of poor people ... affected with the cancer for which this drug is effective. This will have [a] disastrous effect on the society as well'.

[107] *Novartis* v. *India*, para 76.

> the grave risk in creating private monopolies in an area like pharmaceuticals, the abuses to which product patents in pharmaceutical products were vulnerable, and the ploys used by big companies to artificially extend the period of patent [protection] to keep competitors out and keep the prices of the patented product high. It was strongly argued that, while fulfilling its commitment under the TRIPS agreement, the Government must not bring in a patent regime where all the gains achieved by the Indian pharmaceutical industry are dissipated and large sections of Indians and people in other parts of the world are left at the mercy of giant multinational pharmaceutical companies.[108]

As Sunder rightly points out in her commentary on the decision of the Indian Supreme Court in the *Novartis* case,

> The Indian Supreme Court expressly approached its task 'within a very broad framework', considering everything from 'India's obligation to faithfully comply with its commitments under international treaties' to protecting 'India's status as "the pharmacy of the world"'. The court took up its task of interpreting the Indian patent statute, cognisant 'that an error of judgment … will put life-saving drugs beyond the reach of the multitude of ailing humanity not only in this country but in many developing and under-developed countries'.[109]

The Supreme Court's discussion of the legislative history behind section 3(d) indicates that the lawmakers who enacted the provision incorporated a *model of human rights* into the design of section 3(d). The goal of the lawmakers was to ensure that the implementation and enforcement of the Indian Patents Act would not impede the enjoyment of the right to have access to essential medicines at affordable prices. This goal of securing the right to have access to essential medicines was not lost on the courts that adjudicated the *Novartis* case, that is, the Madras High Court, the Indian Intellectual Property Appellate Board, and the Indian Supreme Court. All these courts, directly or indirectly, incorporated a *model of human rights* into their judgments in this case and it is therefore not surprising that the goal of the lawmakers with regard to section 3(d) was fulfilled in this particular case.

108 Ibid., para 79 (emphasis added).

109 Madhavi Sunder, 'Novartis v Myriad: The Indian and US Supreme Courts on Patents and Public Health' (2013) 35 *European Intellectual Property Review* 711, 712. See also *Novartis* v. *India*, para 4, where the Indian Supreme Court noted that, 'The debate took place within a very broad framework. The Court was urged to strike a balance between the need to promote research and development in science and technology and to keep private monopoly (called an "aberration" under our Constitutional scheme) at the minimum. Arguments were made about India's obligation to faithfully comply with its commitments under international treaties and counter arguments were made to protect India's status as "the pharmacy of the world". The Court was reminded of its duty to uphold the rights granted by the statute, and the Court was also reminded that an error of judgment by it will put life-saving drugs beyond the reach of the multitude of ailing humanity not only in this country but in many developing and under-developed countries, dependent on generic drugs from India.'

6.4.2 Natco *v.* Bayer: *Compulsory Licences and the Availability of Patented Drugs at Reasonably Affordable Prices*

The case of *Natco* v. *Bayer*[110] is the first case in India in the post-TRIPS Agreement era where an applicant invoked the relevant provisions of the Indian Patents Act to seek the grant of a compulsory licence. The patentee in this case, Bayer, invented a drug called 'Sorafenib' and obtained an Indian patent for the drug in 2008. The drug is sold under the trade name 'Nexavar' and it is used for the treatment of kidney cancer and liver cancer. The applicant, Natco, an Indian generic drug manufacturer, had initially requested a voluntary licence from Bayer to sell the drug to the public at a cheaper price. Bayer did not grant this request and Natco subsequently applied for a compulsory licence. In granting Natco's request for a compulsory licence, one of the issues considered by the Indian Controller of Patents was the price at which the drug was being sold in India. According to section 84(1)(b) of the Indian Patents Act of 2005, one of the grounds for the grant of a compulsory licence is that 'the patented invention is not available to the public at a reasonably affordable price'.

Natco argued that the price of the drug was 'too high and simply unaffordable by the common man making the product inaccessible and out of reach'.[111] According to Natco, a drug that costs Rs. 280,000 per month 'will push a large proportion of the population into poverty'.[112] In response, Bayer argued, *inter alia*, that 'reasonable' price must mean 'reasonable' to the public and the patentee as well, and that 'the cost of R&D and the cost of manufacture, both have to be taken into account while determining "reasonable affordable price"'.[113] Interestingly, in its arguments, Bayer differentiated between the various categories of people that can constitute the 'public'. According to Bayer, the term 'public' denotes different sections of the public, that is, the 'rich class', the 'middle class', and the 'poor class'.[114] Bayer further contended that a blanket compulsory licence cannot be granted to sell its drug to all sections of the 'public' at the same price.[115] It can be inferred from Bayer's arguments that it was cognisant of the fact that the application of differential pricing to the sale of Nexavar within India would ensure that members of the public, especially those who were in the 'poor class', would have access to the drug. However, Bayer did not adopt a system of differential pricing in its sale of Nexavar.

In deciding to grant the compulsory licence, the Controller agreed that the drug, being sold at a price of Rs. 280,000 per month, was not reasonably affordable to

[110] *Natco* v. *Bayer*, Compulsory License Application No.1 of 2011 (Decision of the Indian Controller of Patents, 9 March 2012).

[111] Ibid., para 11.

[112] Ibid.

[113] Ibid.

[114] Ibid.

[115] Ibid.

members of the public.[116] The Controller disagreed with Bayer's argument that 'reasonable affordable price' should be construed with reference to both the public and the patentee, and held that it has to be construed predominantly with reference to the public.[117] The Controller questioned why Bayer had not engaged in differential pricing based on its argument that the term 'public' should be construed as different sections of the public.[118]

According to the terms of the compulsory licence granted to Natco by the Controller, Natco was required to sell the drug at the price of Rs. 8,880 per month. The sale of Nexavar at Rs. 8,880 per month will reduce the financial burden of poor patients who need the drug. It should be noted that most Indians pay out-of-pocket for health expenses. According to statistics from the World Health Organization, in 2011, out-of-pocket expenditure as a percentage of private expenditure on health in India was 86.3 per cent[119] and it has also been estimated that 70 per cent of out-of-pocket expenditure on health in the country is spent on drugs.[120]

Bayer subsequently lodged an appeal against the decision of the Controller at the Indian Intellectual Property Appellate Board (IPAB). During the pendency of the appeal and before its final determination by IPAB, Bayer sought an order staying the grant of the compulsory licence to Natco. In refusing to grant this interim order, IPAB considered, among other issues, the issue of the affordability of Nexavar in India. IPAB held that the words, 'reasonably affordable' can 'only be understood in the context of the purchasing power of the public' and that 'the question is not whether Bayer can afford to sell [Nexavar] at price X, the question is [whether] the public [can] reasonably afford to buy the medicine at price X'.[121] According to IPAB, 'prima facie there is no error in the Controller fixing the price at Rs. 8,880/- per month' because it will enable more Indians suffering from kidney and liver cancer to buy the drug than when it is sold at Rs. 280,000.[122]

IPAB also incorporated a *model of human rights* into its decision in this regard as it considered the effect that the grant of a stay would have on access to medicines. IPAB stressed the fact that the grant of a stay in this case will have an impact on the right of access to affordable medicines. According to IPAB,

116 Ibid.

117 Ibid.

118 According to the Controller, '[The] Patentee also submitted that affordable to [the] public is required to be considered as affordable to different classes/sections of [the] public. On this point, I fully agree with the Patentee. I only wonder why the Patentee did not execute this concept by offering differential pricing for different classes/sections of [the] public in India' (ibid.).

119 WHO, *World Health Statistics 2014* (2014), 141–51.

120 The Hindu, 'Govt. to Provide Free Generic Drugs at Public Hospitals: Azad' (27 February 2012), available from www.thehindu.com/news/national/govt-to-provide-free-generic-drugs-at-public-hospitals-azad/article2938450.ece (last accessed 27 September 2021).

121 *Bayer* v. *Union of India & Others*, M.P. Nos. 74 to 76 of 2012 in OA/35/2012/PT/MUM, decision of the Indian Intellectual Property Appellate Board, (14 September 2012), para 22.

122 Ibid.

> if [a] stay is granted, it will definitely jeopardise the interest of the public who need the drug ... the right of access to affordable medicine is as much a matter of [the] right to dignity of the patients and to grant [a] stay at this juncture would really affect them ... Though this is not a reason why we are not granting [a] stay, yet this is an additional factor.[123]

In March 2013, IPAB issued its final judgment and it dismissed Bayer's appeal against the grant of the compulsory licence.[124] IPAB upheld the order of the Controller of Patents though it increased the rate of royalty to be paid by Natco to Bayer from 6 to 7 per cent.[125] In its final judgment, IPAB referred to section 83 of the Indian Patents Act which contains the general principles applicable to the working of patented inventions in India. Specifically, section 83(c) provides that patents should not impede the protection of public health. Section 83(g) further states that patents are granted to make the benefit of the patented invention available at reasonably affordable prices to the public. IPAB noted that it could not 'ignore these markers' in its decision.[126]

In its final decision in the *Bayer* case, IPAB equally incorporated a *model of human rights* into its judgment. IPAB's final decision in this case indicates that it was mindful of the need to protect the right to health and the right to have access to medicines. In its judgment, reference was made to the Doha Declaration on the TRIPS Agreement and Public Health of 2001.[127] The Doha Declaration provides, *inter alia*, that the TRIPS Agreement 'does not and should not prevent members from taking measures to protect public health ... [and] that the Agreement can and should be interpreted and implemented in a manner supportive of WTO members' right to protect public health and, in particular, to promote access to medicines for all'.[128] Importantly, IPAB noted that, under the Doha Declaration, countries 'affirmed their full right to use the TRIPS flexibilities ... especially in connection with [their] right to protect public health and in particular, to promote access to medicines for all'.[129] This led IPAB to the conclusion that the running theme is 'public health and access to medicine, a facet of [the] right to life'.[130] IPAB's statement, that public health and access to medicine is a facet of the right to life, definitely implies an awareness on the part of IPAB that it was dealing with a matter that involved the right to health.

[123] Ibid., para 34.
[124] See *Bayer* v. *Union of India & Others*, OA/35/2012/PT/MUM, decision of the Indian Intellectual Property Appellate Board (4 March 2013).
[125] Ibid., para 54.
[126] Ibid., para 22.
[127] WTO Ministerial Conference, 'Declaration on the TRIPS Agreement and Public Health', Adopted on 14 November 2001, WT/MIN(01)/DEC/2 (20 November 2001).
[128] Ibid., para 4.
[129] *Bayer* v. *Union of India & Others*, OA/35/2012/PT/MUM, decision of the Indian Intellectual Property Appellate Board (4 March 2013), para 20.
[130] Ibid.

IPAB therefore held that 'the reasonably affordable price necessarily has to be fixed from the view point of the public and the word, "afford" itself indicates whether the public can afford to buy the drug ... and the price definitely is the factor that will determine whether the public will reach out for a particular invention'.[131] IPAB further held that 'the Controller was right in holding that the sales of the drug by the appellant at the price of about [Rs.] 280,000 ... considering the purchasing capacity of the public ... was not reasonably affordable to the public'.[132]

6.4.3 Bayer Corporation *v.* Union of India: *(Refusal to Recognize) Patent Linkage*

Patent linkage has been described as a procedure that 'requires that applicants for drug registration declare whether their product has infringed a valid patent and ... [to] assume liability for patent infringement'.[133] It 'links (and conditions) the market approval of a drug to the status of potentially blocking patents'.[134] Essentially, it is a procedure that ensures that producers of generic drugs are prevented from obtaining regulatory or marketing approval prior to the expiration of the patent on a brand name drug.[135] In the absence of patent linkage, the usual procedure for preventing a generic drug from being sold when a patent is still in force is by going to court and seeking an order to prevent patent infringement. However, patent linkage ensures that a generic drug producer is unable to obtain the requisite approval from the drug regulatory authorities until the expiration of the patent, thus obviating the need to engage in patent litigation.

Apparently in a bid to encourage the early introduction of generic drugs into the market, the European Union and most developing countries do not adopt the practice of patent linkage. This ensures that generic drug producers can apply for marketing approval at any time prior to the expiration of a patent on a brand name drug (though usually they cannot begin to sell the generic drugs until the patent expires but it allows them to launch their generic drugs immediately the patent expires). Patent linkage is practiced in the United States (the first country to adopt patent linkage), Canada, and China. There is no patent linkage in India, Kenya, or

[131] Ibid., para 40.

[132] Ibid., para 44. The decision of IPAB in this case was affirmed by the Bombay High Court in 2014. See *Bayer Corporation* v. *Union of India and Ors.*, Writ Petition No. 1323 of 2013 (Decision of the Bombay High Court, 15 July 2014). Bayer's subsequent petition to the Indian Supreme Court for a special leave to appeal against the judgment of the Bombay High Court was dismissed by the Supreme Court. See *Bayer Corporation* v. *Union of India & Ors.*, Petition(s) for Special Leave to Appeal (C) NO(S). 30145/2014 (Decision of the Indian Supreme Court, 12 December 2014).

[133] Yahong Li, *Imitation to Innovation in China: The Role of Patents in Biotechnology and Pharmaceutical Industries* (Edward Elgar, 2010), 144.

[134] Benjamin P. Liu, 'Fighting Poison with Poison? The Chinese Experience with Pharmaceutical Patent Linkage' (2012) 11 *The John Marshall Review of Intellectual Property Law* 623, 625.

[135] Ibid., 627.

South Africa, and the TRIPS Agreement does not mandate countries to adopt patent linkage.

Two multinational pharmaceutical companies (Bristol-Myers Squibb and Bayer) have each instituted separate cases in Indian courts to seek judicial interpretation to the effect that patent linkage can be inferred from the provisions of the Indian Drugs and Cosmetics Act of 1940. The Act, however, only empowers the Drug Controller General of India to grant marketing approval to drugs and the basic requirement is that the drug must be fit for introduction into the Indian market.[136] In the first case, *Bristol-Myers Squibb Co.* v. *Dr BPS Reddy and others*,[137] Bristol-Myers was successful in obtaining an ex-parte injunction preventing the Drug Controller General from approving a generic version of its cancer drug Dasatinib. In this case, the Delhi High Court ruled that 'It is expected that the Drug Controller General of India while performing statutory functions will not allow any party to infringe any laws and if the drug for which approval has been sought by the defendants is in breach of the patent of the plaintiffs, the approval ought not be granted to the defendants'.[138]

This decision is however contrary to the provisions of section 107A(a) of the Indian Patents Act which expressly provides that 'any act of making, constructing, using, selling or importing a patented invention solely for uses reasonably related to the development and submission of information required under any law ... that regulates the manufacture, construction, use, sale or import of any product ... shall not be considered as an infringement of patent rights'. This provision, which is a regulatory review exemption (or *Bolar* exemption), anticipates that producers of generic drugs can take steps to obtain regulatory approval for generic versions of patented drugs before the expiration of the patent terms on the patented drugs. Furthermore, it is not really the responsibility of the Drug Controller General of India to police and enforce patent rights. The main responsibility of the Drug Controller is to grant regulatory approval to drugs that meet the stipulated standards.

It is particularly striking that in this case, the court did not incorporate a *model of human rights* into its reasoning before deciding to grant the ex-parte injunction. Besides the fact that patent linkage has no legal grounding in Indian law, the court should have considered the impact that an ex-parte injunction could have on the production of cheaper generic versions of the patented cancer drug. Having failed to incorporate a *model of human rights* into its decision in this case, it is not surprising that the court restrained the defendants from 'manufacturing, selling, distributing, advertising, exporting, offering for sale, or in any manner dealing directly or indirectly in any product infringing the plaintiffs' patent subject matter'.[139] Thus, through

[136] Anshul Mittal, 'Patent Linkage in India: Current Scenario and Need for Deliberation' (2010) 15 *Journal of Intellectual Property Rights* 187, 188.

[137] *Bristol-Myers Squibb Co.* v. *Dr BPS Reddy and others*, CS(OS)No. 2680/2008 (High Court of Delhi, 12 December 2008).

[138] Ibid., 3.

[139] Ibid.

this ex-parte order, the court judicially introduced and enforced the practice of patent linkage. It is noteworthy that the court could even grant an injunction that could potentially infringe the right to health of several poor patients without listening to arguments from the defendants.

In the subsequent case of *Bayer Corporation* v. *Union of India*[140] (decided in 2009), Bayer Corporation brought an action challenging Cipla's attempt to seek regulatory approval for a generic version of Bayer's patented drug. The Delhi High Court rejected Bayer's argument for patent linkage and it held that patent linkage will undermine the regulatory review exemption contained in the Indian patent law and have a negative impact on efforts to address India's public health challenges.[141] In this case, the Delhi High Court highlighted the distinction between the roles of the patent office and the drug regulatory agency.[142]

The court noted that if it were to establish or decree a patent linkage system as demanded by Bayer in this case, 'it would not only be making a policy choice, [which was] avoided by Parliament, but [the court would be] overstepping its obvious interpretive bounds'.[143] Besides noting that patent linkage would clothe drug regulatory authorities (which are solely concerned with scientific quality, efficacy, and safety issues) with completely new powers and compel them to delve into areas where they lack expertise such as policing patent rights, the court was mindful of the impact that patent linkage could have on access to medicines.[144] According to the court, patent linkage undermines the regulatory review exemption contained in section 107A(a) of the Indian Patents Act, which encourages 'quick access to the post patent markets for generic medicines', and this is 'a major public policy consideration in India, which faces a host of public health challenges'.[145]

The decision of the court was upheld on appeal by a panel of two Judges of the Division Bench of the Delhi High Court.[146] Recognizing the potential impact of

[140] *Bayer Corporation* v. *Union of India*, WP(C) No.7833/2008 (Delhi High Court, August 2009).

[141] Ibid., para 44.

[142] According to the court, 'The Controller of Patents and other officers are experts at judging whether claimed products or processes are patentable. This expertise is not only in respect of pharmaceutical products, but other specialized areas, such as engineering goods, components, accessories and other processes and articles that have industrial applications. This expertise depends upon adjudging, on an objective basis, whether a product or process is novel, or contains an inventive step. Such expertise does not necessarily exist in the case of officials under the Drugs Act, who are required to test the safety of the product, and ensure that it conforms to the therapeutic claim put forward. Whether it involves an inventive step, or is novel, is not within the domain of the Drugs Act authorities and officials. To invest these regulatory authorities with functions that are exclusive to other enactments would be beyond [the] intendment of the Drugs Act. Conversely, the authority to police Patent standards is exclusively that of the authorities under the Patent Act' (ibid., para 37).

[143] Ibid., para 41.

[144] Ibid., para 44.

[145] Ibid.

[146] See *Bayer Corporation* v. *Union of India*, LPA 443/2009 (Delhi High Court, 9 February 2010).

patent linkage on access to medicines, the Division Bench also incorporated a *model of human rights* into its decision in this case. According to the court,

> There are other problems in accepting the submission of Bayer. If the patent holder in respect of a life saving drug decides only to seek marketing approval and not manufacturing approval, it would mean that it will be importing into the country that drug which will consequently be priced very high. Accepting on the other hand, Bayer's contention would mean that the patent holder would be able to block off all generic manufacturers who might have been able to make the drug available in the market at affordable prices, subject of course to their being able to successfully resist injunctions in infringement suits instituted by the patent holder. If the patent holder does not apply for even a marketing approval, then the drug will be virtually unavailable in India till such time [as] the patent holder decides [that] it should be available. Although the Patents Act recognises the monopoly of the patent holder for a period of three years, after which the compulsory licensing route opens up, the question of preventing the [Drug Controller General from granting] marketing approval for the generic version of the drug during that period is not envisaged by the provisions of the [Drugs and Cosmetics Act] as they presently stand.[147]

6.4.4 Hoffmann-La Roche Ltd *v.* Cipla Ltd: *Interim Injunctions, Balance of Convenience, and the Model of Human Rights*

Incorporating a *model of human rights* can be helpful when a court is considering the balance of convenience in a case where a pharmaceutical company is trying to obtain an injunction to prohibit or delay the production of cheaper generic drugs. For instance, in the case of *Hoffmann-La Roche Ltd.* v. *Cipla Ltd.*,[148] the Delhi High Court incorporated a *model of human rights* into its decision when it refused to grant an injunction sought by Roche against Cipla for the latter's production of 'Erloticip' (a generic version of Roche's patented anti-cancer drug known as 'Erlotinib'). The Delhi High Court noted that:

> [T]he Court cannot be unmindful of the right of the general public to access life saving drugs which are available and for which such access would be denied if the injunction were granted . . . The degree of harm in such eventuality is absolute; the chances of improvement of life expectancy; even chances of recovery in some cases would be snuffed out altogether, if [an] injunction [were to be] granted . . . Another way of viewing it is that if the injunction in the case of a life saving drug were to be granted, the Court would in effect be stifling Article 21 [of the Indian Constitution,

[147] Ibid., para 29. Bayer Corporation lodged a further appeal to the Indian Supreme Court but this appeal was dismissed in December 2010. See *Bayer Corporation & Anor.* v. *Union of India & Ors*, Supreme Court of India (DC 6540/2010).

[148] *Hoffmann-La Roche Ltd.* v. *Cipla Ltd.*, I.A. 642/2008 in CS(OS) 89/2008 (Delhi High Court, 19 March 2008).

> which provides for the right to life and which forms the bedrock of the right to health in India] so far as those [who] would have or could have access to Erloticip are concerned.[149]

According to the Delhi High Court, 'as between the two competing public interests, that is, the public interest in granting an injunction to affirm a patent during the pendency of an infringement action, as opposed to the public interest in access for people to a life saving drug, the balance has to be tilted in favour of the latter'.[150] The court observed that the damage that would be suffered by Roche (the patent owner) in this case can be assessed in monetary terms but the 'injury to the public which would be deprived of the defendants product, which may lead to shortening of lives of several unknown persons, who are not parties to the suit, and which damage cannot be restituted in monetary terms, is not only uncompensatable, it is irreparable'.[151]

The decision of the Delhi High Court in this case was upheld on appeal by the Division Bench of the Delhi High Court.[152] In concurring with the trial court, the Division Bench held that,

> [I]n a country like India where [the] question of general public access to life saving drugs assumes great significance, the adverse impact on such access which the grant of [an] injunction in a case like the instant one is likely to have, would have to be accounted for. [Erloticip] is the Indian equivalent produced by the defendant in India as a generic drug manufacturer. It is priced at Rs. 1,600 per tablet. Even if this does not make it inexpensive, the question of [the] greater availability of such [a] drug in the market assumes significance.[153]

However, it should be noted that the incorporation of a *model of human rights* may not always result in the denial of an injunction to a pharmaceutical company that owns a patent on a pharmaceutical product if there is no credible challenge to the validity of the patent. For instance, in *Novartis* v. *Cipla Ltd*,[154] the Delhi High Court ruled against Cipla Ltd by granting an injunction restraining it from infringing Novartis' patent on Indacaterol (a drug used in the treatment of chronic obstructive pulmonary disease (COPD)). In this case, Cipla had, in October 2014, filed an application with the Department of Industrial Policy and Promotion (DIPP) of the Government of India seeking to revoke Novartis' patent on Indacaterol. However, without waiting for the determination of its application, Cipla went ahead to launch

149 Ibid., para 85.
150 Ibid., para 86.
151 Ibid.
152 See *Hoffmann-La Roche* v. *Cipla*, FAO (OS) 188/2008 (Delhi High Court Division Bench, 24 April 2009).
153 Ibid., para 81.
154 *Novartis* v. *Cipla Ltd.*, I.A. No. 24863/2014 in CS(OS) 3812/2014 (Delhi High Court, 9 January 2015).

its own version of the patented drug. Novartis therefore brought an application for an injunction restraining Cipla from infringing its patent rights on Indacaterol.

In response to Novartis' application for an injunction, Cipla argued, *inter alia*, that Novartis had failed to make the patented drug available to the patient population in India.[155] Cipla also contended that Novartis did not provide any reason for not manufacturing the patented drug in India by itself or through an assignee or licensee.[156] Cipla also argued that Novartis provided no reason for not importing sufficient quantities of the patented drug into India and for not making the patented drug available to patients at affordable prices.[157] Cipla stated that, while Novartis' drug was being sold at Rs. 677, it was selling its own version at Rs. 130.[158]

Essentially, Cipla based its arguments on the grounds for the grant of a compulsory licence contained in section 84 of the Indian Patents Act, that is, the reasonable requirements of the public with respect to the patented invention has not been satisfied; the patented drug is not available to the public at a reasonable price; and the patent was not being worked in India.[159] It is, however, curious to note that, rather than apply for the grant of a compulsory licence, Cipla chose to infringe the patent rights of Novartis by launching its own version of the patented drug.

Cipla incorporated a *model of human rights* into its arguments in this case as it argued that the right granted to a patentee is always to be exercised in a manner which protects, preserves, and promotes the 'Constitutional intent to promote the right to life and not in a manner contrary thereto'.[160] Cipla noted that the right to life contained in Article 21 of the Indian Constitution has been interpreted by the Indian Supreme Court to include the right to health.[161] Cipla also offered to pay royalties in lieu of an injunction.[162]

Novartis however argued, *inter alia*, that it had supplied the patented drug according to the market demand raised on it and that it was ready and willing to increase its supply whenever the need arises.[163] Interestingly, Novartis also responded to the arguments on human rights by contending that it had 'contributed to public health, public interest and [the] right to [a] better quality of life enshrined in Article 21 of the Constitution by disclosing its invention in India by way of the patent application which will go into [the] public domain on expiry of the patent in less than 6 years' and it had also 'fulfilled [the] public interest by actually supplying the [patented] drugs as per the demand in [the] Indian market' and it was 'committed to additional supply of the [patented pharmaceutical] product ... if there is [an]

155 Ibid., para 11.
156 Ibid., para 16.
157 Ibid., para 16.
158 Ibid., para 29(iv).
159 Ibid., para 29(i).
160 Ibid., para 20.
161 Ibid., para 20.
162 Ibid., para 22.
163 Ibid., para 25(iv).

unfulfilled requirement'.[164] Novartis submitted that it respects the Indian Constitution and also that it is 'fully alive to the sanctity which is to [be] accorded to [the] right to life and dignity' and that as a patentee, it 'is conscious of its responsibility towards supplying drugs to the public in India'.[165] Novartis equally alleged that Cipla was really fighting for its own business interest and not the public interest.[166] Novartis assured the court that it was not only willing to increase its supply of the drug if there was an increase in demand, 'the price would also be reworked in accordance with the market demand'.[167]

In its decision, the Delhi High Court distinguished the present case from that of *Roche* v. *Cipla*. According to the court,

> . . . Unless there is a credible challenge to the validity of the patent itself, the Courts will not include any alleged public interest as a factor to exercise discretion. It was observed in the judgment of [*Hoffmann-La Roche Ltd.* v. *Cipla Ltd*] . . . cited by the Defendant, that the Plaintiff failed to establish [a] prima facie case of infringement and on the contrary, defendant successfully raised [a] credible challenge to the validity of the patent and the Courts . . . accepted the plea of the defendant in that case on the basis of [the] defence raised. However, such circumstances are missing in the present case.[168]

The court stated that Novartis had established a *prima facie* case for the validity of its patent and that Cipla has merely urged grounds of invalidity by relying on documents which according to Cipla constitutes prior art 'without explaining to the court and to the other side . . . how these documents can be categorized as [prior art]'.[169] The court further stated that Novartis, on the other hand, provided the points of distinction between the earlier patents relied upon as prior art and its own patent.[170] The court held that, 'if [a] patent is valid, the defendant has failed to establish [a] prima facie credible defence and the case of infringement is made out by the patentee, the patentee may be entitled [to an] injunction'.[171]

The ruling of the Delhi High Court in this case shows the importance of the need to ensure that the *model of human rights* is not misused or abused in disputes

164 Ibid., para 25(iv).
165 Ibid., para 25(xii).
166 According to Novartis, 'The Defendant [i.e. Cipla] has a huge business interest in the patented compound . . . which led to [the] filing of several patent applications. However, having failed to overcome the hurdle of establishing . . . inventive step, [it] abandoned some of the applications and filed the representation before [the] DIPP for its commercial interest under the garb of public interest and public need. This court ought to take a serious note of . . . the intent behind raising such frivolous plea of public interest and [the misuse of] the forum for . . . [Cipla's] business interest' (ibid., para 25(xxiii)).
167 Ibid., para 27(iv).
168 Ibid., para 74.
169 Ibid., para 83.
170 Ibid.
171 Ibid., para 87.

involving pharmaceutical patent rights. According to the court, Cipla's reliance on the right to life contained in Article 21 of the Indian Constitution is misplaced and it stated that 'Article 21 cannot be pressed into service by an infringer seeking to justify the infringement of a valid patent and the statutory rights conferred by the statute'.[172] The court further stated that if Cipla was 'so very much concerned about the welfare of [the] public ... and its grounds are genuine and correct, it could have filed [an] application for [the] grant of [a] Compulsory Licence'.[173] The court stated that Cipla is free to apply for a compulsory licence and it can approach the court for the modification of the injunction if it successfully obtains a compulsory licence.[174]

6.5 CONCLUSION

Thus, Indian courts have, to a large extent, preserved the Indian patent policy space and facilitated greater access to essential medicines at affordable prices for poor patients in India by incorporating a *model of human rights* into their decisions in cases involving disputes on pharmaceutical patent rights. The combined effect of the liberal interpretative approach adopted with regard to the constitutional right to life and the incorporation of a *model of human rights* into their decisions in pharmaceutical patent cases has enabled Indian courts to safeguard and protect the enjoyment of the human right to health in India.

[172] Ibid., para 89.

[173] Ibid., para 91.

[174] According to the court, '... the defendant can always seek [a] compulsory license before the appropriate forum under the provisions of section 83 and 84 of the Act ... by urging the grounds urged before this court for non working of the patent or inability of the plaintiff to comply with demands or monopoly by way of importation etc. Accordingly, the defendant can pursue its remedies if the defendant has [a] good case on the grounds of compulsory license and in which case the appropriate forum may allow the defendant to manufacture the patented products if the case of the defendant is found to be plausible by the appropriate forum and the defendant can always approach this court for modification of the interim order in case the compulsory licensing tribunal comes to the said conclusion' (ibid., para 86).

7

Conclusion

In its critical examination of the problem of access to affordable medicines in three developing countries, this book has addressed two key questions: (1) How should the relationship between patent rights and human rights be conceptualized?; and (2) In resolving the tension between patent rights and the right to health and in trying to discharge their right to health responsibilities, what should inform the design, implementation, interpretation, and enforcement of patent rights by the organs of the state in developing countries?

In response to the first question, this book has argued that patent rights cannot be considered as human rights under international human rights law. Moreover, in relation to the second question, this book contends that a *model of human rights* should be incorporated into the design, implementation, interpretation, and enforcement of patent rights at the national level. The book equally critically evaluates the extent to which the national courts and tribunals in Kenya, South Africa, and India, respectively, have incorporated a *model of human rights* into their decisions when adjudicating disputes that involve a tension between patent rights and the right to health. The cases examined in Chapters 4–6 demonstrate that the incorporation of a *model of human rights* into the adjudication of such disputes can be useful in preserving patent policy space and securing access to medicines.

7.1 THE MODEL OF HUMAN RIGHTS

From a socio-centric perspective, it is better to describe intellectual property as a policy instrument or set of laws meant to define and regulate the grant of exclusive rights to creators. This helps to shift the focus of patent rights from a creator-centric perspective to a broader socio-centric perspective. Since inventors rely and build on the pre-existing body of knowledge in society, it is reasonable to demand that the interests of the society should equally be protected by patent laws. Patent laws should equally recognize and protect the interests of other 'users' of the patent system in society such as medical doctors, manufacturers of generic drugs, and poor patients who require access to medicines at affordable prices.

The regulatory theory of patent law, which adopts a socio-centric approach to patent law, permits the incorporation of a *model of human rights* into a country's patent law system. The *model of human rights* demands that any regulatory instrument implemented by a state must not constitute a breach of its international human rights obligations. Thus, any country that is a party to the International Covenant on Economic, Social and Cultural Rights (ICESCR) has an obligation to ensure that its patent law system does not impede the enjoyment of the human right to health in its country. Since patent rights are not human rights, there is no reason why developing countries cannot insist on the primacy of human rights obligations when designing, implementing, interpreting, or enforcing their national patent laws.

Besides, paragraph 4 of the Doha Declaration on the TRIPS Agreement and Public Health, by providing that the TRIPS Agreement should be interpreted and implemented in a manner that supports the right of countries to promote access to medicines, sanctions the incorporation of a right to health perspective, and invariably the incorporation of a *model of human rights*, into the design, implementation, interpretation, and enforcement of a country's patent law. Thus, the TRIPS Agreement, read together with the Doha Declaration, does not prohibit countries from incorporating a *model of human rights* into their national patent laws.

7.2 THE ROLE OF STATES IN PRESERVING PATENT POLICY SPACE AND SECURING ACCESS TO MEDICINES

Since states bear the primary responsibility to respect, protect, and fulfil the right to health and secure access to medicines, countries that are parties to the ICESCR have an obligation to preserve their patent policy space in order to ensure that access to affordable medicines is not impeded by the implementation and enforcement of excessively high levels of patent protection. Since patent rights are not human rights, such countries should ensure that their patent law system is structured in a way that facilitates the production and distribution of affordable drugs. This can be done by incorporating a *model of human rights* into the design, implementation, interpretation, and enforcement of patent laws at the national level.

As argued in Chapter 3, the incorporation of a *model of human rights* into a country's national patent law system will not be in conflict with its obligations under the TRIPS Agreement. Thus, the use of flexibilities such as the exclusion of new forms of known drugs from patent protection, compulsory licences, parallel importation, and regulatory review exemptions, pursuant to a *model of human rights* is compatible with the text of the TRIPS Agreement. The incorporation of a *model of human rights* into a country's patent law system provides a stronger normative basis for the utilization of the flexibilities in the TRIPS Agreement by a country that is willing to facilitate access to medicines and protect the right to health of its citizens.

However, with regard to the incorporation of a *model of human rights* into the adjudication of disputes on pharmaceutical patent rights, it is imperative to emphasize that the incorporation of *a model of human rights* does not necessarily translate to the abrogation of patent rights, it only means that the courts should not permit patent rights on pharmaceutical products to be exercised and enforced in a manner that impedes the enjoyment of the human right to health. Where there is no risk that the exercise or the enforcement of patent rights will impede the enjoyment of the right to health, there is no need to prevent a patentee from exercising or enforcing its patent rights.

In summary, states (in this context, developing countries), as the bearers of the responsibility to respect, protect, and fulfil the right to health, should incorporate a *model of human rights* into the design, implementation, interpretation, and enforcement of their national patent laws. This should help developing countries to preserve their patent policy space and secure access to affordable medicines for poor patients in their countries.

Index

For EU product safety concerns, contact us at Calle de José Abascal, 56–1°,
28003 Madrid, Spain or eugpsr@cambridge.org.

www.ingramcontent.com/pod-product-compliance
Lightning Source LLC
LaVergne TN
LVHW022217200926
848481LV00006B/2008
* 9 7 8 1 1 0 8 4 5 8 9 8 6 *